Practical Appreciative Inquiry

Practical Appreciative Inquiry

A Toolkit for Applying Appreciative Inquiry to Organisational Challenges, Opportunities, and Aspiration

Sarah Lewis

WILEY Blackwell

This edition first published 2025
© 2025 John Wiley & Sons Ltd

All rights reserved, including rights for text and data mining and training of artificial technologies or similar technologies. [For any titles with third-party copyright holders, replace the previous sentence with: All rights reserved.] No part of this publication may be reproduced, stored in a retrieval system, or transmitted, in any form or by any means, electronic, mechanical, photocopying, recording or otherwise, except as permitted by law. Advice on how to obtain permission to reuse material from this title is available at http://www.wiley.com/go/permissions.

The right of Sarah Lewis to be identified as the author of this work has been asserted in accordance with law.

Registered Office(s)
John Wiley & Sons, Inc., 111 River Street, Hoboken, NJ 07030, USA
John Wiley & Sons Ltd, The Atrium, Southern Gate, Chichester, West Sussex, PO19 8SQ, UK

For details of our global editorial offices, customer services, and more information about Wiley products visit us at www.wiley.com.

Wiley also publishes its books in a variety of electronic formats and by print-on-demand. Some content that appears in standard print versions of this book may not be available in other formats.

Trademarks: Wiley and the Wiley logo are trademarks or registered trademarks of John Wiley & Sons, Inc. and/or its affiliates in the United States and other countries and may not be used without written permission. All other trademarks are the property of their respective owners. John Wiley & Sons, Inc. is not associated with any product or vendor mentioned in this book.

Limit of Liability/Disclaimer of Warranty
While the publisher and authors have used their best efforts in preparing this work, they make no representations or warranties with respect to the accuracy or completeness of the contents of this work and specifically disclaim all warranties, including without limitation any implied warranties of merchantability or fitness for a particular purpose. No warranty may be created or extended by sales representatives, written sales materials or promotional statements for this work. This work is sold with the understanding that the publisher is not engaged in rendering professional services. The advice and strategies contained herein may not be suitable for your situation. You should consult with a specialist where appropriate. The fact that an organization, website, or product is referred to in this work as a citation and/or potential source of further information does not mean that the publisher and authors endorse the information or services the organization, website, or product may provide or recommendations it may make. Further, readers should be aware that websites listed in this work may have changed or disappeared between when this work was written and when it is read. Neither the publisher nor authors shall be liable for any loss of profit or any other commercial damages, including but not limited to special, incidental, consequential, or other damages.

Library of Congress Cataloging-in-Publication Data Applied for:

Paperback ISBN: 9781394198122

Cover Design: Wiley
Cover Image: © Hispanolistic/Getty Images

Set in 10.5/13pt Minion by Straive, Pondicherry, India
SKY10092604_120324

Contents

About the Author	xii
Foreword	xiii
Preface	xv
Acknowledgements	xvii

Part One: Background and Practice Theory	**1**
1 What Is Appreciative Inquiry?	**3**
What Are the Origins of Appreciative Inquiry?	4
How Is Appreciative Inquiry Different to Other Change Methodologies?	5
How Does Appreciative Inquiry Engage with Organisational Problems?	7
What Is Dialogic Organisational Development?	8
How Can We Ensure That Our Appreciative Inquiry Practice with Organisations Is Evidence-Based?	11
Critiquing Appreciative Inquiry	12
Conclusion	14
Learning Points	14
Discussion Questions	15
Teaching Practice	15
Resources and Further Reading	15
Notes	16
References	16
2 The Appreciative Inquiry Summit	**18**
Introducing the 5D Model of Appreciative Inquiry	18
The Principles of Appreciative Inquiry	24
Narrative, Stories and Sensemaking in Appreciative Inquiry	26

Research that Supports Appreciative Inquiry as a Practice	30
The Effectiveness of Appreciative Inquiry in Transformational Change	30
Conclusion	31
Learning Points	31
Discussion Questions	31
Teaching Exercises	32
Helpful Resources and Further Reading	32
Notes	33
References	33
3 Preparing, Delivering and Following-up an Event	**34**
Contraindications for an Appreciative Inquiry Event	34
Common Myths Attached to Appreciative Inquiry	36
Preparing for an Appreciative Inquiry Event	38
Delivering the Event	40
The Quality of Conversation	41
The Quality of the Questions	44
The Volunteer Principle in Appreciative Inquiry	45
After the Event	46
Conclusion	46
Learning Points	47
Discussion Questions	47
Teaching Exercise	47
Further Reading and Resources	47
References	48
4 Creating the Appreciative Inquiry Commission, Psychological Safety and Equality, Diversity and Inclusion	**49**
Developing an Appreciative Inquiry Commission	50
Frequently Encountered Pushbacks Against Adopting an Appreciative Inquiry Approach	55
Practice Design Principles	55
Ethical Practice	57
How Appreciative Practice Can Support Equality, Diversity and Inclusion	58
Case Studies Using Appreciative Inquiry to Enhance Diversity, Equality and Inclusion	62
Conclusion	63

Learning Points	64
Discussion Questions	64
Teaching Exercises	64
Helpful Resources	64
Notes	65
References	66

Part Two: Applications — 67

5 Appreciative Inquiry for Flourishing Organisations, SOAR and I-IPOD — 69

Appreciative Practice and the Flourishing Organisation	69
Strengths and the Organisational Power Zone	73
The SOAR Model of Strategy Development	74
Case Study: Using SOAR to Return to the Power Zone	75
Case-Study: A Community System I-IPOD Appreciative Intervention	80
Conclusion	82
Learning Points	82
Discussion Questions	83
Teaching Exercise	83
Helpful Resources and Further Reading	83
Notes	84
References	84

6 Appreciative Leadership — 86

Leadership Actions That Can Undermine an Appreciative Inquiry Event	87
The Leadership Mindset Required for Appreciative Inquiry	88
Leadership Conversations that Include or Exclude	89
Leading Through Uncertainty	93
Case Study: Appreciative Leadership in Action	93
Conclusion	96
Learning Points	97
Discussion Questions	97
Teaching Exercise	97
Further Resources	97
Notes	98
References	98

7 Building Resilience for People and Organisations — 99
Appreciative Inquiry and Organisational Resilience — 100
Appreciative Inquiry and Personal Resilience — 102
The Resilience Boosting Effects of Strengths — 104
Case Study: A Positive Approach to Difficult Issues — 105
Case Study: Bringing Appreciative Inquiry to the Disruption of Organisational Change — 109
Conclusion — 111
Learning Points — 112
Discussion Questions — 112
Teaching Exercise — 112
Helpful Resources — 112
Notes — 113
References — 113

8 Engaging with the Particular Challenges of Project Management — 115
The Psychology of Project-Craft — 115
Taking an Appreciative Approach to Team Member Diversity — 118
Applying Appreciative Inquiry to Project Management — 120
Case Study: A Project Team-Based Large-System Change — 121
Conclusion — 126
Learning Points — 126
Discussion Questions — 126
Teaching Exercise — 127
Further Resources — 127
Notes — 127
References — 127

9 Boosting Innovation and Creativity — 128
Understanding Innovation and Creativity as Generativity — 128
How the Appreciative Inquiry Process Generates Ideas and Energy — 129
Working Generatively with Discovery Stories — 131
Inquiring into Creativity — 133
The Relationship Between Appreciative Inquiry and Improvisational Theatre — 135
Case Study: An Organisation Adapting to Market Changes — 135
Case Study: Creativity for Business Growth — 136
Conclusion — 137

Learning Points	137
Discussion Questions	137
Teaching Exercises	138
Helpful Resources	138
Notes	138
References	139

10 Challenging the Silo Mentality — 140
Why the Siloed Organisation Is Popular and How It Becomes Dysfunctional	141
The Nature of Organisational Energy	143
What Does Appreciative Inquiry Bring to the Challenge?	144
Case Study: A Merged Organisation	145
Conclusion	153
Learning Points	154
Discussion Questions and Practical Exercise	154
Teaching Exercises	154
Helpful Resources On and Offline	154
Notes	155
References	155

11 Motivating Performance with PRISMM Coaching — 156
The Importance of a Performance Culture	157
Appreciative PRISMM Coaching	159
Case Study: An Inquiry into Creating a Great Performance Management Culture	162
Conclusion	172
Learning Points	172
Discussion Questions	173
Teaching Exercise	173
Helpful Resources	173
Notes	174
References	174

12 Releasing the Synergy of Teams — 175
What Is a Team?	176
What Makes a Successful Team?	176
Creating Team Positivity	177
When Teams Get Stuck	178

Case Study: Working with a Stuck Team	179
Conclusion	186
Learning Points	186
Discussion Questions	187
Teaching Exercises	187
Helpful Resources	187
Note	187
Reference	188

13 Virtual, Remote and Hybrid Working — 189

Some of the Challenges of Remote Working for the Individual	190
Applying Appreciative Inquiry to the Challenges of Remote Working	190
Hosting an Appreciative Inquiry Online	196
Effects of Remote Working on the Workplace	197
Hybrid Working	198
Case Study of Hybrid Working Challenges	200
Conclusion	203
Learning Points	203
Discussion Questions	204
Teaching Exercise	204
Helpful Resources and Further Reading	204
Notes	204
References	205

14 Reviewing and Evaluating Practice — 206

Why Evaluate Activity?	207
Meaningless Measurement Points and the Reflective Ritual Review	208
Appreciative-Informed Evaluation of Leadership or Management	208
Appreciative Process for Management Performance Assessment	209
Case Study: Introducing Appreciative Peer Reviews to a Regional Health Team	211
Conclusion	218
Learning Points	218
Discussion Questions	219
Teaching Exercise	219
Helpful Resources and Further Reading	219
Notes	219
References	220

15 Supporting Planned Change Processes — 221
- The Challenges of Wholesale Large-Scale Planned Change — 222
- Appreciative Inquiry and the Generation of Hope — 222
- Some General Principles for Bringing Appreciative Inquiry to Planned Change — 224
- The Blended Approach Is Best — 227
- Case Study: From Push to Pull — 229
- Case Study: Impact of a Two-Hour Workshop on Change Practice — 231
- Conclusion — 232
- Learning Points — 233
- Discussion Questions — 233
- Teaching Exercise — 233
- Helpful Resources and Further Reading — 233
- Notes — 234
- References — 234

16 Health and Well-being at Work — 236
- People at Work — 237
- How Organisational Cultures Can Become Toxic — 239
- The Importance of Relationships and Emotional States — 240
- System-level Health and Well-being Intervention — 241
- Psychological Safety in Teams — 243
- Case Study: Working with Respect — 245
- Conclusion — 249
- Learning Points — 249
- Discussion Questions — 249
- Teaching Exercise — 250
- Helpful Resources and Further Reading — 250
- Notes — 250
- References — 250

Index — 253

About the Author

Sarah Lewis is a chartered psychologist, an Associated Fellow of the British Psychological Society, and a founder and principal member of the Association of Business Psychologists. She holds a master's degree in occupational and organisational psychology, attained with distinction, and a certificate in systemic consultation. She is a specialist appreciative inquiry practitioner and an expert at facilitating large group events.

She is the managing director of Appreciating Change and is an experienced organisational consultant and facilitator who has been actively involved in helping people and organisations change their behaviour for over 30 years. Her clients include local government, central government, not-for-profit organisations and private sector clients, particularly in the manufacturing, financial and educational sectors. She works both nationally and internationally.

Sarah lectures at postgraduate level in the UK and continues to be a regular conference presenter in the UK and internationally. She writes regularly for publication and has five previous publications

- *Appreciative Inquiry for Change Management*
- *Positive Psychology at Work*
- *Positive Psychology and Change*
- *Positive Psychology in Business*
- *Creating Energised Commitment to the Dialogic Approach*

Sarah also runs a boutique online shop supplying positive psychology and appreciative inquiry training and development tools at http://www.theppshop.store.

Sarah's work can be viewed on her website: www.acukltd.com, and she can be contacted on ++ 44 (0)7973 782 715 or by emailing sarahlewis@acukltd.com.

Foreword

It is my pleasure to write a foreword to Sarah Lewis's newest book on appreciative inquiry, a powerful method for organisational change. While appreciative inquiry is over 30 years old, it can seem like a new, fuzzy-wuzzy thing for many managers. Nothing could be further from the truth. As Sarah documents throughout the book, appreciative inquiry integrates a great deal of evidence-based research on the psychology of organising and has decades of successful application to draw on.

Sarah is a seasoned practitioner and a good writer. Still, for someone looking to gain insight and expertise in using this powerful change method, the question must arise: Why this book instead of one of the many others on offer?

First, this book rises above many by focusing on principles. These, not recipes, are more likely to help you adopt appreciative inquiry successfully. As I can attest from personal experience, when practitioners adopt new practices in a "paint by numbers" approach, they are just as likely to fail as succeed and not be clear why. This book will help you avoid that pitfall. While the first few chapters introduce you to the standard practices of appreciative inquiry, more importantly, they teach the underlying principles that make these practices powerful. Throughout the book, as Sarah introduces different scenarios and applications, she returns over and over to the foundational principles that make appreciative approaches to leadership and change work. In addition, she goes far beyond the standard 4-D model in offering many other practices that can be usefully integrated into a change process. Helpfully, she is mindful of numerous reasons why one might not want to use an appreciative inquiry in specific situations and offers excellent insights into the traps to avoid as one brings this approach into an organisation.

Second, this a great resource because of Sarah's review of adjacent topics, like project management, diversity and inclusion, organisational resilience, performance management and even conventional, top-down planned change. She shows how appreciative approaches can enhance their effectiveness. In some cases, she even demonstrates how principles drawn from those practices can be applied to improve the effectiveness of appreciative inquiry.

Third is Sarah's exceptional integration of research and practice. Like most books on methods of change, numerous stories of successful practice make the principles come alive. However, more unusual is her references to management research that provide evidence supporting the change principles and practices described. For practitioners trying to convince leaders to try something new, these are valuable resources to draw on.

Finally, I would point to the lively, informal writing style that makes it easy to keep turning the page. Sarah makes complex concepts easy to understand and demonstrates their practical utility through numerous anecdotes, figures, tables and cases. Anyone with experience in the trenches of organisational change will recognize the characters and situations she describes. I appreciate the good-humoured way she identifies the many common, self-defeating mindsets managers can bring to change issues and how to respond to them gently and with respect for the complexities and burdens of leadership.

Gervase R. Bushe
Vancouver, British Columbia, Canada
September 2024

Preface

Once again, I find myself devoting irretrievable hours of my life to writing a book. At this point, with the deadline only days away and my hands tingling with RSI, I can only ask myself: why? What do I have left to say on the subject, and is anyone interested?

Every book has a different gestation. This one was spurred first by my commitment to producing many hours of video recording for an online university course, which necessitated the production of a lot of text; and secondly by the desire to pass on some of what I have learnt about the practice of appreciative inquiry in many different situations. By using the second to shape the first, I hoped to create a legacy document that might prove valuable to others. This is it.

The ambition of this book is to demonstrate the versatility and flexibility of the appreciative inquiry methodology. Primarily, this is a book for practitioners. It is aimed at the general or specialist organisational member looking for ideas and activities they can pick up and use to improve their organisation, as well as at consultants and organisational development experts. Yet it is also important to me that those of a curious mind or with a more academic bent can follow the information presented back to its source: that the theory and science behind the practice be readily available.

These dual ambitions have resulted in the decision not to provide in-text references. Instead, I have chosen to use footnotes. This is in service of creating a smoother reading experience for those looking more for how than why. I believe this may be the point at which to confess that I have been unable to source a few references. I can only apologise for the frustration I know this can cause.

Another ambition is that this book be of value to both experienced practitioners that are looking to extend their practice, and to those new to the field. To assist both audiences, the book is divided into two parts. Part One provides an overview of the theory and science of appreciative inquiry and includes some guidance on creating the commission. Part Two, while including discussion of interesting ideas, is more focused on the 'doing' of appreciative inquiry. To this end the chapters in the latter part of the book are focused on particular areas of intervention.

Key to supporting the practice learning is the provision of case studies. A large proportion of these come from my own practice. They have been selected not on the basis that they were necessarily great pieces of work, but for their value in showing how theory can be put into practice. By exposing my thinking behind the practice design, and by highlighting the compromises made when a model of practice meets a messy situation, I hope to expose the reality of putting the theory into practice, and to provide material for classroom discussions of how to do it better!

In addition, recognising that appreciative inquiry is appearing more frequently in management and organisational education and that a textbook could be helpful, the book provides some teaching aids including suggested discussion topics and a teaching exercise at the end of each chapter.

As someone seemingly wedded to producing books, a particular challenge I face, which gets harder with each new book, is how not to end up repeating myself! I have endeavoured to keep the degree of overlap between this and my previous texts to the necessary minimum while still allowing this book to be a stand-alone read. At the same time, I have indicated where the subject is covered in more depth in a previous text for those who might be interested.

Since I wrote my last Wiley-Blackwell publication, I have set up an online shop that sells positive psychology and appreciative inquiry training and development tools. Most of the products we sell I use in my work. This means that they are referenced both in the case studies at times and in the further resources where I believe knowledge of them may be helpful to practitioners.

And, as a final note, I am pleased to report that no AI (artificial intelligence) has been used in the creation of this text. Although I fear my writing on AI (appreciative inquiry) may have been used to support the creation of an AI (artificial intelligence) capable of having done so had I asked it to!

Acknowledgements

All texts are built on other texts, and this book is no exception. I am indebted to the many appreciative inquiry practitioners by whose work I have been inspired. In particular I owe huge thanks to Anne Radford, a pioneer of appreciative inquiry in the UK, who has been a constant source of inspiration and support.

In addition, Anne was the founder of the online publication *AI Practitioner*, to which I refer extensively throughout this book. Without her dedication to providing a forum for collecting together the developing theory and practice of the field, much of value would have been lost. We all owe her deep appreciation for setting up this legacy repository and for sustaining it as a labour of love for so many years. I personally am grateful to Anne for her lighting of the way, her friendship and for her generous sharing of her deep knowledge of the subject. Anne was also a leading light in the UK AI network.

This network, from which I took much inspiration, is sadly now no more. In its time, it was invaluable as a home for AI practitioners across the UK and, I believe, helped us all raise the level of our game. I found it an invaluable source of expertise and learning. I have also, for many years, been involved in the European AI network, another source of great expertise in both the living and the practice of appreciative inquiry. This, I am pleased to report, is still thriving and can be found at https://www.appreciativeinquiry.eu. To the many dedicated volunteers who ran, or run, both these networks I owe a deep debt and offer heartfelt thanks.

In addition, I am indebted to the many organisations I have worked with over the years honing my skills. Many of them feature, suitably anonymously, in the case studies in the text. In all cases I greatly appreciate the opportunities they created to learn how to apply appreciative inquiry skills in many situations.

Finally, of course, I am grateful to my family. My urge to communicate my passion and to share my learning, at length, through the written word, is as incomprehensible to them as to me, yet every few years they put up with me dedicating myself to writing a book. All that time that could have been spent on other things, such as country walks or redecorating! I am very grateful for their patience, and for my husband's ability and willingness to rustle up drawings for the diagrams I am incapable of creating on a computer. There are three in this text.

My sincere thanks to all involved. And as ever, while any light the text may shine on the practice of appreciative inquiry is due to the sterling work of others on which I have drawn, any errors and mistakes are mine and mine alone.

PART ONE

Background and Practice Theory

PART ONE

Background and Gaelic Ethnos

1

What Is Appreciative Inquiry?

The term *appreciative inquiry* refers to an approach to achieving change in organisations. This approach is, to some extent, codified in a series of models of practice. At the same time it is a philosophical system of beliefs about the nature of truth, knowledge, and reality, and of how change occurs, or not, in human systems. This combination of profundity and practicality is the basis for appreciative inquiry's versatility, flexibility and robustness. That said, it is not a panacea for all ills. It is as important to know when it is not an appropriate approach as when it is.

In this first chapter we briefly consider the development of appreciative inquiry as a change methodology and outline some of the places to find case study accounts of appreciative inquiry practice beyond those recounted in this book. We look at what distinguishes appreciative inquiry as an approach, particularly the view it takes of organisations as living human systems. The chapter then considers how that difference in perspective affects the mode of practice and the approach to creating change. In examining when it is appropriate to use appreciative inquiry, we look at the nature of different organisational problems and the rise of dialogic organisational development as a broad field of distinctive practice within which appreciative inquiry fits. This chapter notes also that appreciative inquiry is a field application supported by scientific theory from academic sources. We look at this though the lens of evidence-based standards of intervention and consider the challenge for field-based practice. Finally we look at, and consider, the validity of some of the critiques of appreciative inquiry since its introduction to the field of organisational development at the end of the 1990s.

Practical Appreciative Inquiry: A Toolkit for Applying Appreciative Inquiry to Organisational Challenges, Opportunities, and Aspiration, First Edition. Sarah Lewis.
© 2025 John Wiley & Sons Ltd. Published 2025 by John Wiley & Sons Ltd.

What Are the Origins of Appreciative Inquiry?

In 1987, as part of his Ph.D. research, supervised by Suresh Srivastva, into organisational change and development, Cooperrider [1] made a serendipitous discovery: that asking about and focusing on the good aspects of organisational life can produce positive change.* His breakthrough realisation was that organisations can positively and effectively engage with problems without necessarily addressing them head on, without even framing them as problems. This continues to be a revolutionary idea in the world of organisational change where it is still widely believed that to solve a problem you need to talk about the problem **as a problem**. Appreciative inquiry suggests that we can address, work on and solve problems while talking about the situation in a different way: in an appreciative way. How does appreciative inquiry work?

Figure 1.1 illustrates the process by which a positive inquiry into a positive experience, a practice which forms the basis of appreciative inquiry practice, has an impact on emotional states, relationships and the ability to

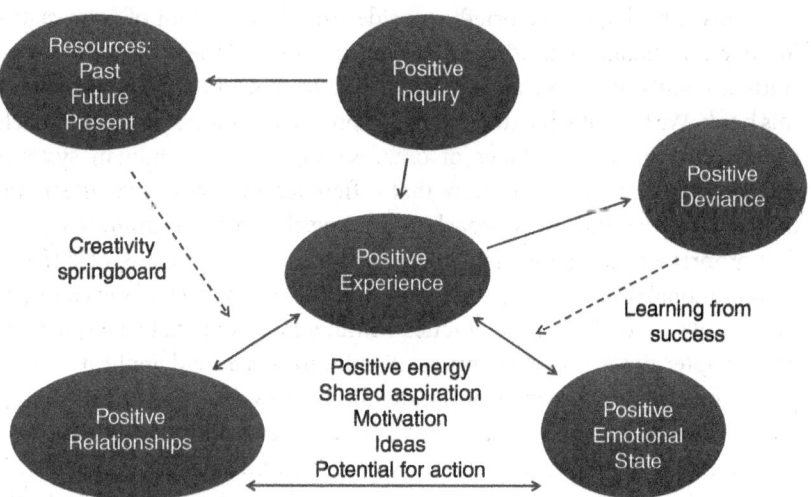

Figure 1.1 Positive Energy: the shared experience and demonstration of positive affect, cognitive arousal agentic behaviour among unit members in their joint pursuit of organisationally salient objectives.

---

* As this book was going to press, I came across this excellent account of how David Coopperrider arrived at the idea and practice of appreciative inquiry: Bushe, G. (2012) Foundations of Appreciative Inquiry: History, Criticism and Potential. AI Practitioner Vol 14, No.1. www.aipractitioner.com

access resources. This process, through the generation of positive energy, shared aspirations, motivation and ideas, creates the potential and impulsion for action. Positive deviance [2] is a positive psychology term that refers to exceptional performance. It's these examples of exceptional performance that appreciative inquiry brings into focus as a resource for organisational learning, growth and development. The diagram below also illustrates how appreciative inquiry generates hope, a key motivational emotion.

Today, Champlain College, which houses the David L. Cooperrider Center for Appreciative Inquiry,[1] lists a variety of organisations using appreciative inquiry. These range from corporations such as Apple, Johnson and Johnson, Coca Cola and Visa, through non-profits such as the United States Navy, American Red Cross and the State of Massachusetts, to global initiatives such as the UN Global Compact. Case studies can also be found in the core practitioner publication *AI Practitioner: The International Journey of Appreciative Inquiry*.[2] Founded by Anne Radford in 1998, it continues to capture and disseminate appreciative inquiry theory and practice across the globe. Further case studies can be found in the book *Appreciative Inquiry for Change Management* [3]. A number of case studies are also shared in this book.

How Is Appreciative Inquiry Different to Other Change Methodologies?

There are many factors that distinguish appreciative inquiry from other change practices, as will become evident throughout the book. However, there are four key practices to highlight at this point. One is the specific kinds of question asked by appreciative inquiry, questions that target exploration of, and expand conversation about, the good and the best. Another is its focus on the conscious and deliberate redirecting of attention away from the problem to the aspiration. The third is the creation of a pull motivation through the lived experience of a more attractive future. And the fourth is the involvement of the whole system from the very beginning of the intervention. These practices are explored throughout this book. In essence, while other approaches essentially ask what has gone wrong here and how can we fix it or prevent more of it, appreciative inquiry asks what is going right here and how can we grow more of it.

Behind these surface differences lie differences in understanding the nature of an organisation. Appreciative inquiry views organisations as psychological spaces, full of psychologically alive and complex people: people who experience emotions, have differing relations with each other, who can be fired up, or depressed, just by their imaginations. People who are motivated by things like loyalty, fair play and a sense of justice or betrayal as well as by logic or greed. Appreciative inquiry understands that all of human drama, all the emotions that fuel comedy and tragedy, are present in organisational life. One might say that it views organisations as Shakespearean theatre. Many other approaches tend to treat organisations more like predictable, logical machines.

There are further differences in the mode of practice. Appreciative inquiry is a co-creative, collaborative methodology, sailing close to the idea of 'no conversation about me without me'. This means that people are involved in conversations that affect their future from the very beginning. The ambition of this upfront investment is to generate energy for change in all levels of the system simultaneously. Obviously, this speeds up the process compared to a more traditional top-down linear 'energy-pumping' approach. Involving everyone from the beginning means that more people are simultaneously available to take the lead on different, forward-focused activities. While this may present challenges of coordination, it means that change can be achieved by a lot of people doing a little, rather than by a few having to do everything. This is a more effective use of organisational energy and makes it less likely any key player will burn-out through work overload.

Possibly the most important difference between appreciative inquiry and other approaches is that appreciative inquiry views organisations through a social constructionist lens [4].[3] Approaching the organisation from this perspective, we view it primarily as a social system that creates, through language, an understanding of itself and of the social world in which it exists. This social world is the context within which possibilities for action do, or don't, exist. As we work to change the social world, through working with perceptions, connections, stories and belief systems, so we work to change the potential for action.

Compared to the facts-and-data approach to change, which owes allegiance to the premises of hard science, appreciative inquiry is more akin to anthropology, ethnology or sociology, all of which are interested in the meaning given to objects, the myths, rituals, group norms and mores, the beliefs held by the group about appropriate behaviour that govern the boundaries of the acceptable, the power structures, and the stories told and their significance. This makes appreciative inquiry as an approach to organisational growth and change particularly interesting to those of us who, as psychologists, were trained in the scientific method, yet who also recognise the validity and effectiveness of a social constructionist perspective. As a practitioner, I feel I spend a lot of time balancing on this edge, living in both world views.

How Does Appreciative Inquiry Engage with Organisational Problems?

This is a frequently encountered, valid question. Let's start by clarifying what we mean by problems and problem-solving.

We solve problems all the time, very effectively, and we tend, as a default linguistic habit, to refer to most challenges in life as problems. When problem-solving we tend to formulate the issue as a question that needs answering, assemble some data, analyse options against some criteria, select the best option and then implement our decision. For example, I have to organise the logistics of my consultant life. Not so long ago I had to get from a full day's delivery in Dublin in Ireland to Truro in Cornwall for the following afternoon. This turned out to be quite complicated. Solving the 'how to get from A to B within a given timetable, ensuring I arrive fresh enough to work' involved researching options to identify the optimal modes of travel, finding overnight accommodation, and paying close attention to all the timings so I didn't miss any connections. It's the kind of challenge that makes my brain melt, but I knew it would be, and it was, solvable with the application of information gathering, logic and brain power. I am sure this kind of logic-based problem-solving is very familiar to you.

Organisations, of course, deal with many problems like this all the time, trying to work out what the profit margin is on item Z, or to ascertain the optimal machinery layout in the floor space available and, on the whole, a logic-based problem-solving approach works very well in these situations. This means that the more traditional change methodologies can be applied here and will help move things forward.

The difficulties arise, in my experience, when the problem under consideration is not of this nature: when it is not a rational, logical, or analytical problem – for example, when the question is not 'What is the most cost-effective way to work?' but rather, 'How are we going to get people to work differently?' Many organisational change and development challenges are of this nature. These include recurring challenges such as, 'How can we boost morale?', 'How do we increase employee engagement?' or 'How can we get departments to work better together?' These are not easily answered through a traditional problem-solving approach because they are essentially psychological and social challenges, not logical challenges.

Joanna Wilde refers to these kinds of challenges as 'wicked' problems' [5]. She defines wicked problems as those that are difficult or impossible to solve because they are social in nature, and they exist in a constantly changing environment. She says, 'A wicked problem is a problem whose social complexity means that it has no determinable stopping point'. In other words, it can be hard to grasp what the challenge actually is, and even if you think you do, the situation is changing all the time, meaning that any 'solution' is likely to be subject to further disruption. Wilde also points that, 'because of complex interdependencies, the effort to solve one aspect of a wicked problem may reveal or create other problems'. In other words, when working with a 'wicked' problem, unexpected outcomes, including new problems, are to be expected.

I think this description of the characteristics of a wicked problem gives a very good flavour of the kind of organisational challenge with which organisations can run into difficulties. They are challenges of a different order, and they require a different approach. This distinction is not always appreciated by organisations who only have one set of change tools at their disposal, often those of traditional problem-solving. Awareness of the mismatch between traditional ways of thinking about helping organisations develop and the basis of approaches such as appreciative inquiry stimulated a questioning of the fundamental thinking behind organisational development as a discipline and practice and led to the emergence of a new approach: dialogic organisational development.

What Is Dialogic Organisational Development?

In 2009 Bushe and Marshak coined the phrase 'dialogic organisational development' to reflect this new understanding of how to work with organisations to achieve change. To help distinguish it from what had gone before, they named the more traditional approaches diagnostic organisational development. In 2015 they brought the different strands of thinking that informed this emerging field of practice together into a seminal book [6], organised a conference, and initiated a conversation about this.[4] Even more recently they have published a series of short practitioner-oriented books each focused on a different aspect of dialogic organisational development.[5] As an emerging field the terrain and boundaries of dialogic organisational development are still being established, but it is clear that appreciative inquiry fits well. Let's explore the difference between the two schools they identify, diagnostic and dialogic, in a little more detail.

The diagnostic approach to organisational development is likely to be familiar to you. This way of thinking, which Bushe calls the conventional mindset, talks about organisations in the abstract, as systems, as things, as parts, that can be moved around and reconfigured. It sees organisations as made up of independent, autonomous, rational individuals and groups. At the centre is the idea of the heroic leader whose vision and wisdom can steer their organisation to success. These leaders believe in rational, analytical ways of making decisions. Perhaps unaware of the importance of context to implementation, they gravitate towards one-size-fits-all solutions. And, while they might be cognizant of uncertainty and ambiguity, they usually act, and encourage others to act, as if there was certainty and predictability. Their actions are predicated on the belief that leaders can control what happens in organisations.

Working from this perspective to achieve change, the process is to name the problem, diagnose the fault, and then fix it. This approach tends to produce logic like: 'Sales have been dropping, why?' 'Because the sales team aren't selling very well'. 'Okay, then we need training for the sales team'. However, a moment's thought reveals there may be any number of reasons sales have fallen, many of which may bear little relation to the selling ability of the sales team. Organisations frequently make these jumps in logic, driven by the need to solve the problem efficiently, that is, with minimum expenditure of time and effort, rather than effectively, that is, in a way that works.

The dialogic approach spreads its net a little wider. In particular it recognises the key role of the processes of sense-making and storytelling within organisations. People engage with what they see, hear and are told in ways that make sense to them in the context of their experience. Dialogic organisational development appreciates that the 'reality' of what is going on from one perspective, and the sense people are making of it from another, may bear only a passing acquaintance; but it also recognises that it is the sense people are making and the explanatory stories they are sharing that fuel their ambitions and actions. Therefore, of key interest is the question, 'How are people making sense of things and what stories do they tell to explain things?' This meaning-making offers a point of intervention to achieve change.

Similarly, in contrast to a common view that people have huge agency in organisations, and that an inability to get things is due to some personal failing, dialogic organisational development recognises people's interdependence and how people constrain and enable each other. It recognises that no one can control what everyone else is choosing to do and that often they can't get much done without the consent of others. It is this aspect of organisations that can be seen to explain why leaders often feel, despite their position of power, powerless to influence their own organisation. The dialogic approach emphasises that change is what emerges from the interplay of all the choices, intentions and strategies of all the stakeholders, and that this can result in both intended and unintended outcomes. Recognising and working with interdependencies is another point of intervention to achieve change.

Dialogic organisational development also argues that that far from being purely rational, people are emotional and that their emotional states, their likes and dislikes, their hopes and anxieties, affect what they believe and how they behave, offering yet another sphere of intervention to achieve change.

Frustrating though it can be for organisations that are used to working in a command-and-control way, when viewed through this dialogic lens situations are understood to be so uncertain and the local contingencies and context so important that generic tools are of very little value; rather the organisational intervention needs to be very context-specific. And instead of the logic for the change being dictated from the top, each person involved needs to go on a personal journey of discovery and change to arrive at a place where the changes make sense and are meaningful and motivating in their own social world. Appreciative inquiry offers a way to do this that is faster, more effective and more sustainable than the time-honoured approach of pushing the change onto the organisation, an approach which often provokes high degrees of foot-dragging resistance or inertia-inducing incomprehension. Appreciative inquiry is one of the most established dialogic organisational development interventions.

To summarise, these two approaches encourage organisations to focus on different things. The diagnostic approach encourages and focuses on problem-solving, creating detailed plans, directing, having the answers, monitoring, fault-finding and rigid control of plan breaches. While, by contrast, the dialogic approach focuses on creating conditions for change, problem-setting (note the difference from problem-solving), co-creating, having questions, coordinating actions, creating coherence, directing the organisation's attention and nurturing growth by amplifying small changes in the right direction. Compared with a more formal problem-solving approach, some of this sounds very fuzzy. In the light of this, given the emphasis on evidence-based practice as the gold standard, it is important to explore how, while working in the field applying dialogic thinking and appreciative inquiry practice to organisational challenges, practitioners can meet these standards.

How Can We Ensure That Our Appreciative Inquiry Practice with Organisations Is Evidence-Based?

Wilde has some very interesting things to say about all this. She argues that the laboratory is about, and works with, controlled problems, while the field, as we have seen, presents us with wicked problems. To bridge the divide, she argues, knowledge needs to change its nature as it moves from research to practice. The emphasis needs to switch from 'know what' to 'know how'. Research-produced knowledge needs to be mobilised in a way that influences policy and practice within organisations, while our understanding of consultancy needs to shift from a knowledge-driven method' to a 'helping-based practice' if we are going to bring the benefits of the research to the field. What she is essentially saying is that telling people about the research, while it may be experienced as interesting, doesn't necessarily lead to change in practices. Many an academic making the switch from working as a lecturer to providing consultancy has discovered this. The slides, dense with details of significance, that may hold essay-encumbered students' attention rarely have the same impact on action-oriented managers and leaders. Instead of boring them to death with highly informative PowerPoints, we have to find a way of putting the knowledge into practice to produce change. We can always supply the underlying research details if requested.

Inexperienced consultants, especially when trying to introduce a new approach such as appreciative inquiry to a leadership team, are often concerned that they need a detailed research case to persuade organisations to adopt this new approach. And in recognition of this request I do provide some of this when teaching appreciative inquiry; no harm having it all up your sleeve. In practice though, most managers aren't academics, and what they're buying isn't your academic knowledge so much as something different, namely your practice expertise.

'Practice', says Wilde, 'is the process by which knowledge from one situation is converted into a different form designed to be effective for the particular situation at hand; it must judge itself by "impact" and not by the "facts" it generates'. And she adds, in a comment I wholeheartedly agree with, 'It is the dynamic nature of translating knowledge into changing complex environments that makes the work [of consulting to organisations] engaging and rewarding'. The beauty of appreciative inquiry, to my mind, is that this is exactly what it does. It provides a ready-to-go practice methodology, based on good science. Meanwhile, positive psychology as a recent research discipline has produced a mountain of research that supports the practice of appreciative inquiry, some of which is introduced in Chapter 2.

Following this, we can see that there is a need to define what we mean by 'evidence-based practice' for working in the field. In this spirit, Barends and colleagues [7] in 2014 suggested that field evidence-based practice can be defined as 'making decisions through the conscientious, explicit and judicious use of four sources of information: practitioner expertise and judgement, evidence from the local context, a critical evaluation of the best available research evidence, and the perspectives of those people who might be affected by the decision'. This sounds like an excellent take on the challenge to me.

Also thinking this way, Jacobs and colleagues [8] noted that the way the change intervention was conducted, what he called the implementation climate, was a critical factor for effectively influencing change. In particular he noted the need to work with staff and managers to co-create expectations. I argue that appreciative inquiry fits these definitions of evidence-based practice from the field. It is a social psychology–based approach to organisational change and development, and as such is predicated on a particular understanding of the nature of both organisations and people, that is delivered in a contextualised way using practitioner expertise and judgement, fully involving those to be affected by decisions made. To be accepted as a robust, evidence-based methodology, appreciative inquiry cannot be presented as the panacea to all organisational ills. It needs to be open to critique.

Critiquing Appreciative Inquiry

An important aspect of being evidence-based is to be able to be critical of both method and findings. Critiques of appreciative inquiry are in short supply, as a number of researchers have noted. For example, Van der Haar and Hosking noted in the early 2000s [9] that within the appreciative inquiry literature at that time both evaluation studies and critical reflections were rare, suggesting that critical reflection needed to become a core practice within appreciative inquiry. Given the paucity of critique I was able to find for this section, I would suggest this is still a valid criticism. Even so, we can identify the application of a critical lens to the theory in the decades after its first announcement.

In 2002 Patton [10] criticised appreciative inquiry for its emphasis on positive stories, suggesting that it was therefore unrealistic and unbalanced. This criticism is alive and kicking, often expressed as a belief that appreciative inquiry ignores or downplays the negative. We address this in detail in Chapter 3, but just to say here that this criticism is associated with a misunderstanding of the true nature of appreciative inquiry practice. Another researcher, Reed [11], argued that there was a danger of appreciative inquiry ignoring power imbalances, and he warned that it should not confuse collaboration with democracy, since without the support of powerful players in an organisation, the outcomes of the appreciative inquiry work risked being sidelined. I learnt the truth of this the hard way and find this to be a very important point of potential weakness. Throughout this book and elsewhere [12][6] I emphasise the need to work closely with leaders and other powerful players in the system. This is addressed in more detail in Chapter 5.

Drew and Wallis [13] argued that appreciative inquiry wouldn't be the first choice in any situation with an urgent need to solve a problem or deal with a crisis. Again this is a sentiment with which I happily concur: if the situation is critical, speed is of the essence, and if people are in such a panic they can barely think, then their greatest need may be to be rescued to a sufficiently safe place that they can once again engage their brains. If I were drowning, I would just want the person on the bank to throw me a rope and tell me to grab it. Only once I was safe would I be able to think about anything beyond my immediate survival. Teams and other organisational systems are, very occasionally, in this state, in which case they are likely to benefit more, in the immediate term, from knowledgeable expert direction.

Schooley [14] also raises a good point, noting that in situations such as public sector government not all stakeholders can be 'brought into the room' or forced to participate in an appreciative inquiry summit. Having made this point, they ask whether it is ethical to agree to follow the consensus of the people who participated in an appreciative inquiry process while ignoring those who chose not to participate. What about the issue of the common good? While there are some problems with the notion of appreciative inquiry being a consensus based decision-making process, it a valid concern, and I think there are ways to address this, which we explore more in Chapter 3.

Rogers and Fraser [15] extended the critique from the process to the practitioner, noting the need for good and particular facilitation and group work skills to manage and guide the process. They warn that without affirmatory facilitation and group work skills to apply the 4D cycle appropriately (as the core appreciative inquiry methodology was commonly known then and which is explained fully in Chapter 2), appreciative inquiry could go dangerously wrong. For example, avoiding hard issues and uncomplimentary data could lead to vacuous, self-congratulatory findings or even worse, could provide a platform for airing vengeful and destructive sentiment. This again is a criticism to take seriously. When I first discovered appreciative inquiry and started practicing it, I underestimated how much my ability in this new approach rested on my many previous years' experience of group work, facilitation, and indeed skills acquired in my previous career as a residential social worker.

However, it is worth noting that appreciative inquiry is a flexible process, and while adherence to the principles that underpin practice is important (these are explained in Chapter 2), there are many ways to work from the appreciative inquiry perspective. The art is to work out how you can bring your particular strengths and skills to support your appreciative practice.

Conclusion

This chapter has introduced appreciative inquiry as a practice, exploring its place in the field of organisational development. It has noted that appreciative inquiry fits within the definition of a dialogic organisational development approach and that it is particularly appropriate for engaging with problems that are 'wicked' in nature. In addition, the chapter has explored the wider issues of ensuring evidence-based practice and of acknowledging and accommodating critiques of appreciative inquiry. In Chapter 2 we build on this by looking in more detail at the core and original practice of appreciative inquiry, the 5D summit.

Learning Points

1. Appreciative inquiry is based in a social constructionist, sense-making view of the social world of organisations.
2. It is suitable for 'wicked' organisational problems.
3. It can be seen as a dialogic organisational development approach.

4. It is an effective container to bring research from science to the field of practice.
5. It can be critiqued, and care must be taken in practice to ensure these potential critiques are addressed.

Discussion Questions

1. How would you characterise the difference between appreciative inquiry and more traditional approaches to change?
2. How would you distinguish dialogic and diagnostic organisational development?
3. What are the challenges of achieving gold-standard evidence-based practice in the field, and how can they be addressed?
4. What might be some of the challenges of introducing appreciative inquiry to an organisation?

Teaching Practice

1. Divide the class into two groups or more. Get each to prepare a brief talk for their colleagues that outlines, for either a dialogic or diagnostic approach to change, the benefits, the risks, and some possible organisational situations or challenges appropriate for its adoption.

Resources and Further Reading

There are many good texts available about appreciative inquiry. See for example:
Lewis, S., Passmore, J., and Cantore, S. (2016). *Appreciative Inquiry for Change Management Using AI to Facilitate Organizational Development*, 2e. London: Kogan Page Chapters 1 and 2.
Watkins, J.M. and Mohr, B.J. (2001). *Appreciative Inquiry: Change at the Speed of Imagination*. San Francisco, CA: Jossey-Bass/Pfeiffer Chapter 2.
Whitney, D. and Trosten-Bloom, A. (2003). *The Power of Appreciative Inquiry: A Practical Guide to Positive Change*. San Francisco: Berrett-Koehler Chapter 4.
Barrett, F.J. and Fry, R. (2005). *Appreciative Inquiry: A Positive Approach to Building Cooperative Capacity*. Chagrin Falls, OH: Taos Institute Publications Chapter 1.

For online resources see

David Cooperrider, Center for Appreciative Inquiry at Champlain College, 251 South Willard Street, Burlington, VT 05401, USA. http://Appreciativeinquiry.champlain.edu
www.aipractitioner.com.

Finally, there are many good resources in the footnotes and references sections. See particularly the Bushe and Marshak text on Dialogic OD, and Joanne Wilde's book on the social psychology of organisations.

Notes

1. David L. Cooperrider Center for Appreciative Inquiry at Champlain College, 251 South Willard Street, Burlington, VT 05401, USA. http://Appreciativeinquiry.champlain.edu.
2. https://aipractitioner.com/
3. Social constructionism is a philosophical approach to the nature of reality and knowledge.
4. The Dialogic Salon Series hosted by the Bushe-Marshak Institute and featuring all the authors in conversation with each other and the audience.
5. The Bushe-Marshak Institute Book Series can be found here https://b-m-institute.com/bmi-series-in-od.
6. As the title suggests, this is all about preparing an organisation for a dialogic intervention, such as appreciative inquiry.

References

1. Cooperrider, D. and Srivastva, S. (2001). Appreciative inquiry in organizational life. In: *Appreciative Inquiry: An Emerging Direction for Organizational Development* (ed. D. Cooperrider, P.F. Sorenson Jnr., T. Yaegar, and D. Whitney). Stipes Publishing L.L.C.
2. Spreitzer, G.M. and Sonenshein, S. (2003). Positive deviance and extraordinary organising. In: *Positive Organizational Scholarship: Foundations of a New Discipline* (ed. K.S. Cameron, J.E. Dutton, and R.E. Quinn), 207–224. Berrett-Koehler.
3. Lewis, S., Passmore, J., and Cantore, S. (2016). *Appreciative Inquiry for Change Management: Using AI to Facilitate Organizational Development*, 2e. London: Kogan Page.
4. Gergen, M. and Gergen, K. (2003). *Social Construction: A Reader*. London: Sage.

5. Wilde, J. (2016). *The Social Psychology of Organizations: Diagnosing Toxicity and Intervening in the Workplace*. London: Routledge All the quotes from Wilde in the text are from this book.
6. Bushe, G.R. and Marshak, R.J. (ed.) (2015). *Dialogic Organisational Development: The Theory and Practice of Organisational Change*. Oakland: Berrett-Koehler.
7. Barends, E., Janssen, B., ten Have, W., and ten Have, S. (2014). Effects of change interventions: what kind of evidence do we really have? *Journal of Applied Behavioral Science* 50 (1): 5–27.
8. Jacobs, S.R., Weiner, B.J., Reeve, B.B. et al. (2015). Determining the predictors of innovation implementation in healthcare: a quantitative analysis of implementation effectiveness. *BMC Health Services Research* 15 (1): 6.
9. Van Der Haar, D. and Hosking, D.M. (2004). Evaluating appreciative inquiry: a relational constructionist perspective. *Human Relations* 57 (8): 1017–1036.
10. Patton, M.Q. (2002). *Qualitative Research and Evaluation Methods*, 3e. Thousand Oaks, CA: Sage.
11. Reed, J. (2007). *Appreciative Inquiry: Research for Change*. Thousand Oaks: Sage.
12. Lewis, S. (2021). *Creating Energized Commitment to the Dialogic Approach: The Change Team's Journey of Discovery*, BMI Series in Dialogic Organisational Development. BMI Publishing.
13. Drew, S.A.W. and Wallis, J.L. (2004). The use of appreciative inquiry in the practices of large-scale organisational change a review and critique. *Journal for General Management* 39 (4): 3–26.
14. Schooley, S.E. (2012). Using appreciative inquiry to engage the citizenry: four potential challenges for public administrators. *International Journal of Public Administration* 35 (5): 340–351.
15. Rogers, P.J. and Fraser, D. (2003). Appreciating appreciative inquiry. In: *Using Appreciative Inquiry in Evaluation* (ed. H. Preskill and A.T. Coghlan), 75–84. San Francisco, CA: Jossey-Bass.

2

The Appreciative Inquiry Summit

Appreciative inquiry can perhaps be summarised as a process that works to refocus people's attention; generate new information and new perspectives; create new mental maps and connections; grow more of what is wanted in the organisation; *dis*-solve rather than *re*-solve problems; and affirm the best in people and situations using a remarkably flexible, robust and adaptable core model.

This chapter introduces the core 5D model[1] (see Figure 2.1), which acts as a guide to undertaking an appreciative inquiry intervention. The five stages of the model are usually named as define, discover, dream, design and destiny, although some practitioners have added further Ds, such as drumming, dancing and doing, to better fit their philosophy, client group or mode of working. Each of the core 5Ds will be explained from a practice-oriented perspective to create some initial understanding of how the intervention works.

In addition, this chapter introduces the principles of practice, thoroughly explaining the philosophical ideas that support their efficacy. The chapter concludes with a consideration of some of the research that supports appreciative inquiry as an effective change process.

Introducing the 5D Model of Appreciative Inquiry

1. Stage one: *defining the topic of inquiry*

The first step in an appreciative inquiry process is to define the topic of inquiry. Deciding what this might be often involves creating a 'flip' in the conversation from the original presenting issue, which is usually a problem

---

Practical Appreciative Inquiry: A Toolkit for Applying Appreciative Inquiry to Organisational Challenges, Opportunities, and Aspiration, First Edition. Sarah Lewis.
© 2025 John Wiley & Sons Ltd. Published 2025 by John Wiley & Sons Ltd.

The Appreciative Inquiry 5D Model of Practice

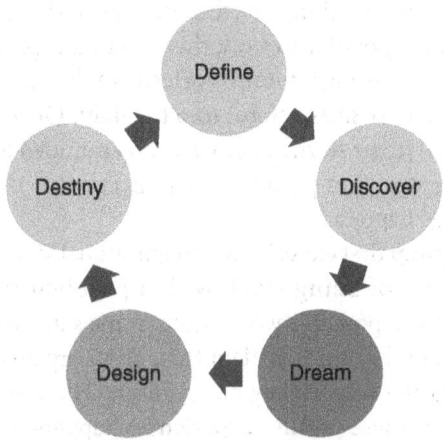

Figure 2.1 The 5D model of appreciative inquiry.

statement, towards the articulation of an aspiration. If this step is omitted, and the problem statement continues to be the focus of attention, then the unintentional effect can be to amplify the problem as the magnifying beam of concentrated attention acts to enlarge it in our field of view.

For example, an organisation might identify that a lack of teamwork across organisational boundaries is causing problems. Typically, they would start to investigate the depth, scale, impact etc. of the problem. Taking an appreciative inquiry approach, however, the organisation would say to itself 'If that is what we don't want, what is it we do want? What do we want more of?' In this instance the answer might be: 'We want more effective interdepartmental communication and problem-solving at the lowest organisational level possible. We want issues to be addressed between departments as and when they arise. More than that, we want departments to proactively consult with each other about plans they have that might impact on another department'. This answer gives a sense of the organisational aspirations and so ideas for defining the topic of inquiry. In this instance the topic for inquiry might be 'excellent interdepartmental working and effective low-level problem solving'.

2. Stage two: discovering the best of the present

This stage is about revealing current great practice from which the future can be imaginatively created. For example in the hypothetical case above, we would ask people about their best experiences of working across organisational boundaries. Questions might include asking people to share their best experiences of working like this, then exploring what difference it made, or what made it possible to work this way in this particular situation. Asking such questions brings untold stories (untold because no one ever asked about these experiences before) into the light. Once in the light they can be shared, added to the stories of others, and examined for their learning. As more and more stories of positive experiences come to light, a number of interesting things happen.

Generally, the group first experiences an emotional shift from the doom-and-gloom position of being stuck with a problem to a more joyful sentiment of hope and possibility. Secondly, at the same time their view of the present shifts as it becomes evident that, as an organisation, they have more resources to call on than they had realised. The stories are evidence, but until the inquiry, these positive experiences happened in an unnoticed, isolated, and unconnected way. Thirdly, the stories provide data of what is needed to enable such cooperation to occur; and finally, they offer a springboard of hope and possibility.

Before going on to consider the rest of the 5D model, it is worth pausing to notice the power for change inherent in just asking about and connecting stories of the positive in organisations. The discovery interview is a highly versatile approach that can be taken into many areas of organisational life as outlined in Figure 2.2 below.

Throughout this chapter we will be looking at the evidence base for appreciative inquiry. Positive psychology in particular proves to be a good

---

Further Uses of Discovery Interviews

To create, raise or change mood so positively affecting morale and enhancing change abilities

To access personal resources so increasing individual or group resourcefulness

To discover differences that make a difference by comparing with not quite so great experiences

To boost confidence by the naming of abilities

To boost resilience through generating memories of success

To boost problem solving abilities by bringing previous solutions found to light

To identify strengths which helps with performance, confidence, self-esteem

To identify success factors from the past that might be useful for the current challenges

---

Figure 2.2 Further uses of discovery interviews.

source of supporting research. For example, the discovery process is supported by research into positive deviance, strengths, positive affect, flow, psychological capital, high quality connections, constructive responding and mindfulness.[2]

3. Stage three: dreaming of a better future

The dream phase of the model is focused on creating attractive images of the future towards which the organisation might grow. One of the things that makes appreciative inquiry different from other change processes is that the imagined future state is developed from the known reality of what is possible. In this sense it is not 'blue sky thinking', it is more a form of grounded dreaming, an expansion of the actual into the possible. Essentially the dreaming stage of appreciative inquiry asks, 'How would our world be if more of these good things were happening more of the time? What would I be doing the same or differently? What conversations would I be having with whom and about what?' In this way the group or organisation can co-create positive aspirations for the future based on growing more of the best of the present.

The dreaming phase is very important, and yet often it's the phase people struggle most to get to grips with. I think it is partly the terminology 'dreaming' and partly the nature of the exercise. The terminology question is an easy one to address: there is no imperative to announce, 'We are now going to do some dreaming', if such an assertion would be detrimental to the event. Appreciative inquiry is a context specific methodology; therefore adapting such things as the words used to describe the activity to the local context is totally appropriate. Different words mean different things in different contexts; pick those that work in yours.

The second challenge is the nature of the activity. The dreaming phase is essentially an exercise in imagination, and done well, it releases an energy of playfulness. Organisations are sometimes concerned that their people may not be able to engage in such frivolities. They feel that somehow to ask engineers, accountants, or senior managers to use their imaginations and to be playful is not appropriate, or may even be disrespectful. The thing to appreciate is that this is not a role-play exercise; it is a 'social group' exercise. Play is a very important aspect of social groups whether families or sport teams, and it is key to social bonding. Neurodiversity notwithstanding, we all have the power of imagination. What might be unusual is the request that people access this ability in a work context. However, the transformational power of the dream process lies as much in this deviation from 'work as usual' as in the building of a much denser picture of possible and desirable futures.

The ambition of the dream phase is to help the group co-create images of the best possible future based on the known best of the past, and then to find engaging ways to share their dreams. Personally, I have used collage materials, drawing, postcards and stickers, pipe cleaners, playlets, plasticine, raps, poems and Lego with groups to encourage a creative, connected and engaging expression of their dream. Other practitioners, to my knowledge, have used sandboxes, music, dance, photography and film. The variety of creative possibilities is immense.

Once again, we can identify the positive psychology research that supports this activity. I would suggest that in the dream stage we are inducing playfulness, a positive emotional state. The dream phase also encourages the creation of dense future zones with stories of the future that reveal strengths and resources, and it creates desirable goals, connected to the idea of a worthwhile life and positive energy networks. At the same, it builds social capital and relational reserves. Dreaming is a highly creative activity, but how to select amongst the possibilities produced and how to make them real? These challenges are addressed through the design and destiny phases.

4. Stage four: designing for better futures

In the design phase consideration is given to what needs to be different in the present to increase the likelihood that the organisation will develop in the direction of the imagined attractive futures. One approach is to review the architecture of the organisation to see which design aspects are key to creating different futures. For example, there may be a realisation that recruitment needs to be done differently, that key decision-making board memberships need shaking up, or that everyone needs an easily accessible directory of the people in the organisation.

As explained earlier, the dream phase encourages people to immerse themselves in an imagined best future, and this makes it easier for people to quickly focus in on the key things that are likely to make an important difference. For example, asking them while they are still enmeshed in their dreams of the future to look back and identify the changes that allowed this new future to emerge from the old past makes it possible to create a 'path of possibility' from the present to the desired future.

In this way, the plan of change is created from two sources: what can be built on what is already working and what needs creating. Research into the positive emotional states of innovation, creativity, hope, mental flexibility, intellectual curiosity and concordant goals supports the effectiveness of the design activities.

5. Stage five: achieving our destiny

The final of the 5Ds is destiny. Destiny is what happens next, and, as the word implies, is dependent on what has gone before. In other words, the quality of the collective event is key to the power of the afterlife of the event. It is very important to grasp that the event is not just a prelude to the 'real action' that happens when everyone 'goes back into the organisation'. It *is* the action. However, of course, at some point the event ends and the organisation reverts to its usual pattern.

Destiny is about what happens at this point, about how the energy, ideas and momentum for change created by the event are sustained and brought into the 'business as usual' of organisational life. There are generally two key ways this happens. Firstly individuals, through the experience of the event, will have developed new relationships with their colleagues and will have experienced them differently as they have worked together through the process. They will have developed their own motivation to move towards their attractive future and so will probably go away inspired to do different things and do things differently. In addition, groups of people may well have coalesced around particular projects that they are fired up to make happen, and so work groups or project groups may emerge out of the event. As Bushe says, one of the characteristics of the generative effect of appreciative inquiry is that 'few arrive wanting more work: few leave without having volunteered for cooperative action'.[3] This phenomenon is part of the excitement and magic of appreciative inquiry processes; they work at a very human level to inspire collective action towards shared goals.

Positive psychology research into strengths, social relationships and worthwhile goals supports this phase. In addition, working with the volunteer principle (more on this in Chapter 3) enacts self-determination theory, that is, generates autonomy, intrinsic motivation and relatedness. The 5D cycle, and the practice of appreciative inquiry in a more general sense, is built on some key principles.

The Principles of Appreciative Inquiry

Understanding the principles is key to being able to practice appreciative inquiry flexibly and responsively. Once they are understood, it is possible to bring an appreciative approach to many different organisational challenges. As with the model, the original five principles articulated by Cooperrider and Whitney [1][4] have been expanded upon by others. Please see both the original and some additional principles in Figure 2.3. Seven of these are expanded upon below.

1. The poetic principle

The poetic principle highlights our understanding of organisations as groups of people collectively involved in making sense of the world, and of then acting into that understanding. The choice of the word *poetic* is to emphasis the idea that our social world, or our organisation, is created in language, that as members of an organisation we co-author stories about it or the story of it. It suggests that understanding, or sense-making, is a social endeavour, and no one has a complete picture of reality. From this perspective, it can be seen that knowledge of 'reality' or 'truth' is always partial, and that people are continually having to make judgements about what might be the best thing to do from within an imperfect understanding of the situation. The poetic principle encourages an understanding of the organisation as a living human system, generated by those within it, that is open to creativity and growth, rather than as an inanimate machine following predetermined procedures and routines. The collective sense-making necessary to achieve coordination and growth is enhanced by the appreciative principle of wholeness.

2. The wholeness principle

Appreciative inquiry suggests that, contrary to normal practice, it is much more efficient and effective to have everyone party to any proposed change present from the very beginning, taking part in discussions and influencing ideas for the future as they unfold. This is because, firstly, bringing everyone together means more of the pieces of the puzzle are available, resulting in better informed decisions. Secondly, it reduces the challenge of 'selling' the outcome to those who were absent, speeding up the process of change. And

The original five principles

The Poetic Principle views the organization as a living system, meaning that the organization is a social creation. Each day people breathe life into the structures and processes of the organization and co-create the lived reality. The stories we tell about our organization and ourselves affect our future actions.

The Constructionist Principle captures the understanding that what we focus on becomes our reality: that reality is socially constructed. We have choices about what we inquire into, where we focus our attention and how we talk together. All these choices influence what is brought into the light and what remains hidden in our shared reality.

The Simultaneity Principle recognises that everything is connected. The data gathered is determined by the questions asked. The actions taken are determined by the conversations held. We live in a systemic world where talk and action or question and intervention are intimately connected.

The Anticipatory Principle focuses on the importance of creating visions of what is desired before making decisions about how to achieve it. Attractive images of the future are powerful motivators for change that draw us forward through challenges and difficulties. The richer the picture of the best possible future we create for ourselves, the greater the likelihood that we will grow towards it.

The Positive Principle recognises that change takes energy and that energy is a renewable and depletable resource. Positive energy is generated by the desire to achieve attractive futures. It can be created and recreated by imagining positive futures and by reliving positive moments from the past and in this way is a sustainable form of energy.

Five additional principles

The Narrative Principle recognises that we live in a storied world where we continually construct stories about our lives, the world and our place in it. Changing the story creates the potential for further change, affects future possibilities and can, in that way, become transformational.

The Enactment Principle encourages us to do what we can now to embody the change we want to see rather than deferring action to some future point of perfect knowledge. It encourages us to engage in sense-making rather than decision-making, to try things out and learn by doing. It is associated with the idea of running prototypes of ideas for change.

The Wholeness Principle reminds us of the importance of having the whole system in the room when working to achieve change. It recognises that wholeness provides more expansive thinking than reductionism, leading to greater creativity. It recognizes that people both influence, and are influenced by, what is emerging in the whole system.

The Free Choice Principle is another way of stating the idea of the volunteer principle, which recognizes that when people are able to engaged through free choice with the process as a whole and every part of it, their engagement is much more likely to be constructive, energized, motivated and meaningful.

The Awareness Principle asks us to be mindful in understanding and integrating the appreciative inquiry principles in our practice, to recognize that context is always important and always coming into being. Appreciative inquiry is an aware practice, not a recipe. This principle encourages us to practice cycles of action and reflection, where we act, reflect, and then act again with reflective awareness

Figure 2.3 Principles.

thirdly, the shared mental maps developed at appreciative inquiry events help people coordinate their post-event activities, reducing implementation costs.

One of appreciative inquiry's most powerful insights is the realisation that to effect change in the inevitably incomplete mental maps that drive our behaviour is to create change 'in reality'. The new thinking that results as maps shift is often captured in a metaphor that encapsulates something of importance for the group. Metaphors and ideas that a group generate for themselves are likely to be highly inspiring and motivating. We explore this generative process, and its close relative creativity, further in Chapter 9. This emphasis on sense-making leads us to think about the nature of stories, narrative and storytelling in organisations. The role of storytelling, creating accounts of what is going on, is key to the process of appreciative inquiry. Let us explore that further by looking at the narrative principle.

Narrative, Stories and Sensemaking in Appreciative Inquiry

3. The narrative principle

A story can also be thought of as a narrative. Boje [2] presents some very interesting ideas about something he refers to as 'ante-narrative', that is, 'the fragmented, non-linear, incoherent, collective, unplotted pre-narrative speculation'. This, I believe, can be understood as the undigested life-in-the-organisation experience, the raw untold experience, the state of experience before it has been wrangled into some account of what's happening, or has happened, an account capable of being told and shared. In other words, before a story of incidents or events has been created, the situation is in a state of ante-narrative, and it is this ante-narrative state that is the fuel for the stories told about organisational life. This is a state of huge potentiality, when many possible ways of articulating the experience are available for selection and enhancement. Those stories not selected usually quickly wither and die and, very soon, the story told becomes the only possible story. This, being repeated and embellished, quickly becomes the truth; all potential alternatives are lost to view. However, any social grouping is likely to contain more than one version of 'the truth'. The creation of a 'true' narrative is something people do continually, and these narratives do not always align.

Stories or narrative are created from ante-narrative when people 'give account' of themselves, when they are called to explain what happened, or what they are doing. Stories are created out of the flowing river of lived experience. They are about making sense. On a different day, or if something changes, they might tell a different story, or the story differently. It is this *dynamic* nature of stories that we work with in organisations when we work in an appreciative way, as we encourage people to 'give account' of experiences they have not shared before. We want to work at the edge between the ante-narrative and the narrative, the point at which sense is being made. This is where the opportunity for creativity, and change, can lie.

However, organisations often do not like this edge, and instead put a lot of energy into trying to form a grand metanarrative, under which all the organisation's stories can fall. You can hear this when people say things like, 'Let's get this straight, let's get our ducks in a row on this. Let's make sure we are all singing from the same hymn sheet'. The problem is that many stories circulating in the organisation will not fit this grand metanarrative, so they get pushed underground, out of view, or are seen as oppositional to the metanarrative and so impermissible. People who persist in holding these stories are often labelled as resistant or as uncomprehending. We explore the role of storytelling in appreciative inquiry further in Chapter 9.

4. *The anticipatory principle*

One of the underpinning assumptions of appreciative inquiry is that human systems grow towards attractive images of the future and that such images are motivating. Most people, at an instinctive level know this, and daydreaming about potential achievements encourages us to keep going. The dream phase of the 5D cycle is this principle in action, helping people create positive, anticipatory stories of the future. The anticipatory principle also underpins the idea of flipping the conversation, as we discussed earlier, from what they do not want to what they do want, or perhaps from conversations about the past to those about the future. In all these situations the ambition is to help people create images of what they want to move towards: to create the pull motivation for change.

5. *The simultaneity principle*

The simultaneity principle is expressed succinctly through the statement that 'the inquiry is the intervention'. What is not always evident is that, while the question is the intervention, it can be ineffective in bringing about change if it only reinforces the current stories of the organisation.

Questions that do not bring something new to the conversation are much less likely to be impactful. It is the questions that inquire into unfamiliar territory that are most likely to be highly impactful by producing new stories or accounts of organisational life. In many organisations just being asked about things that work, rather than the problems, is sufficiently different to normal organisational discourse to produce new conversation, connection, insight and emotional states. We look at the nature of impactful appreciative questions more fully in Chapter 3.

6. The positivity principle

The positivity principle states that change takes energy and that positive energy, created by positive emotional states such as enthusiasm, joy, hope, possibility, passion, trust and engagement, is more effective than negatively charged energy in producing sustainable change.

Positive energy is created by reliving positive experiences from the past (discovery phase) and by creating positive, or inspiring, views of the future (dreaming phase). It is these positive future images that ignite energy for change. Motivation of this nature, known as 'pull' motivation, may initially be a slower burn than negatively charged motivation, but it is much more sustainable and indeed can become self-sustaining as the positive effects of the changes made become apparent. By contrast the power of escape or 'push' motivation fades as the threat starts to retreat.

Positive emotional states help build resourcefulness and resilience [3]. When people experience positive emotions they are likely to be relaxed and to feel safe and stress-free enough to engage with and explore the world, broadening their repertoire of skills, knowledge, resources and relationships. Then, when they once again face hard times, they have more resources of all kinds to call on because they have built up their ability to cope.

Meanwhile neuropsychologists have discovered that positive emotional states result in a release of the neurotransmitters serotonin and dopamine, both of which enable the brain to work better and faster and to be more widely connected. In brief this means better information retention and recall, more creativity and the ability to link information better and to better manage complexity. In this way, appreciative inquiry creates the conditions for people to be both working at their cognitive best, and to be in a state where they are more willing and able to relate well to others.

7. The constructionist principle

Another key assumption of the appreciative inquiry approach is that the sensory stream from the outside world has to be sorted in some way. It is not possible to take in everything that is going on in the world around us. People manage the potential sensory overload by searching out some things and ignoring others. What is noticed, amongst all the options, is a reflection of an existing view of what is important in the world. What is found to be important is driven to some extent by an individual's particular focus, which in turn determines the content of their conversation (internal and external). It's a circular process: the more people talk about, think about, and focus on something particular, the more they notice it in the environment. In this way the world is socially constructed; people live, in a very real sense, in the world that they construct in their social interactions.

From these many perspectives that exist in any human system we constantly strive to socially construct, or more accurately to socially co-construct, a sufficiently shared understanding of the world to allow for coordinated, conjoint, coherent action both in the world and in our relationships. And we do this through the medium of language and communication. This leads us to a very useful definition of organisations as 'patterns of communication and meaning' [4].[5] It is these patterns that we work to change when we work dialogically with appreciative inquiry.

This last principle takes us to the heart of appreciative inquiry practice: by focusing on (inquiring into) what we want more of (what we appreciate) we can change the (social) world. And when this is done by a whole system, then the collective accounts of reality are changed. This effectively means the organisation is changed because actions are predicated on an understanding of reality: change the understanding of reality and the possibilities for action are changed. This is often summarised in phrases such as 'we see what we talk about' and 'we can grow more of what we want through inquiring into it'. Appreciative inquiry recognises that if the focus is on problem spotting, problems will be found. Conversely, if the focus is on excellence, excellence will be found.

It is well recognised that attempts to explain how appreciative inquiry works, such as this here, can sound very woolly and 'woo-woo.' And in 2017 Cantore [5] set out to identify supporting evidence for the effectiveness of appreciative inquiry in an attempt to create a firmer research base to support claims of its effectiveness.

Research that Supports Appreciative Inquiry as a Practice

Cantore found that the evidence base needs to be drawn from a wide range of sources and that other areas of research can act as proxy support, as we have seen above with the references to positive psychology research. For example, he cites research suggesting that the ability of an organisation to develop a culture of organisational citizenship behaviour is related to its ability to effect change. Since appreciative inquiry develops a strong collective vision and an innovation climate that encourages psychological empowerment, and since these two things are seen as being the markers of organisational citizenship behaviour, we can argue for its efficacy in effecting change by reference to this research.

More generally, a lot of the literature supporting the effectiveness of appreciative inquiry is case study based. There are many reasons for this, and of course such literature can be criticised on many levels, especially when it is frequently written up by the consultants who undertook the intervention. Even so, case studies may offer useful guidance. Cantore found a number of case studies where appreciative inquiry was found to support the development of excellent nursing practice. He also reports that appreciative inquiry was found to have strengthened the collaborative capacity of the US Marine Environment Agency. He also uncovers evidence that appreciative inquiry has been used successfully to support school reform and in adult learning environments, while yet more researchers relate how appreciative inquiry was used to transform the culture of a US drug offences court. All this suggests there is a rich trove of case studies, which, along with articles in *AI Practitioner*, can be seen to form a good practice base, if not gold standard evidence, of effectiveness.

The Effectiveness of Appreciative Inquiry in Transformational Change

Lastly, Bushe and Kassam [6] undertook a meta-analysis of appreciative inquiry research, in which they found that if appreciative inquiry was used as a transactional change process (i.e. a step change programme, focused on improving what already existed) then it was as effective as any other conventional change process. However, when the process was intentionally transformational, they found that using appreciative inquiry supported the emergence of new thinking and generative images and led to desired shifts that the organisations themselves would consider transformational.

Conclusion

In this chapter we have outlined the key 5D model that is at the heart of the appreciative inquiry process and of which you will find many variations over the coming chapters. We've also looked at seven core principles that underpin both the model and appreciative inquiry in general. Finally, we have seen how appreciative inquiry is supported by the science of positive psychology, and by some empirical case studies. This chapter is of necessity an overview of all these areas. However, there is a wealth of information about the core model and practice of appreciative inquiry freely available on the web. We explore the practicalities of running an appreciative inquiry event in the next chapter.

Learning Points

1. Appreciative inquiry practice is supported by a model and principles.
2. Its efficacy is further supported by research from positive psychology, general psychology and case studies.
3. It is firmly located in a social constructionist understanding of the social world.
4. Key concepts include: mental maps, narrative, story and sense-making.

Discussion Questions

1. What do you find attractive about this way of working with organisations?
2. What do you find confusing?
3. How might you try to introduce these ideas to an organisation?
4. What other psychological research or theory can you think of that might support or refute this model's efficacy?

Teaching Exercises

1. In your next meeting, notice how many questions are devoted towards the positive and how many towards the negative. What impact do these questions have on the way the conversation goes? See if you can frame a question that redirects attention to the positive.
2. Split the group into pairs and have them conduct discovery interviews with each other.

Helpful Resources and Further Reading

For more on the positive psychology that supports appreciative inquiry go to

Lewis, S. (2011). *Positive Psychology at Work: How Positive Leadership and Appreciative Inquiry Create Inspiring Organizations.* Chichester: Wiley Blackwell.

The following texts also give explanations of the 5D model and the principles, as indicated:

Lewis, S., Passmore, J., and Cantore, S. (2016). *Appreciative Inquiry for Change Management: Using AI to Facilitate Organizational Development,* 2e. London: Kogan Page Chapters 4 and 9.

Watkins, J.M. and Mohr, B.J. (2001). *Appreciative Inquiry: Change at the Speed of Imagination.* San Francisco, CA: Jossey-Bass/Pfeiffer Chapter 4.

Whitney, D. and Trosten-Bloom, A. (2003). *The Power of Appreciative Inquiry: A Practical Guide to Positive Change,* 6–10. San Francisco: Berrett-Koehler Chapter 3.

Barrett, F.J. and Fry, R. (2005). *Appreciative Inquiry: A Positive Approach to Building Cooperative Capacity.* Chagrin Falls, OH: Taos Institute Publications Chapters 6 and 7.

Stavros, J.M., Torres, C., and Cooperrider, D.L. (2018). *Conversations Worth Having: Using Appreciative Inquiry to Fuel Productive and Meaningful Engagement.* Berrett-Koehler Publishers Chapter 4.

Both teachers and practitioners might also find the following resources helpful:

- Positive Organisational Development Cards. These contain and briefly explain 20 positive organisational psychology concepts including many of those referred to in the text
- Appreciative Inquiry Cards. These introduce the model, complete with inquiry questions, the principles and a series of image and quote cards

- Positive Emotion Cards. This card set consists of 30 positive emotions. They are explained as are the benefits of experiencing each emotion for the individual and for the workplace

All of these are available from http://www.theppshop.store, and from Amazon in some parts of the world.

Notes

1. The Appreciative Inquiry Model was originally a 4D model, as introduced by Cooperrider and Whitney, as below. It is more common these days to use a five, or even more, D model. The 5D model as presented in this chapter is my preferred model.
2. For more on these positive psychology concepts, and others mentioned in this chapter, see my book *Positive Psychology at Work*.
3. I believe this to be a quote from Gervase Bushe, but I am unable to trace it back to its source. He agrees he is the likely source, but also can't locate where it might be written!
4. This text contains a lot of the original writing and research on appreciative inquiry.
5. Once again, while I cannot be sure of the author of this phrase, I suspect it to be Christine Oliver, and in any case if you are interested in this idea, I highly recommend her text.

References

1. Cooperrider, D. and Whitney, D. (2001). A positive revolution in change: appreciative inquiry. In: *Appreciative Inquiry: An Emerging Direction for Organizational Development* (ed. D. Cooperrider, P.F. Sorenson, T. Yaegar, and D. Whitney). Stipes Publishing L.L.C.
2. Boje, D.M. (2001). *Narrative Methods for Organizational and Communication Research*. Sage.
3. Fredrickson, B. (1998). What good are positive emotions? *Review of General Psychology* 2 (3): 300–319.
4. Oliver, C. (2018). *Reflexive Inquiry: A Framework for Consultancy Practice*. Oxon: Routledge.
5. Cantore, S. (2017). Positive approaches to organizational change. In: *The Psychology of Positivity and Strengths-Based Approaches at Work* (ed. L.G. Oades, M.F. Steger, A. Delle Fave, and J. Passmore), 272–296. Wiley Blackwell.
6. Bushe, G.R. and Kassam, A.F. (2005). When is appreciative inquiry transformational? A meta-case analysis. *Journal of Applied Behavioral Science* 41 (2): 161–181.

3

Preparing, Delivering and Following-up an Event

In broad terms there are three phases to an appreciative inquiry event or summit: before, during and after. Each of these is important to the effectiveness and success of the event. This chapter outlines areas of consideration important to the preparation, delivery and follow-up of an intervention. Important success factors such as careful matching of the appreciative topic to the available participants, the principle of self-organisation, decision-making processes, recording the event, the role of the facilitator, the quality of conversation including the important consideration of psychological safety, the nature of appreciative questions and sticking to the volunteer principle will all be discussed. But first we must remember that appreciative inquiry isn't the answer to all organisational ills and that being alert to contraindications is part of the preparation process, as is recognising and responding to some of the prevalent myths about appreciative inquiry.

Contraindications for an Appreciative Inquiry Event

As an appreciative inquiry practitioner it is important to be aware of the signs that an appreciative inquiry approach is not advisable and to be able to identify the contraindications.

One such situation is when the sponsor or commissioner or other most powerful person in the system believes they have the answer, the only answer, and the right answer to the challenge. Appreciative inquiry is a co-creative process: the way forward emerges from the combined input of knowledge, perspective, resource and aspiration in discussion within a

---

Practical Appreciative Inquiry: A Toolkit for Applying Appreciative Inquiry to Organisational Challenges, Opportunities, and Aspiration, First Edition. Sarah Lewis.
© 2025 John Wiley & Sons Ltd. Published 2025 by John Wiley & Sons Ltd.

structured, containing process. Lots of people may believe they know what needs to be done, but they are not in a position to impose their solution; they have to persuade, which also opens them to persuasion. Leaders, of course, are in a position to ignore the outcome of the process and to instead impose their view.

The general principle is that when someone powerful strongly believes they have the answer, then appreciative inquiry is highly unlikely to be successful. Instead, it can lead straight to cynicism and disaffection in the workforce, making it doubly hard for the next person who attempts a genuine co-creative intervention to garner support and enthusiasm. Personally, I have walked away from potential engagements when it is clear that this is the situation and that what is really being requested is a process that leads everyone to the foregone conclusion, for which, by definition, they have so far been unable to create much enthusiasm, hence their request for a group process to produce the required 'buy-in'. My advice is to be very wary of getting caught up in this scenario.

Another situation that deserves some examination before committing to engagement is when it is apparent that there is a deep level of distrust, or an entrenched schism, in the organisation. Of course, this isn't always easy to spot early in an engagement. And it is a judgement call as to how much distrust is too much distrust. It is because of potentially hidden hazards like this that it is important to feel your way forward with an organisation into creating a context-sensitive intervention, rather than just plonking a standard template of appreciative inquiry over whatever the organisation offers. Over the years I've learn to pick up some of the hidden hazard indications. Sometimes it's the language used, or the way people talk about others in the organisation; sometimes it's a sudden unexpected hostile or highly resistant reaction to ideas of 'whole system', or 'co-creation' or even the sharing of conversations at the event. When I begin to feel that there is a danger of some unresolved dispute erupting in the middle of the event, or of people compliantly attending but passively going through the motions, then alarm bells ring. My suggestion here is to make your reservations clear and to offer to do some remedial or preparatory work to move the organisation to a suitable place to work creatively together. The organisational reaction to these suggestions is often very informative, helping to confirm or relieve your concerns.

Another indication that appreciative inquiry may not be the way forward is when people or an organisation are in some sort of crisis and are panicking. In this situation it may be helpful to refer them to an expert for clear direction. Once they are out of the immediate danger, and again capable of taking time and giving thought to addressing the future, appreciative inquiry may well be very suitable.

I would also always be wary and engage carefully when it is clear that the people you are being asked to work with, or the organisation as a whole, are exhausted or overwhelmed. Appreciative inquiry takes, as well as creates, energy. In this instance restorative work takes a priority, and other interventions that address workload or well-being may well be more suitable initially. Of course, appreciative interventions themselves can be highly restorative, so, as ever, it's a judgement call.

Other signals to watch out for is when it's the 'wrong' topic or when the topic and the system are poorly matched. It is not uncommon for a system, for example a team, to want to address an issue that extends beyond their organisational boundary. For example, they want to address the relationship they have with some other team or division in the organisation. It is very hard to make effective and sustainable relationship improvements without having the other group involved. Sometimes it's possible to increase participation in the event; at other times though, it is necessary to adapt the topic to fit within the boundaries of what the group can actually influence or change.

In a similar vein, although appreciative inquiry is generally interested in working with existing group resources, sometimes the resources or knowledge needed to have good conversations and make good decisions about the future just aren't in the system. In this case it may well be possible to proceed with an appreciative inquiry, but the resource base would benefit from being broadened by incorporating additional knowledge or information.

Even if there are no contraindications, organisations can present arguments that appreciative inquiry may not be a good approach in their situation. While some may be valid, many are variations on prevalent myths about appreciative inquiry. These myths, while commonly encountered at early stages of the engagement, can arise at any point throughout the engagement.

Common Myths Attached to Appreciative Inquiry

1. Turkeys won't vote for Christmas

This is an argument against co-creative events. It arises regularly but particularly when the answer to the challenge under inquiry appears to be downsizing. I know of two ways to engage with this challenge. One, if the situation might warrant downsizing but it is possible there may be other ways forward, then appreciative inquiry could be a very powerful way to address the challenge. On the other hand, if the decision has been made to downsize, then the appreciative inquiry can be focused on that very challenge. In which case the appreciative topic of inquiry might be something like: 'How can we do this downsizing the best way possible for everyone?' or 'How can we best celebrate the past while preparing for our future?' I have run a few events of this nature, either with teams that are going to fold or with an organisation that is facing a round of redundancies, and have found it to be very powerful.

2. Adults don't do play

This pushback usually occurs when the conversation turns to working creatively, for instance doing collage or drawing pictures, particularly if the work being commissioned is with professional groups like accountant or engineers. There are a few answers to this. Firstly, one can refer back to the volunteer principle, no one is going to be made to do anything. As a compromise, I have frequently said, 'Well, I'll bring some creative materials along just in case anyone feels like using them', only to have the whole lot snatched up by eager participants at the first opportunity. Secondly, the worried person can be reminded that the people concerned may be very creative in other areas of their life outside of work. I have repeatedly been amazed at the range of creative skills motley groups of people possess. And finally, it can be useful to think about providing materials and possible ways of sharing their dream vision that are a good fit to the group. For example, I have successfully used Lego with groups of engineers, while a local authority group happily presented short dramas they had devised to represent their dreams of how the future could be.

3. Appreciative inquiry ignores the bad

Appreciative inquiry does not ignore the bad; it reframes the conversation around the issue to a more productive one. However, it is important to note that there is a transition from the bad to the good. That is, people's difficult experiences around the topic mustn't be ignored or brushed over. Rather they need to have their experience acknowledged and to feel understood. However, this needs to be done without amplifying the negative emotions and accounts in any way. Once the person concerned feels seen, heard and acknowledged, it is usually possible to flip the conversation into a more productive space.

4. The language is off-putting

This may well be true in many contexts: the idea of dreaming particularly doesn't sit well everywhere. It is not necessary to use the formal language of the 5D cycle to explain the approach and the process. If particular words cause difficulties, find others.

5. It's all woo-woo

As demonstrated in Chapter 2 and throughout this text, appreciative inquiry is actually based on good science.

Preparing for an Appreciative Inquiry Event

Some early choices and decisions that need to be addressed are outlined below. This stage of the process is mostly about facilitating topic and design decisions.

1. Identifying the appreciative topic

The first stage in the 5D model is to define the appreciative topic of inquiry. Here the organisation is helped to identify an area of organisational life or functioning into which they wish to appreciatively inquire. In broad terms this means something positive they want to 'grow more of', grow towards or otherwise do better. The challenge, when supporting the organisation in this task, is both to make sure the topic is truly an affirmative one and to make sure it resonates with the organisation as a whole. One way to ensure this is to work with a holographic planning team [1] from as early as possible in the programme, preferably while the event still has a 'holding' or 'working' title and is open to further refinement. By holographic I mean one that is the organisation in microcosm, varied by hierarchical position, job role, division and protected characteristics. Working with a group like this gives a good chance of alighting on a topic that is positive, affirmative, business critical, attractive and meaningful to all.

> Event organisers need to invite people with
> - Authority to Act – decision-makers
> - Resources – time, money, contacts
> - Expertise – relevant knowledge
> - Information – relevant to the topic
> - Need – need to be involved as they will be affected by the outcome and can speak to the consequences

Figure 3.1 The ARE IN model of participants for appreciative events.

2. Who should be there, and how to get them there?

To identify who needs to be at an event, the ARE IN acronym can be helpful (Figure 3.1).

A debate that often arises at this point is about the status of the invitation. Should it be compulsory or voluntary? For a smaller group, like a team, the issue tends not to arise. But for anything larger, where people are being asked to come together in an unfamiliar configuration, it can become a big debating point. I always lobby strongly for the event to be based on voluntary attendance for various reasons as outlined later in the chapter.

3. How to run the event

Many different event designs are shared throughout this text, so I won't say much more here, except that essentially the design needs to be based on an affirmative topic, allow for generative co-creation, and embody the principles whether or not it follows a 5D summit format.

4. Managing groupings within the event

Whatever the design, there will be a need to plan how to manage the groupings within the event, deciding, for example, when people are to work within their own teams and when they will work in groups across organisational boundaries. There can be benefits to both groupings at different parts of the process.

As a general principle it is good practice to let people self-organise, but around what criteria? It needs to be possible to identify who people are, what department they work in and so on. Of course, name badges can be used but that points back to 'the usual' in most organisations and works against making clear that this event is different to 'the usual'. Creative ways of solving this challenge are suggested in Chapter 4.

5. How will decisions be made?

Most importantly, there needs to be clarity about the decision-making process. As a broad rule of thumb, it is desirable to have action decisions as close as possible, if not incorporated into, the event. When the whole system is present at the event, and their proposed post-event actions are, as they should be, focused on things within the group's sphere of influence or control, then it should be perfectly possible to make decisions on the day about which activities will be taken forward and about who is doing what after the event. At the other extreme, one of the worst arrangements is an agreement that 'recommendations' will be sent off from the event to some other decision-making body to ratify at some indeterminate point in the future. Experience suggests this is a good recipe for an enjoyable event that achieves very little.

6. Capturing and recording the event and its outcomes

Another thing to think about before the event is how things will be captured and recorded. Beyond the basic flip-chart record, which should not be overlooked and is frequently sufficient, consideration can also be given to using graphic recorders, making a photographic record or capturing key moments and stories on video. Such recordings can be used after the event to produce a video, a booklet or a newsletter that serves as both a record and a celebration.

Other information it might be helpful to capture could include a map of the positive core, for example, a map of 'when we are at our best' and the dream creations. Bear in mind they might be 3D constructions, or transitory in nature, like acted sketches, dances and so on. And it is helpful to capture commitments to action, both personal and collective, including first steps, desired ultimate outcome, timescale and who has volunteered to help with, or lead, any projects that have emerged.

Delivering the Event

With a good event design in place, this part of the process is mostly about facilitation.

1. The influence of the facilitator

Even though appreciative inquiry is an amazingly robust process, how the facilitator shows up does make a difference. Through experience, I have discovered that I need to be fresh and rested to be at my best as host and facilitator: listening well, quick to process what is happening, able to be creative as necessary and to have the capacity to handle the relational elements with grace and elegance. I can assure you these outcomes don't happen, for me anyway, by happy accident! The job of the facilitator, or as some prefer, host, is to do everything possible to help people engage positively with the possibilities the event offers and to create something great. This desire and effort notwithstanding, it is worth emphasising that the facilitator cannot be responsible for the choices attendees make of how to engage with or react to what is being offered.

To support the ambition for the event, embedded in the design, the facilitator needs to be attending to energy levels, ensuring that everyone present is productively engaged, and, if they aren't, using their skill and resource to help them shift position. That means that, without denying people's realities, they will be working to reframe deficit dialogue into affirmative possibilities, possibly by employing the flip: if that's what you don't want, tell me what you do want.

The Quality of Conversation

In many workplaces conversation is regarded as an adjunct to the real work of getting stuff done. All too often a request for a conversation is experienced as an interruption, a distraction from real work. Seen as a necessary evil, the objective is to complete the conversation as quickly as possible so all involved can get back to work. In other instances, while the *topic* of conversation may be regarded as important, the importance of attending to the *quality* of conversation doesn't even register. This is very unfortunate as the quality of any conversation will have an impact beyond the moment.

The quality of conversation affects people's emotional state, their ability to learn or take advice, their creativity in problem-solving or generating initiative, their motivation and their action potential, for example, the likelihood of them doing something appropriate and useful after the conversation. It will also affect their willingness to engage in future conversations. In this way every conversation is potentially an investment in the culture, creativity and productivity of the organisation. This means every conversation has an impact on the quality of organisational life.

Each conversation while a small thing in itself is part of a huge construction: the organisational culture. How it feels to be a member of the organisation, to work in the organisation, to attempt to improve the organisation is determined by our day-to-day interactions: our daily work conversations.

So, it is wise to give some thought to the nature of conversation in organisations in general and particularly with regard to appreciative interventions. Conversations, and conversational contributions, in the workplace can be classified along two key dimensions or axis: inquiry to statement and appreciative to depreciative [2]. Each combination of dimensions generates a different quality of conversation (Figure 3.2).

In general terms, conversations conducted from an *appreciative* stance are likely to add value as people share ideas and build on the ideas of others. In addition, people's contributions will be acknowledged, opportunities will be identified, new perspectives will be generated and possibilities for action created. Such conversations create upwards spirals of confidence and optimism. These conversations serve to strengthen connections, enhance relationships and expand awareness. People experience meaningful engagement.

By contrast conversations conducted from a *depreciative* perspective, where people advocate for their own ideas and ignore or actively criticise those of others, are likely to be experienced as belittling and critical. In such conversations people are focused on pointing out why things won't work.

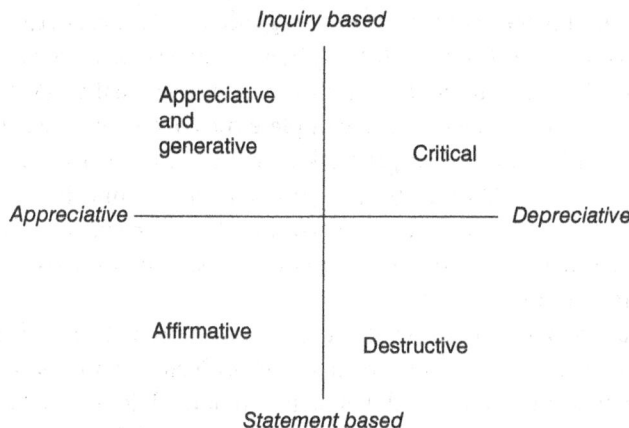

Figure 3.2 Different types of conversation. Developed from *Conversations Worth Having* by Jackie Stavros and Cheri Torres.

They may be dominated by a few strong characters. Such conversations are likely to weaken connections and strain relationships, to reinforce existing assumptions and to eclipse people's potential, that is, to limit possibility and forward movement.

Inquiry-based conversations are based on questions. Conducted from an *appreciative* perspective, the aim of the questions is to generate information and to reveal hidden assumptions, perspectives or knowledge or to expand awareness. They aim to make room for the emergence of possibility and opportunity or to deepen understanding and initiate change. Such conversations are likely to build relationships, awareness and connections. People are likely to feel valued in such conversations. This is where the practice of appreciative inquiry is located. From a *depreciative* perspective such inquiry conversations are likely to consist of rhetorical and negative questions that are pejorative. People are likely to feel that they and their efforts are devalued in such a conversation.

Statement-based conversations consist mostly of comments. Offered from an *appreciative* perspective these are likely to be experienced as affirming. The comments will be positive. They are likely to be experienced as validating and to have a positive impact on people and situations. Statement-based conversations conducted from a *depreciative* perspective are likely to be focused on criticism and blame, and they are likely to be a nonvalidating experience.

In general, the two appreciative-focused conversations are likely to be more beneficial to individuals and the organisation, while *appreciative* and *generative* conversations are more likely to result in change. Table 3.1 outlines the different characteristics of these two appreciatively oriented

Table 3.1 Characteristics of appreciatively oriented conversations. Developed from *Conversations Worth Having* by Jackie Stavros and Cheri Torres.

Appreciative and generative	Affirmative
Meaningful	Genuine, mutual admiration
Mutually enlivening and engaging	Acknowledgement
Geared to generating information, knowledge and possibility	Focused on identifying the positives in plans and aspirations
Solution or outcome focused	Motivating and encouraging
Uplifting and energising	Feel good
Positive	Reinforcing positive relationships
Productive	Unlikely to generate new knowledge or innovation

conversations. The difference in impact lies in the power of questions to promote change in thinking and action.

Appreciative conversations are much more likely to create conditions of psychological safety in participants, which, as explained in Chapter 4, is key to genuine participation and generativity.

The Quality of the Questions

One of the key determinants of the quality of the conversation is the quality of the questions. Appreciative questions direct attention towards the positive and are focused on enabling those involved to learn from success and from peak experiences. They bring into view resources that can be used as a springboard to new futures. When creating appreciative questions peak-moment-emotion phrases such as, 'the most moving', 'the proudest' or 'the best experience of …' are often employed to draw out stories of great moments and experiences and to access the exceptional best.

The ambition is that the questions encourage the sharing of generative stories, those with the potential to change the dialogue. Appreciative questions should bring new, previously untold, at least in this context, stories about the resources and best experiences in the organisation into the conversation. It is this introduction and sharing of new accounts of life in the organisation that allows new ideas, possibilities and visions to flourish. Questions that haven't been asked before bring stories that haven't been told before into the conversation.

A good appreciative question directs people to go looking for examples of the 'best of'. They look harder and see things they didn't see before. Then, as they share their stories, and hear the stories of others, their awareness of the presence of the topic of inquiry in their life, or the social world, or the organisation, grows.

Appreciative questions can also be used to bring different aspects of organisational life into focus. When considering what to inquiry into, think about what people *aren't* talking about, what *isn't* being noticed right now. This is where some of the new accounts, knowledge and perceptual shifts might lie. Very often this is achieved simply by focusing on the positive or the positive potential in any situation, but it can also be induced by focusing on the future rather than the past, credit rather than blame, hope rather than fear and so on.

> Tell me about a time when – the essential discovery interview question
>
> If you had three wishes for this organization/system, what would they be?
>
> If by a miracle we woke up tomorrow and the system was running as we dream, how would we know, what would we notice?
>
> Tell me about how we got from there to here, what was the first thing that changed?
>
> What is the smallest thing we could change that would make a difference?
>
> What is the unimaginable thing we could do?
>
> If we could absolutely do what needs doing, what would we do?
>
> How will our customer know things are changing here?
>
> If our success were completely guaranteed, what bold steps might we choose?

Figure 3.3 A sample of generic appreciative inquiry type questions.

Most importantly, we need to make sure our appreciative questions are context specific, resonating with language meaningful to the organisation. While I am about to share some generic question shapes, the most impactful questions are tailored to the context, carefully crafted for the particular situation, connecting to the organisational language or 'grammar', as I hope will be evident in the second part of this book (Figure 3.3).

Another factor that is likely to affect the success of an appreciative inquiry event is the status of the participants.

The Volunteer Principle in Appreciative Inquiry

This is also known as the free-choice principle. As mentioned in the chapter 2, this is often a topic of debate, particularly with larger events. As far as possible, I would argue that attendance at, and engagement in, the appreciative inquiry should be a voluntary activity. This means active choice occurs in three parts of the process.

Firstly, ideally, people are invited, rather than directed, to attend the appreciative inquiry event. The event topic, the nature of the event and the invitation have to be sufficiently compelling that people prioritise being there of their own volition. At the team level this isn't usually an issue; however, for a large system intervention it is a key task of the planning team. Making attendance voluntary means the team really have to work to create a compelling event addressing a business-critical issue, designed in such a way that people have real belief, or at least strong hope, that they can influence the outcome of the event, that is, the future.

Secondly, this voluntarism principle needs to extend to participation in any and every particular activity or discussion that is planned for the process or event. The facilitator can't know what may be going on in people's lives that makes some topic of discussion unbearable or some exercise untenable. To feel psychologically safe, participants have to be able to call this shot.

Thirdly, towards the end of most events there is a shift to decision-making and action planning. Often this involves forming project or work groups to make progress. The desire to contribute to changing things for the future needs to stem from the motivation and community built during the day. It is either there or it isn't, and different people will be motivated by different proposed actions. Group membership needs to be voluntary. Be warned, this can be a hard pill for some managers and leaders to swallow.

After the Event

After the event, the facilitator or the organisation may need to communicate outcomes to various audiences including absent attendees and other interested parties. The facilitator, or the organisation, may need to offer support to any action or innovation teams. Leadership often needs support or encouragement to attend to the action groups, broadcast their successes, make it clear they appreciate their efforts, inquire into how things are going and generally help them along. It's also a good idea to have a celebration and success event a few months after the summit.

Conclusion

In this chapter we have walked through some of the key points to think about when preparing for and delivering an appreciative inquiry event. A large part of the success of an appreciative inquiry process lies in the preparation. There is lots to be thought about and negotiated, and working with an internal planning team for larger events is highly recommended.

Learning Points

1. There are some situations in which appreciative inquiry may not be suitable.
2. There are myths about appreciative inquiry that may need to be addressed.
3. Appreciative inquiry is a process not just an event.
4. Various elements particularly influence the outcome of appreciative inquiry beyond the application of the principles and the 5D cycle.

Discussion Questions

1. When might appreciative inquiry not be appropriate?
2. What are some of the common myths about appreciative inquiry, and how might they be overcome?
3. What do we mean by quality of conversation?
4. What are the defining features of an appreciative question?

Teaching Exercise

1. Help the group practice creating appreciative topics of inquiry from initial problem statements.

Further Reading and Resources

Lewis, S., Passmore, J., and Cantore, S. (2016). *Appreciative Inquiry for Change Management: Using AI to Facilitate Organizational Development*, 2e. London: Kogan Page Chapters 3, 5, 6, 10.

Lewis, S. (2016). *Positive Psychology and Change: How Leadership, Collaboration, and Appreciative Inquiry Create Transformational Results*. Chichester: Wiley-Blackwell Chapter 6.

Ludema, J.D., Whitney, D., Mohr, B.J., and Griffin, T.J. (2003). *The Appreciative Inquiry Summit: A Practitioner's Guide to Leading Large Group Change*. San Francisco: Berrett-Koehler Chapters 2 and 3.

Stavros, J.M., Torres, C., and Cooperrider, D.L. (2018). *Conversations Worth Having: Using Appreciative Inquiry to Fuel Productive and Meaningful Engagement*. Berrett-Koehler Chapter 2.

Hammond, S. (1996). *The Thin Book of Appreciative Inquiry.* Lima, OH: CSS Publishing.

McQuaid, M. and Cooperrider, D. (2018). *Your Change Blueprint: How to Design and Deliver an AI Summit.* NSW Australia: Michelle McQuaid Chapter 5.

Lewis, S. (2021). *Co-creating Planning Teams for Dialogic OD: From Entry to Event,* BMI Series in Dialogic Organisational Development. BMI Publishing.

References

1. Lewis, S. (2021). *Creating Energised Commitment to the Dialogic Approach: The Change Team's Journey of Discovery,* BMI Series in Dialogic Organisational Development. BMI Publishing.
2. Stavros, J.M., Torres, C., and Cooperrider, D.L. (2018). *Conversations Worth Having: Using Appreciative Inquiry to Fuel Productive and Meaningful Engagement.* Berrett-Koehler.

4

Creating the Appreciative Inquiry Commission, Psychological Safety and Equality, Diversity and Inclusion

An awareness by an organisation of the need for change can come from many sources. For example, regular ongoing organisational activity such as staff surveys, internal quality reviews, customer surveys or similar assessment activity undertaken by a particular department can all reveal problem areas. Sometimes the request for help might be based on an analysis of needs identified by performance reviews, changing training demands, or sales data. At other times it is driven by external factors such as a change in regulations. The challenge for the appreciative inquiry practitioner is how to develop such problem-identified requests for help into a request for appreciative inquiry.

In this chapter we look at the nature of these different requests for help and identify the need to create a shift in the commissioner's mindset if they are to be able to respond from an appreciative inquiry perspective. We consider the elements of an appreciative conversation with the commissioner and the possible pushbacks against using appreciative inquiry to move the identified issue forward. We introduce some practice principles of appreciative inquiry that underlie our responses to some of the commonly encountered pushbacks.

This chapter also considers the place of ethics in appreciative practice and how appreciative inquiry creates psychological safety. It considers how appreciative inquiry is particularly well suited to enhancing the diversity, equality and inclusion culture, with particular regard to its ability to elicit and effectively utilise the tacit knowledge of many diverse participants. The chapter concludes with a couple of case studies that illuminate how appreciative inquiry has been used in specific contexts to improve organisational culture.

Practical Appreciative Inquiry: A Toolkit for Applying Appreciative Inquiry to Organisational Challenges, Opportunities, and Aspiration, First Edition. Sarah Lewis.
© 2025 John Wiley & Sons Ltd. Published 2025 by John Wiley & Sons Ltd.

Developing an Appreciative Inquiry Commission

Assessments of need that stem from the sources outlined above tend to be past-focused, blame-focused and diagnostic in nature, and so lead to a concentration on problem-fixing with the assumed adoption of a diagnostic planned problem-solving intervention. Converting such a request for help into an opportunity to work with appreciative inquiry rests on the ability to create a shift in the commissioner's understanding of what a fruitful way to move things forward might look like.

The good news is that while these sources identify the negative need for change (what we want to get away from) they can be interrogated to identify positive needs (what we want to move towards), and so act as a springboard to an appreciative intervention. To achieve this switch in perspective and understanding, the facilitator needs to help the commissioner shift from a belief that the information they have is a true and full picture to a recognition that they have a partial and biased view of the situation. This can be done by exploring other accounts of the current context by asking, for example, how someone in a particular department or a frontline position might describe what is going on. It can also be done by picking up on underdescribed parts of the story.

The facilitator also needs to help them to shift from being past-focused to being future-focused and from concentrating on finding the solution to focusing on framing the question. The story of the past is important for what it tells us about present organisational thinking and the framing of past events. However, this is not the part of the conversation we want to amplify, rather we want to help them start constructing a story about the future. The flip question 'If that's what you don't want, what is it you do want?' can be useful throughout to get them off talking about the problem and on to talking about the aspiration.

The facilitator needs to help shift the focus of the intervention from something that is of peripheral concern of some to something that is of central concern of all. They need to peel back to the business dilemma at the root of what is worrying the organisation: the existential threat. When pursuing these questions, the ambition is be able to frame a 'How can we…?' type question that captures their puzzle, as opposed to working with a 'What we need is…' statement. This is the basis of being able to achieve a large voluntary attendance: once people start to believe that at this event, about this important topic that is going to affect their future, they will have a voice and influence, they are likely to want to be there.

At the same time, these early conversations present an opportunity to gather some essential information about the organisation, the challenge and their existing ideas about how change happens. Listening carefully to these stories, the facilitator can spot opportunities to ask an appreciative question and open up ways to connect.

Throughout these conversations, the facilitator is listening for cues as to how aware, or not, the commissioner is of this more emergent, positive, appreciative, dialogic way of working, and how receptive they might be to it. For example, how do they respond to the idea of exploring positive experiences or the power of the imagination in relation to change? Have they had prior experience of related approaches like world café or open space? One way people try to make sense of what the appreciative practitioner is suggesting is to connect what they are being told to what they already know. In this case they might say something like, 'That sounds a bit like NLP' or 'Is that like solutions-focused therapy?' There are points of connection with these fields of practice, and the skill is to acknowledge and emphasise these, and to then explain how appreciative inquiry takes that idea and embeds it in a different model. Moments like this offer an ideal opportunity to move the perception of how the commissioned intervention might look closer to that of an appreciative event.

Another challenge that often arises in these early conversations is that of preserving the integrity of the appreciative approach. Commissioners sometimes see having the whole system together as an opportunity not to be missed. It occurs to them that they could meet some of their other objectives, such sharing as their business expansion vision or getting each director to share a progress report. They might also baulk at the cost of bringing the whole system together and suggest instead an event made up of representatives. These suggestions will seriously dilute the efficacy of the event and should be resisted as strongly as possible.

The facilitator needs, throughout the conversation, to create the sense that they understand the commissioner by connecting with and reflecting their concerns, and then move to extending their thinking by offering a path that takes the possibilities for the intervention somewhere a little different. This can be done by directing their attention to the positives, strengths or opportunities present in the story, which can then be amplified. Asking these questions signals the aspects of the story in which, as an appreciative practitioner, the facilitator is interested. This starts to seed the idea that it can be valuable and productive to look into exceptional experiences of achievement or success, as well as attending to problem areas.

It's important to note that this is not about ignoring what's wrong – that is being attended to – but rather it's about nudging them to expand their focus in the situation to include what is going right.

I find it fascinating that while wanting to develop a workforce that is empowered, self-motivated, innovative and well-connected, commissioners often intend to hold an event that is highly managed and directed, and indeed replicates the current organisational structures and culture. It's important to help the commissioner understand that the way the event is conducted is as important as the outcome and that the experience of the event can give people a taste of a possible future way of working together, that is, being empowered to make decisions, being encouraged to be creative and working collaboratively across organisational boundaries towards a co-created idea of a positive future. It's worth noting that the commisioning process can be initiated in a number of different ways, and can involve more than one person. See Table 4.1. for an outline of possible roles you may need to engage with while securing your commission.

The ambition is that the possibilities offered throughout the conversation are sufficiently enticing, intriguing, exciting and persuasive that as the conversation progresses the commissioner becomes interested and ready to do something different. Sometimes it is helpful to give people a direct experience of what you are proposing by running a mini-appreciative inquiry with the commissioner or the group. On other occasions a short webinar that presents both the more usual 'planned change approach' and the appreciative approach, examining the differences between them and pointing up the benefits and costs of each, can be helpful to people struggling to understand exactly what is being offered. This approach honours what they know, are familiar with, probably have experience with and works to move them from there to a new place. Table 4.2 outlines some of the key differences it is helpful to get across in such a process.

Table 4.1 Roles in the commissioning process.

Initial caller: the person who issues the initial call for help for their system
Commissioner: the person who has the authority to commission the work
Contractor: the person who contracts with you to do the work
Your sponsor: the person who leads the initiative within the organization
Direct client: the people you will be directly working with; the leader of this group is, obviously, particularly important
Note these roles can all be held by one person or may be distributed amongst a number of people.

Table 4.2 Contrasting traditional and appreciative inquiry approaches to change.

Assumptions and Beliefs	Traditional approaches to change	Appreciative inquiry approach to change
Organisational change stems from...	Problem-solution achieved by the cognitive application of logical, rational problem-solving skills	The development of strongly felt, shared, common aspirations and a shift in the organizational dynamics
The underpinning metaphor of organization is of...	The organization as machine, meaning that change is to be engineered	The organization as a living system, meaning that change is to be grown
Change events are organised...	By providing clear direction (much micro-managing within process)	By providing robust process (much self-organising within process)
At the event, there is an emphasis on...	The problem statement, solution generation, and applying problem-solving skills and techniques	Discovery through conversation, convergence of aspirations for action, the generation of emotional energy and the emergence of energised ideas
The discussion is centred on...	Particular topics	Particular questions
There is an emphasis on understanding...	The problem	The system
The agenda is...	Developed from the initial problem statement. Topics are predetermined; people are allocated or self-select into static limited size topic groups	Developed by participants within the process – people work on things important to them
Pattern of the day looks like...	People work in same 'stream' or brainstorming group most of the day. Regular, full briefs from groups. People have special roles as scribe, time-keeper etc.	Organic, continual mixing of groupings, much self-selection into groups. Creative ways of sharing information, such as marketplace. No special roles except facilitator

(*Continued*)

Table 4.2 (Continued)

Assumptions and Beliefs	Traditional approaches to change	Appreciative inquiry approach to change
Convergence of ideas/ commitment to action happens through...	A process for evaluating proposed solutions from those available against specific criteria. Each group must produce a solution. People assigned to project groups.	The emergence of key ideas that people converge on and are energized to pursue. Voluntary commitment to working together to make something happen.
Decision-making happens by...	Ideas from day being taken to a smaller decision-making forum for further work and ratification	Decision-makers being present. There is an emphasis on decisions being made on that day if at all possible.
What happens next?	Ideas are ratified, drawn into a plan, implemented in due course.	People are 'empowered' to take immediate action within the agreements of the day, both individually and in groups.
Follow-through takes the form of...	Driving change: process-tracking and monitoring progress. Key tool is programme and project management.	Growing change by fanning the first sparks of change, and by amplifying and broadcasting early signs of positive impact. Key tool is leadership attention and interest.

As demonstrated above, it can take some conscious thought and effort to convert the normal invitation to help an organisation into an invitation that can be worked with from an appreciative inquiry perspective, and every conversation that is part of the commissioning process is an opportunity to achieve these shifts. Pushbacks will continue to be met along the way as the inquiry progresses, particularly, for example, at the event or intervention design stage. For a smaller event, this might just be when the team leader is presented with a design. For large initiatives, we may need to influence a whole a steering or managing group [1].

Creating the Appreciative Inquiry Commission

Table 4.3 Some common concerns and frequently suggested solutions.

Challenge	Suggested solution
People won't speak up in front of their managers.	We should exclude managers from events.
People can't be trusted to follow simple instructions.	Everyone must be directed at all times.
People can't be trusted to follow a process.	Every conversation must be facilitated.
People won't understand how it works and won't come.	We need to tell them what to talk about and how action will happen.
People will just pursue personal vendettas.	We need to manage group membership and police every conversation.
People won't be brave enough to name what needs to be named.	We must do that, and tell them what they must talk about.
If we include open space, people won't put forward topics.	We must name some topics beforehand, or have some in our back pocket.
Our people are too sophisticated for your silly games.	Let's stick to bullet points and report-outs.

Frequently Encountered Pushbacks Against Adopting an Appreciative Inquiry Approach

See Table 4.3 for some of the concerns commonly raised in these early conversations and the potential solutions often presented by commissioners or steering group members. All these concerns or fears are valid, but the proffered solutions run against the process and spirit of appreciative inquiry. Most of them can be responded to by reference to some key principles of design. These are useful to keep in mind throughout the intervention, as guiding stars for navigating the process.

Practice Design Principles

A good starting point for thinking about the principles that support appreciative inquiry designs is, of course, the core principles and the 5D cycle explained in Chapter 1. Over the years I have found a few additional ideas useful to help manage my responses to these kinds of concerns and inappropriate design suggestions, for example, the principle of self-organisation and the volunteer principle mentioned in Chapter 3. I have also found it helps to bear in mind that the event can often be thought of as a time-travel capsule where, for a limited period, the organisation experiences the way it aims to be in future. For example, if the organisation wants a culture of greater engagement across organisational boundaries, then, to create an experience of this, the event needs to break up the usual structural pattern and get people engaged with each other, which means that people need to talk about, and work on, what is engaging to them and not just with the usual suspects. Furthermore, if the ambition is for staff to be more empowered, then the process must be empowering, which means encouraging self-organisation and decision-making.

It can also be helpful to remember that the aim of an appreciative event is to create commitment to achieving the identified future. Commitment is a qualitatively different motivation to compliance. Many organisations run on compliance and so the need to organise a choiceful, proactive day may not be self-evident to them. But it is these features of the day that start to build that sense of commitment, along with adherence to the other principles, particularly that of self-organisation.

This principle can come under threat very early in the conversations as people, exercising their usual habits, start to plan, in minute detail, the composition of each and every group that will be formed during the day. It is worth noting that self-organisation does rely on people being able to identify each other so that they can comply with instructions such as, 'Find five people to work with from departments different to yours'. Issuing standard name and department badges is counterindicated as it replicates the current culture; what is wanted is something different. Creative ways to do this might include using symbols for departmental membership or, to encourage random pairing up, badges that split common phrases such as 'eggs and bacon'. Here the invitation would be to find the person who completed the phrase on your event badge.

Habitual ways of thinking and working can lead people to suggest that the event be structured around content rather than questions, or that, for efficiency's sake, groups work in the same formation throughout the event. Both of these are incompatible with an appreciative inquiry. Firstly, the inquiring nature of the event means the content is generated live on the day in response to the inquiry. This process creates contemporary, fresh, relevant and dynamic content. Secondly, the ambition almost always is to help the organisation connect as a whole system. Inviting groups to form and dissolve throughout the event encourages greater creativity, the building of new relationships and social bonds and allows ideas to flow naturally around the group.

By seeking points of connection, pushing back gently on ideas contrary to the process and by sticking to the core appreciative inquiry principles, the facilitator enables commissioners and others to maintain an appreciative approach.

Ethical Practice

I have written elsewhere about my strong belief that organisational development is a values-based activity that should be grounded in clear ethical practice [2]. There are various sources one can draw on to develop a personal code. One is the codes of conduct drawn up by various professional organisations. For others, the evidence base that underpins their interventions is what renders their actions ethical. Some people subscribe to the Hippocratic Oath to 'first do no harm' and find that sufficient, while others are guided by religious strictures about behaviour. Personally, I'm drawn to the idea of accountability: I need to be able to account for my actions by drawing on a set of psychological beliefs, underpinned by scientific evidence, of what benefits and harms people. All of these offer a place to start and many of us practice from a combination of all of them. I have found that my ethical boundaries become clearer as I encounter threats to them.

For example, many years ago an organisation that had asked me in to help explained that what they wanted was for me to redesign their organisation as if it were starting from scratch. This new organisational design would act as a basis for restructuring the organisation and as a rationale for probable redundancies. I do not know what was behind the request, but I expect it was one or more troublesome staff that they wanted to be rid of. But even as it was being explained I knew there was something 'off' about this potential commission.

Essentially, I was being asked to undertake a paper exercise as if it would not affect existing people. Yet there were existing people, and what I provided could easily be used to justify real action. I found the thought of being this unconnected 'voice of authority' a very uncomfortable proposition: this assignment was not for me. The key point is to be reasonably clear on where your own boundaries lie and to be able to justify actions you take by some ethical criteria. Some of the key ideas I adhere to, which allow me, I believe, to practice in an ethical manner, are outlined below in the hope that they might be helpful to others (Table 4.4).

Table 4.4 Reflecting principles of appreciative inquiry in your practice.

1. Being open and transparent with your commissioner, and the work participants, on your design for engaging with the challenge.
2. Being willing, and able, to share the theory and research that supports the approach and any specific intervention.
3. Being alert to the contraindications for this approach, and check for them in early-stage engagement activities.
4. Honour the, potentially differing, realities of all participants in the process.
5. Endeavour to create and maintain sufficient psychological safety for the work.
6. Know the boundaries of your role as a facilitator (or coach, or consultant, mediator etc.).
7. Respect client and participant confidentialities, and contract about this at various stages in the process.
8. Assume people are acting from good intent, however destructive their behaviour might appear, and work to bring that good intent into the light.
9. Seek out peoples' and groups' strengths.
10. Practice with an appreciative eye and ear.
11. Be willing to push a little to achieve or maintain optimal conditions for the work to proceed, while also being flexible and adaptable in the face of less than ideal conditions.

How Appreciative Practice Can Support Equality, Diversity and Inclusion

For the majority of people and organisations (at least I fondly believe), it is important to be fair, and fairness includes making sure that equality, diversity and inclusion are practiced. Interestingly, the business case for creating a work environment that is inclusive, that honours and makes good use of diversity and that manages itself in such a way that all employees feel they are fairly treated, has long been made.[1] The challenge is how to achieve such an environment. Appreciative inquiry can be seen to support the development of inclusive, diverse and equitable cultures in two key ways. Firstly, the very process of appreciative inquiry creates the conditions both for psychological safety and for other conditions that enhance diversity, equality and inclusion, as we shall explore below. Secondly, one can, of course, conduct an appreciative inquiry into diversity, equality and inclusion in the workplace as we shall see in the case studies.

1. How appreciative inquiry as a methodology helps with the creation of diversity, equality and inclusion in workplace cultures

Appreciative inquiry as a change process is predicated on inclusion, on getting the whole system in the room. This means that people who might not usually get invited to 'change decision' events are included right from the beginning. From very early in the process they have the opportunity to influence events. This propensity towards inclusion can be further activated by conscious actions and decisions, for example, when selecting subgroups for preliminary interviews or for the planning board. In addition, inclusion is enhanced by drawing the organisation's attention to groups that are on the periphery of the organisation and might be discounted as part of the system. This can include groups like teachers' assistants, temporary, contract or agency workers, part-time staff or those who work offsite or remotely. Making efforts to expand the manager's sense of the boundaries of the system under consideration to include such groups helps with inclusion, diversity and equality. These actions often positively diversify the race ethnic, gender and class mix in the room. However, while presence is a predeterminant of the possibility of inclusion, it is another thing to ensure that all those involved have a voice at the event or during the process.

An appreciative inquiry intervention is deliberately structured to ensure that everyone present has a voice. This is achieved not by putting people under a spotlight in a mandatory 'round robin' for instance, but by using lots of practices like small groups and pairs to encourage people to find their voice. Quiet, shy, reticent-to-speak people are more likely find their voice when the topic is of interest, pertinent to their own lives and something they feel passionate about, especially if they are amongst a small group of people and when they feel psychologically safe.

2. How appreciative practice can support psychological safety

Psychological safety refers to an environment where people believe they will not be punished or humiliated for speaking up with ideas, questions, concerns or for making mistakes, and that it is safe to take interpersonal risks [3]. It's a prerequisite for quality conversations, and from research, it is known that good quality conversation is more likely to happen in a positive atmosphere.[2] A positive atmosphere is one where people are focusing on finding commonality, where they appreciate each other's strengths and are focused on learning together and sharing successes.

However, many meetings and conversations are conducted in quite a different atmosphere. When the conversation is focused on competitive idea pitching, destroying the ideas of others and on establishing the superiority of the intellectual apparatus of one person to that of another, then many present are less likely to feel safe to speak out. A working culture of this nature tends to create a high degree of compliance to the dominant idea expressed by the most powerful person in the room. Dissent becomes dangerous and can unleash a highly critical attack focused on dismantling any such opposition. Those of equal power to the speaker may relish this, seeing it as the cut and thrust of debate, but others are likely to be silenced, even just by witnessing another being attacked in this manner.[3]

Appreciative inquiry, by contrast, is interested in difference, which is seen as bringing value and resource to the group, indeed, exploration of difference is seen as key to the process of discovering attractive ways forward. This creates space for the sharing of tacit as well as intellectual knowledge.

3. The importance of tacit knowledge to organisational growth and development

Tacit knowledge is the embodied understanding of things born from experience that may not be readily accessible to others, or indeed easily transmitted. For example, I recently read an interesting story about something called a TEA laser.[4]

This laser, and how to construct it, had been comprehensively documented in the physics literature, but research laboratories assembling theirs for the first time were unable to get it to work. A researcher discovered that nobody could make the laser work unless they had spent time in a laboratory that already had a working one. Anyone who tried to put one together just using the written articles failed. They had something that looked like a laser on their bench, but it would not lase.

The explanation of why it would not work gets a bit technical, but essentially the common-sense way of assembling this thing, 'putting it on a bench', meant that 'the lead from the capacitor to the top electrode would be too long and have too high an inductance for the laser to work.' Yep, me neither. But the point is clear: you had to have the experience to truly understand what was necessary to get the thing to work. This was because the knowledge about the lead length limitation was just 'how you set it up,' and it did not occur to anyone to add it to the instructions. It was a crucial bit of knowledge that had not been codified in a portable way: it remained tacit knowledge residing only in those who had had previous direct experience. Food recipes are also famous for not being able to include the tacit knowledge of the originator, as anyone who has struggled with identifying the setting point for jam will know.

Tacit knowledge produces a much higher level of resonance than 'book learning'. This is something people know with their bodies as well as their brains; they were there, they lived through it, it is embodied knowledge. Such knowledge has a different quality of depth, passion and belief and is also shared with a different quality of expression. People speak of their lived experience with passion and emotion, which has a different effect on an audience than a dispassionate disquisition on the topic. Emotion speaks to emotion. To be clear, there is nothing wrong with knowing 10 factors that are essential to great team performance, it's just that getting a group to recite them does not have the same impact on motivation to change as learning from their lived experience. It's the difference between we 'should' and we 'ought', expressions of obligation, and 'I want' and 'I feel' expressions of desire. The point is that everyone has access to tacit knowledge, to their life's experience, and when we focus on this we reduce the privilege given to particular codified forms of knowledge to which not everyone has access, making room for a greater diversity of experience to be valued.

When working with groups in the organisation, people with different backgrounds, experiences and cultural understanding from the dominant group can potentially bring such tacit knowledge, gained from their lived experience, into the room. However, whether they get to share such knowledge is a different matter. They are more likely to be able to do so when they feel psychologically safe, as opposed when they do not, in which situation the priority becomes to 'fit in',[5] which usually involves minimising different perspectives and experiences. In this way, a valuable diversity of experience is lost to the group. As well as fostering conditions of psychological safety that encourage such sharing, appreciative inquiry is explicitly interested to know about people's tacit learnt-from-experience knowledge rather more than their intellectual book-learnt knowledge, meaning it supports active inclusion of knowledge from varied life experience.

To help create this atmosphere of psychological safety that enables the sharing of tacit knowledge, time should be invested in the early stages of the event explaining how the event will run and offering suggestions for how people might want to work together to help everyone feel able to fully listen and contribute. The facilitator can then invite small group discussions to reflect on what has been said and to bring up for discussion anything that is still interfering with people's ability to both contribute to, and benefit from, the day.

Case Studies Using Appreciative Inquiry to Enhance Diversity, Equality and Inclusion

Joana Dos Santos [4], a consultant and coach, worked on developing organisational values at her college in response to a student request for racial justice to be central in their education. First, she formed a diverse core team to lead the project. Using the 5D model, they held an appreciative inquiry process. The core group involved was excited and surprised to find that by focusing on what was already working, they could start addressing systemic oppression and move towards an organisational culture built on a diversity, equality and inclusion foundation. The team found that using appreciative inquiry to create college values rooted in social justice and diversity, equality and inclusion was a natural synergy. She notes how, as argued above, appreciative inquiry promotes having a diversity of voices across the organisation involved in the core group and in the organisational change process as a whole, meaning that the approach lends itself to work of this nature.

Elsewhere Sharon Thompson-Tan [5] extended the familiar diversity, equality and inclusion frame to include justice, so creating the JEDI (justice, equality, diversity and inclusion) frame for developing organisational culture. As they worked with organisations to embed a JEDI culture, they came to realise that creating such a culture was fundamentally about how people interacted, how they paid attention to one another, and about how they gave and took space to create the psychological safety necessary to risk being authentic and being heard. And as they realised this, they learned to be patient and accept who they were. Thompson-Tan said that 'listening allowed our people to exhale and decompress from the tensions built up over a rather long period of conflicts that grew from not paying attention to the needs of the people in the organization'. She is at pains to point out that this realisation is not to discount the importance of strategic planning and implementation around external and internal diversity, equality and inclusion measures, but rather that for these structural differences to have impact there needs to be an accompanying shift in the quality of person-to-person interaction to allow new ways of being together to emerge. She goes on to say, 'By adopting an appreciative rather than a deficiency approach, we were able to come together to discuss what the situation was now and what was possible'.

Jeanie Cockell and Joan McArthur-Blair [6] bring a slightly different perspective to this discussion, as they are interested in the challenge of navigating privilege amongst diverse groups. They point out that putting this into practice means paying attention to who gets invited to participate in all aspects of an appreciative inquiry, always asking, 'Is this process privileging certain voices?', as well as ensuring that diverse facilitation teams are created. They note the importance of being strong enough to not allow racism, sexism or homophobia, in a phrase I really like, to 'drift into conversations unchecked'. I like this phrase because I think it captures that sense one sometimes encounters in the buzz of a conversation that something just said was 'off'. As one is puzzling why the particular contribution did not sit well, the conversation moves on. By the time the brain has caught up with the emotional reaction and identified what was 'off' about the comment, it takes courage to stop the conversation and take it back to address something that could easily have slipped under the radar.

Finally, we can look to Florence Delacour Le Petit [7], a consultant and coach, who undertook an assignment to investigate the underrepresentation of women in senior management, with a view to improving their presence at the level of chief officer particularly. As part of an appreciative inquiry approach, she undertook a discovery with both men and women across the company. This allowed her to move from focusing on the barriers to women's mobility to understanding the levers of success for chief officer–level women. In this way she changed the organisational question from what stops women from being successful to what makes women successful in the chief officer-level applications. This was a small but highly significant shift in emphasis.

Conclusion

In this chapter we have looked at how to create an appreciative inquiry commission from the many and varied problem-oriented requests for help that might arise. We have looked at some of the pushbacks that might be experienced in commissioning conversations and have identified some design principles we can call on to inform our response. We moved on to consider the importance of an ethical approach to practice and within that discussion looked at how appreciative inquiry helps to create psychological safety which, along with other features of appreciative inquiry, supports equality, diversity and inclusion good practice. We concluded by looking at some examples of how appreciative inquiry has been used more directly to help cultivate positive diversity, equality and inclusion cultures.

Learning Points

1. Many appreciative inquiry commissions have to be created from initial problem-statement requests for help.
2. Early conversations with the organisation are very important for creating an appreciative inquiry commission.
3. Pushbacks are to be expected as people engage with a new idea.
4. Sticking to design principles will help preserve the process.
5. Appreciative inquiry can be seen as an approach that creates psychological safety and is particularly well suited to creating environments of equality, diversity and inclusion.

Discussion Questions

1. How does appreciative inquiry support work in diversity, equality and inclusion. What must the facilitator attend to with particular vigour?
2. What are some of the common pushbacks appreciative inquiry practitioners are likely to encounter, and how can they be addressed without sacrificing the essence of appreciative inquiry?

Teaching Exercises

1. Distribute the common pushbacks encountered amongst the class in groups to think about how they would work with them using the design principles; then share ideas amongst the group as a whole.
2. Work together to design an appreciative inquiry process to enhance diversity, equality and inclusion within an organisation.

Helpful Resources

For more on developing a deeper understanding of diversity, equality and inclusion issues in the workplace I particularly recommend.

Kandola, B. (2018). *Racism at Work*. Oxford: Pearn Kandola.
Chamorro-Premuzic, T. (2019). *Why Do So Many Incompetent Men Become Leaders? (and How to Fix It)*. Boston: Harvard Business Review Press.

Whitney, D. and Trosten-Bloom, A. (2003). *The Power of Appreciative Inquiry: A Practical Guide to Positive Change*. San Francisco: Berrett-Koehler Chapter 5.

I also found these articles interesting

Sayegh-Moccand, S. (2023). Seven Creative Ways to Attract Top Talent. Achievers. http://www.achievers.com/blog/diversity-and-inclusion Accessed 7 Nov. 2023.

Zaidi, S. (2022). Integrating psychological safety: using the all-in method to cultivate belonging and understanding in diversity and inclusion. *AI Practitioner* 24 (4): 37–42.

While for help with creating a commission these texts all have something to offer

Lewis, S., Passmore, J., and Cantore, S. (2016). *Appreciative Inquiry for Change Management: Using AI to Facilitate Organizational Development*, 2e. London: Kogan Page Chapter 12: How to introduce Appreciative Inquiry and related approaches to your organization.

Lewis, S. (2021). *Co-creating Planning Teams for Dialogic OD. From Entry to Event*, BMI Series in Dialogic Organisational Development. BMI Publishing.

Ludema, J.D., Whitney, D., Mohr, B.J., and Griffin, T.J. (2003). *The Appreciative Inquiry Summit: A Practitioner's Guide to Leading Large Group Change*. San Francisco: Berrett-Koehler Chapter 4.

For specific resources I recommend

The Appreciative Inquiry Card Pack which contains many useful ways of explaining some of the beliefs that underpin appreciative practice.

And the Psychological Safety cards that can help a team explore its working culture.

Both of these are obtainable from http://www.theppshop.store and amazon in some parts of the world.

Notes

1. https://www.achievers.com/blog/diversity-and-inclusion. This blog by S. Sayegh-Moccand quotes research: 'According to Deloitte, diverse companies enjoy 2.3 times higher cash flow per employee and Gartner found that inclusive teams improve team performance by up to 30% in high-diversity environments. Yet only 40% of employees agree that their manager fosters an inclusive environment'.
2. There are a number of chapters about conversation in Lewis, S. et al., 2016, *Appreciative Inquiry for Change Management*.

3. Speaker at ABP conference 2022. Details unfortunately lost and seemingly irretrievable. My apologies.
4. This story is taken from the article 'Everyone Wants Their Chips Served Quickly, but It Turns Out You Need a Special Sauce' by John Naughton in *The Guardian*. Print edition UK. 22.10.23. p. 21.
5. Natasha Brown's novel *Assembly* is a very accessible exposure to the strain of 'fitting in'.

References

1. Lewis, S. (2021). *Co-creating Planning Teams for Dialogic OD: From Entry to Event*, BMI Series in Dialogic Organisational Development. BMI Publishing.
2. Lewis, S. (2016). *Positive Psychology at Work*. Wiley-Blackwell Chapter 1.
3. Edmondson, A. (1999). Psychological safety and learning behavior in work teams. *Administrative Science Quarterly* 44 (2): 350–383.
4. Dos Santos, J. (2022). Using appreciative inquiry to develop organizational values rooted in social justice and diversity, equality and inclusion. *AI Practitioner* 24 (4): 12–17.
5. Thompson-Tan, S. (2022). Breakdowns and breakthroughs in intercultural JEDI work in a non-profit organization. *AI Practitioner* 24 (4): 18–24.
6. Cockell, J. and McArthur-Blair, J. (2022). Navigating privilege as we do and be appreciative inquiry. *AI Practitioner* 24 (4): 25–29.
7. Delacour Le Petit, F. (2022). A possible pathway to the C-suite for every woman. *AI Practitioner* 24 (4): 50–55.

PART TWO

Applications

5

Appreciative Inquiry for Flourishing Organisations, SOAR and I-IPOD

In this chapter we look at how appreciative practices support individual and organisational flourishing. While exploring this, we examine a model of the flourishing organisation and the appreciative practices that can support and maintain its development. The idea of the power zone is introduced as a model that helps explain what can happen to people during organisational change. Later in the chapter, two specific adaptations of appreciative inquiry are introduced: SOAR (Strengths, Opportunities, Aspiration and Results) and I-IPOD (Innovation – Inspired Positive Organisational Development). SOAR is explained and illuminated with a case study, and a second case study illuminates how I-IPOD can be used to great effect with a big community system.

Appreciative Practice and the Flourishing Organisation

1. What is organisational flourishing?

Organisational flourishing was identified by Kim Cameron [1] as an organisational culture that is good for people and for business. In particular he identified three attributes of flourishing organisations. Firstly, they have an affirmation bias, which essentially means they actively look for the good, for strengths and other attributes that can be affirmed and appreciated. Secondly, they have an active interest in positive deviance, that is, learning from the best. And thirdly, they have a culture that allows for the practice of valued or virtuous behaviour, by which he means such things as patience,

---

Practical Appreciative Inquiry: A Toolkit for Applying Appreciative Inquiry to Organisational Challenges, Opportunities, and Aspiration, First Edition. Sarah Lewis.
© 2025 John Wiley & Sons Ltd. Published 2025 by John Wiley & Sons Ltd.

forgiveness, helpfulness and humility. This does not mean they do not address poor performance, engage with problems and so on; rather, they spend more time and energy than most organisations in focusing on these three other behaviours. I hope it's clear that appreciative inquiry resonates with this model. It encourages the awareness of and learning from positive deviance, it looks for features of people and organisations worthy of affirmation and, by encouraging positive emotional states, it increases the likelihood of the expression of virtuous behaviour.

2. How appreciative practices can support organisational flourishing

Appreciative practice can be applied in many areas of organisational life to create and sustain organisational flourishing. Appreciative practice refers to the ability to take the key principles of appreciative inquiry and practice, going beyond the 5D model, and to apply them in many different ways in a variety of contexts. Many practitioners have developed specific appreciative processes and models for different challenges and situations. I believe we now have enough knowledge and expertise in applying appreciative inquiry, supported by findings and practice from positive psychology, to create a full model of the practices that can support the development of the flourishing organization. These are outlined Figure 5.1 below.

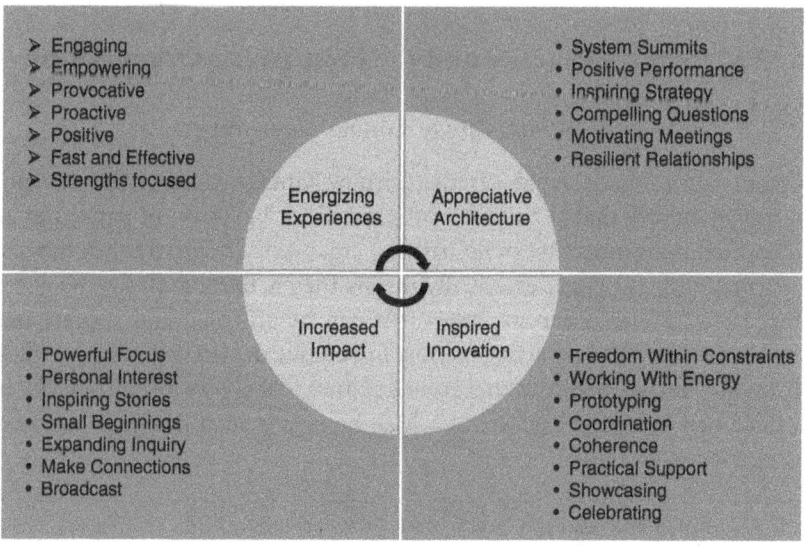

Figure 5.1 Appreciative inquiry for flourishing organisations.

This model pulls together areas of practice knowledge from appreciative inquiry and positive organisational development into four key pillars. These represent domains of knowledge and practice that we can call on to grow flourishing organisations: appreciative architecture, inspired innovation, increased impact and energising experiences. Let us take an overview of these four pillars and their components of practice.

3. Appreciative architecture

Appreciative architecture refers to the systems and processes with which we can build, design, sustain and grow organisations. The core of this, of course, is the appreciative inquiry *system summit* process, itself grounded, as we have seen in previous chapters, in good positive psychology science. Meanwhile, researchers have developed *positive performance* management processes [2, 3][1] that take appreciative inquiry principles and transform performance appraisal into conversations based on stories and aspirations, and the identification of strengths. The conversation becomes focused on using strengths to best effect and the creation of a growth-inspiring future.

The SOAR [4] process, developed by Stavros, which is explained in more detail below, is a process for developing *inspiring strategy*. A basic appreciative inquiry skill is that of creating *compelling questions* as will be evident in the many case studies in this text. This, along with other appreciative skills, can be used to ensure, for example, that *meetings are motivating* for attendees.[2] From positive psychology we know that sharing good news [5],[3] as appreciative inquiry encourages us to do, enhances relationship building. Meanwhile the whole-system collaboration at the heart of appreciative inquiry supports the creation of *resilient relationships*. In this way the first pillar, appreciative architecture, embraces appreciative inquiry, appreciative performance, compelling questions, motivating meetings, SOAR and resilience.

4. Inspired innovation

For inspired innovation there is a whole suite of knowledge about what helps organisations to continually grow and evolve in positive directions, some of which is explored in more detail in Chapter 9. For example, from appreciative inquiry we understand how to create *freedom within constraints* in a way that enables people to innovate and generate new ideas. An understanding of how to create positive energy for change supports the ambition of *working with energy*. Appreciative inquiry as an emergent change process understands the need to *prototype* new ideas, that is, to be experimental, tentative and provisional before deciding on wholesale direction changes. From an understanding of the organisation as a living system, the role of leaders is seen to be about creating *coordination* and *coherence* between energised groups and emerging projects, rather than solely focusing on adherence and control.

Importantly, appreciative inquiry gives us a key understanding of the part played in growth and development by the direction of attention. Leaders need to be alert to, and then share and broadcast, the early signs and signals that things are moving in the new desired direction, rather than waiting for the job to be completed. Some of the ways they can do this are through *showcasing* early signs of growth, change or achievement, and *celebrating* small and large successes along the way. They can also help by providing the *practical support* that new ideas often need when being led by junior organisational members, or when they go against the organisational grain. In this way, we have a full understanding of what is needed to help organisations become constantly innovative and adaptive to rapidly changing environments.

5. Increased impact

The processes above lead, in turn, to increased impact as good ideas, early innovations, early signs of growth, exceptional experiences and performance, and particular breakthroughs are magnified and shared across organisational barriers. People pay attention to what leaders appear to be interested in, which means a *powerful focus* of leadership attention (in a positive way!) will encourage the organisation to also focus its attention in that area. Leadership taking a *personal interest* makes a big difference to the life, energy and sustainability of people's efforts to achieve change.

We also know that sharing and *broadcasting inspiring stories* has an elevation [6] effect on others, who become inspired in turn. We know that by nurturing and cultivating *small beginnings* we can grow larger change. If we *expand our areas of inquiry* and *make connections* between different areas of endeavour, we can increase the impact of activity; and the more we share and broadcast successes, particularly early successes in areas of change, the more we amplify the effect of all the other processes I have just mentioned.

6. Energising experiences

Finally, appreciative inquiry is the perfect tool to create energising experiences for people. Maintaining engagement is a key challenge for organisations, especially when they aren't in a position to offer promotions or exciting new work. By using appreciative practices leaders can create *engaging* interactions. By providing experiences that are *empowering*, that ask *provocative* questions, that allow people to *be proactive*, that are *positive*, that result in *fast and effective* action, and that are *strengths-focused*, the conditions are created for high levels of energy.

I want to pick up on this last idea of strengths as a source of organisational energy and flourishing, by looking at an idea of Mayerson and Chairman's [7] that I came across in a book about strengths by Niemiec [8, 9].

Strengths and the Organisational Power Zone

Figure 5.2 presents a four-quadrant model of the relationship between, performance, competence, and the use of core strengths. It's developed from research[4] which suggests very clearly that knowledge, understanding, and use of strengths is connected to flourishing or thriving at work. The model offers a useful framework for considering the effect of changes at work on strengths use, performance and morale, and for considering how to help improve thriving and motivation at work.

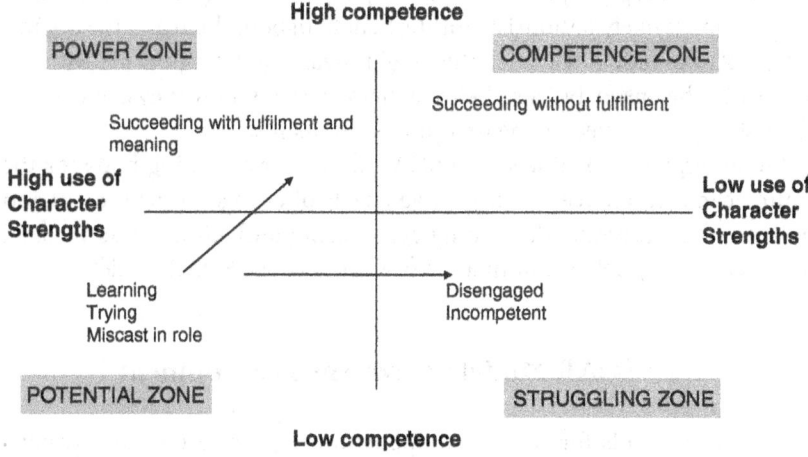

Figure 5.2 The power zone. Extended from Niemiec write-up of Mayerson and Chairman [7].

The quadrant the flourishing organisation wants people to be in is the top left section, the power zone.[5] This is the zone where people experience success and find fulfilment and meaning in their work, which is pretty much the definition of flourishing at work. People are likely to experience this thriving state when they are able to exercise both competency (high skill) and their strengths. The other three quadrants describe other experiences of performance and thriving (or not) at work.

One way this model can be used is to illuminate how organisational change can cause an unintended shift from one state to another. It also gives us ideas about how organisations can proactively help people move from one state to another. For example, we can hypothesise that sometimes during organisational change, people get 'thrown' from one quadrant to another as their job or work changes. From this, various outcomes may follow.

For example, people thrown in the potential zone, where their previous competence is mismatched to the current task, might be on a learning curve, ready to move back to the power zone. On the other hand, if they are not helped with developing their competence, they might instead find themselves in the struggling zone. Once here, and I have seen this quite often, when people feel deskilled and are no longer able to use their core strengths to support their execution of the role, and they are left to struggle, they can start to feel like they are failing. This can lead to disengagement.

The ambition during the disruptions of change should be to help the organisation keep people in, or restore people to, the power zone, where they are more likely to flourish, for the benefit of both them and the organisation. At the individual level, this might mean equipping people with the new skills they need, but also helping them work out how they can best use their strengths to execute the new job requirements.

On an organisational level the SOAR process, by creating hope for the future, can help reduce the disruptive effects of change in the present and enhance organisational flourishing even during difficult times as we shall see in case study below. But first, let us introduce the SOAR model.

The SOAR Model of Strategy Development

SOAR [10][6] stands for strengths, opportunities, aspirations and results. The figures below show the model and the thinking behind it (Figures 5.3 and 5.4).

Appreciative Inquiry for Flourishing Organisations

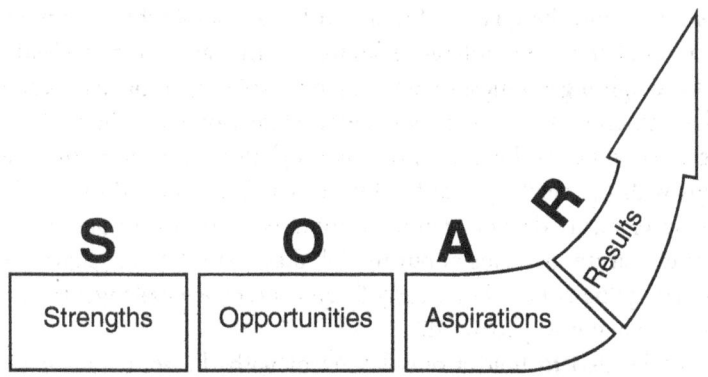

Figure 5.3 Model of SOAR. First developed by Jackie Stavros and Gina Hinrichs.

- The nature of capacity building is multi-level. In other words, every level of the system needs to be part of the process
- There is no one formula for success, so the framework must be flexible, dynamic and able to integrate with other approaches
- Capacity building is relational; dialogue and collaboration build trust and shared objectives
- Capabilities must be identified to start and support the capacity building process, beginning with those in the system
- Capacity building results in participatory learning processes for those involved
- Appreciative Inquiry facilitates capacity building

Figure 5.4 The basis for the development of the SOAR model: capacity building for whole-system change. Source: Adapted from Stavros [10].

In the case study below, focusing on just the initial event, in what turned out to be a larger project, means we get into the detail of the day, noting its effect on motivation, morale, team effectiveness and performance. I'm hoping it will be clear how working in this way, with a team in the struggling zone, kickstarted a move back to the power zone and replenished flourishing. This case study also illustrates how you can combine appreciative inquiry with other methodologies.

Case Study: Using SOAR to Return to the Power Zone

The senior leadership team of an ailing division within an engineering company were facing an uncertain future. The order book was dwindling with no replacement source of orders in sight. The workforce was becoming demoralised, and the quality of their work was measurably declining with rising rates of errors and tolerance failures. At the same time, the leadership team were fighting amongst themselves, busy solving problems in each other's departments rather than their own, while worrying about their own futures. Everyone was busy solving yesterday's problems rather than getting to grips with the challenges of the future. The way ahead threatened to be one of accelerating decline, demoralisation, workforce dropout and failure to secure a future. In terms of our model, they were showing signs of being in the struggling zone. They clearly faced a strategic challenge: How could they forge a better way forward?

It was decided to hold a one-day event with the senior team to help answer this question. Before we got into practicing SOAR, I held an introductory round, following Nancy Kline's 'time to think' practice [11]. Here I asked each senior manager, in turn, to talk about 'Something I am doing right now that I feel good about and that gives me hope.' And to continue by addressing: 'What is the most compelling vision I have for the future of the division and what do we need to focus on to make that happen?'

The 'time to think' model is a tightly managed round robin which ensures that, firstly, everyone gets the chance to address the question, and secondly, that they are enabled to talk, uninterrupted, until they have said all they want to say on the matter. This proved to be quite a challenge with this lively, banter-driven group of men. At the beginning I had to make frequent interruptions to silence enthusiastic comments of affirmation or contradiction, including sounds rather than words. Once I had established the practice of listening in complete silence though they caught on, and the quality of contribution just got better and deeper. The quality of listening grew deeper and denser. Once everyone had heard everyone else, they were then each asked to make a comment, in the same format of a listening round, that started 'Listening to everyone, I'm inspired by...' I did this before we took a break to capitalise on the immediacy of the experience and the quality of connectedness the group was experiencing right then.

This is an example of taking another methodology and combining it with an appreciative inquiry approach. Note how this opening does not ask each person to reflect on 'What's the problem?' Instead, applying appreciative inquiry awareness of the potency of creating positive affect for problem-solving, and of appreciatively framed questions to generate new information, everyone is asked about, and talks about, their moments of pride, their hopes for the future, what they think needs to change (which is subtly and importantly different to what's wrong?) and what they have found inspiring in each other's contributions. As an aside, the physical manifestation of the impact of the process was highly interesting. Before they spoke, everyone was leaning in the circle. As each person finished speaking, they leaned back in the chair clearly indicating a readiness to listen to others. It was like watching a fan open and was prompted, I believe, by the feeling that they really had, for once, been enabled to talk until they had truly said what they wanted to say, and of being truly, deeply heard.

The mood in the room after this initial opening conversation was completely different. This jokey, lively group of vocal men who constantly interrupted each other had become grounded, thoughtful and reflective. They were profoundly affected by the experience of really listening to each other, of being listened to and of being asked a different kind of question. Their comments reflected this as they spoke about how affected they had been by what others said, how much they had learnt about themselves as a management team in just an hour, how much some things resonated with them, how they really heard some things for the first time and took on the full import of the words, even though they had 'heard' that person say those things before.

In this way we change the organisation 'in the moment', producing new patterns of communication and relationship that allow new and different things to happen. For the remainder of the day, we worked our way through the SOAR process, working in small groups as well as the large group.

The first area of SOAR is strengths, and the initial questions for this round were:

- As a division what strengths do we have, what are we really good at?
- What makes us unique, what can we be best at in our world?
- How do we use our strengths to get results?
- How do our strengths fit with the realities of the marketplace?
- What do we provide that is world class for our customers, industry and other potential stakeholders?

These questions can be seen as creating the discovery process.

I hope you can see here how, although the focus of the question is on strengths, the challenge of threats and weaknesses is also addressed but obliquely, in a manner that does not detract from the positive energy the discussion was likely to generate. As indeed it did. It became clear that the division held many strengths that should be valuable to the marketplace if only they could maintain them (remember the division was already showing signs of demoralisation and deterioration) and showcase them to the market.

The next SOAR-based questions, focusing on opportunities were:

- What opportunities do we think are out there?
- What opportunities does the changing world of (our particular industry) create?
- What does the world need from us?
- If we aren't close enough to the market to know, who is? Can we get closer ourselves?

These questions encouraged the group to look forward and outward, to shift their focus from the day-to-day problems to the wider world and its possibilities. The group recognised that there were opportunities, but they needed to be hunted down, lured into orbit. Most significantly they realised that their managing director, who had great connections, needed to be free to create and pursue these opportunities, which he could not do if bogged down in sorting out interdepartmental warfare, or being asked to sign off on every tiny expenditure. He needed to be released to operate in his power zone. It became clear the senior team needed to step up and stop micromanaging (which also meant they needed to get, or let, their underutilised frontline managers to step-up, a challenge we addressed in other events).

We then addressed aspirations:

- What are we deeply passionate about? What matters to us?
- Where is the sustainable energy for growth and change – the positive aspiration the whole division can relate to?
- Reflecting on strengths and opportunities – who are we, who should we become, where should we go in the future?

Here the motivating 'dream' from appreciative inquiry is asking them to create a vision of the division operating in the power zone.

By then it was after lunch, and I sent them off in small groups on a 'walk and talk' with the commission to come back ready to create a team shield that addressed the findings of the day so far and their aspirations, including a team motto. This particular exercise, as well as being fun and engaging, produced metaphors in the form of drawings on their shields and generative images of who and what they were. I hope this illustrates how as a facilitator you can bring your existing tool kit into the process as long as it can work within the appreciative frame. Some of the comments made it clear that they were developing trust in the leader's ability to seek out new opportunities, and that they needed to free him to be able to do so while they led a revitalisation of the system.

They were further asked to address these questions:

- How do we build this aspiration into every interaction/process/meeting we have?
- If we truly believed we could become this, how would we be behaving differently now?

I hope you can see how this conversation relates to the design phase of appreciative inquiry, that is, thinking about what we need to do differently now. This round invited the group to build dreams (based on identified strengths and opportunities and their aspiration) to pull them forward. They were passionately proud of their work and skills, and they felt a strong affinity for the machines they worked with. They believed this should, and could, be of value still. All this created the emotion of hope. Hope about the future; hope about possibilities. Hope is a highly motivating emotion. Yet notice how the idea of hope is transformed into enacted behaviour [12][7] as the question asks how a belief in the achievability of this aspiration would show in everyday work. So, for example, if the aspiration is to be 'world-beating', then asking what we would be doing differently NOW if we truly believed we could be world-beating transforms an aspiration for the future into action in the present, powerfully connecting the present to the future.

Finally, thinking about results, we moved on to ask:

- What meaningful measures would indicate that we are on track to achieve our goals?
- What are three–five indicators that would create a scorecard that addresses a triple line of people, planet and profit?
- What are the best rewards available to support those who achieve our goals?

By the end of this one-day event, the group had resolved to operate differently amongst themselves in the future; they were clear that they needed to act as a senior team that could release the managing director to chase possibilities; that they needed to get their own direct reports to step up; that they needed to bring the rest of the workforce to similar states of optimism, hope and aspiration; that things they did every day had a direct bearing on the possibilities for the future; and that they could have a future. This wasn't the end of the story, but it was a highly impactful start.

One of the things this case study illustrates is that whole-system interventions can begin in different ways. From this small beginning this grew into a much larger project. I never could negotiate to get the whole division together in an ideal way, so, over time, we worked with the whole system in a piecemeal and iterative way. The process emerged: from each event others were born. It would have been almost impossible to have sold this in advance. Instead, the process sold itself, each impactful event breeding an appetite for more.

Case-Study: A Community System I-IPOD Appreciative Intervention

For our second case study let us turn now to an account kindly shared by Fialkov and colleagues [13] who used appreciative inquiry to produce a flourishing community in a very different environment using a very different process. It is a very good example of working through ever-expanding spheres of influence. In this way a small group can have a positive impact on a large system.

Following a period of political violence in Kenya, a local NGO and USA consultancy came together to address the question: 'When communities live under conditions of continuous stress, what methods are best to help develop positive capacity?' The local NGO was operating in an ongoing context of ethnic clashes, displaced families and marginalised communities following earlier violent political activity. To bring hope and positive change to the community, they adopted I-IPOD (Innovation – Inspired Positive Organisational Development), an appreciative inquiry–based process first developed by Cooperrider and Godwin [14]. This model comprises three phases. The first is to elevate human strengths, the second is to magnify them and the third is to refract them out into the world or community (Figure 5.5).

The joint team started by sharing their own strengths and values and building trust and a sense of safety, which is the first circle: elevation of strengths. They structured dialogic processes to address the question: *How do we take our strengths outwards from ourselves and our families to workplace teams and communities?* which addresses the second circle,

Appreciative Inquiry for Flourishing Organisations

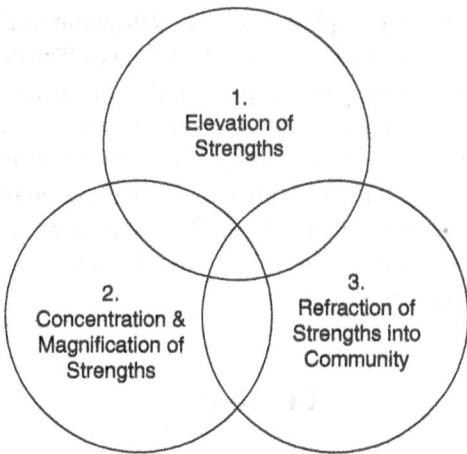

Figure 5.5 The I-IPOD model.

concentration and magnification of strengths and the third circle, refraction of strengths into the community.

Inspired by their answers to these questions they ran various counselling and community-action programmes for local groups such as those orphaned by HIV/AIDS or at risk of drug abuse. The ambition was to help those in direct contact with these vulnerable and often maligned groups to see the good, the valuable and the potential in both the people and their situations and so produce change for the better.

They developed a cascade process where each layer of the community project management teams themselves spent time identifying their strengths and working together to build trust and safety, to ready themselves to be courageous enough to use their strengths to work in a different way with their staff and community leaders. The process, spreading out like ripples in a pond, was based extensively on structured dialogue which is described in very helpful detail in the original articles. In brief, they developed tools such as strengths assessment, a set of dialogic practice guideposts known as Walking the Journey Together, trust interviews, and a story-telling and reflective practice tool. Through this process and the feedback loops created, stories emerged of how identified strengths had been engaged to create change.

In one example, a strength of teamwork had been activated to bring community members together to transform a hotspot of violence and crime by a river into a therapeutic play area for children. This initiative transformed the area to the extent that people were able to walk about freely in the evening without fear of being harmed by vigilantes or thieves. The previously threatening youths transformed into the peace and security ambassadors, while the elderly, previously targeted as vulnerable, became a source of wisdom. The full article gives many more examples of the positive outcomes as well as describing the process in much greater detail. But even in the necessarily abbreviated account, we can see the shift from a languishing community under threat from its own members, to one that is flourishing, promoting the well-being of all.

Conclusion

In this chapter we have examined a model of the flourishing organisation which pulls together some of the many appreciative practices that continue to emerge from the practitioner base. We have also looked at the idea of the power zone, identifying it as a helpful tool to think about what can happen to people during change. From here, the chapter moved to explore the SOAR model and illuminated its practice with a detailed case study. The final case study showcased an example of flourishing community development based on the IPOD model.

Learning Points

1. Appreciative inquiry is a highly flexible and versatile approach to creating flourishing in organisations and wider systems, which can be adapted to many different situations and contexts.
2. Other methodologies can be integrated into an appreciative intervention, assuming they are conducted through an appreciative lens.
3. Appreciative inquiry as a practice has been extended into other models, such as SOAR and I-IPOD.
4. Appreciative inquiry can be used with both commercial and non-profit organisations, and for both organisational and community systems.
5. It can be delivered in its original form, working with the whole system in the room, but also in other configurations such as sequentially or through a cascading pattern, as demonstrated here.

Discussion Questions

1. Given that some of the activity might seem very similar to conventional activity, e.g., talking in small groups and doing exercises together, what ensures it is an appreciative inquiry process?
2. What might be some of the advantages and disadvantages of the two approaches, as illuminated in the case studies, to achieving large system change outlined here?
3. How convincing or otherwise do you find the model of appreciative inquiry for flourishing organisations? What might be the challenges in creating such an organisational culture?

Teaching Exercise

1. Using the four quadrants of the power zone model, ask participants in pairs or small groups to consider firstly where they would place themselves, and secondly, where they would place the wider unit within which they work. Use findings as the basis for coaching conversations either about how they could move to the power zone (if not already there) or about how they would set about helping the organisation.

Helpful Resources and Further Reading

Fialkov et al., 'Tukae Tusemesane – Let's Sit Down and Reason Together,' *AI Practitioner*, 15 August 2015, for those who are interested to learn more about this particular application of appreciative inquiry to a community-based change initiative.

Stavros, J. and Hinrichs, G. (2009). *The Thin Book of SOAR: Building Strengths Based Strategy*. The Thin Book Publishing Company.

Stavros, J. (2020). SOAR 2020 and beyond: strategy, systems innovation and stakeholder engagement. *AI Practitioner* 22 (2): 70–91.

Cooperrider, D. and Godwin, L. (2012). Positive organization development: innovation-inspired change in an economy and ecology of strengths. In: *The Oxford Handbook of Positive Organizational Scholarship* (ed. K.S. Cameron and G.M. Spreitzer), 737–750. New York: Oxford University Press.

Notes

1. See these two articles for more on appreciative based performance appraisals.
2. This is explained more fully in my Udemy video: Six Steps That Lead to Productive Meetings, https://www.acukltd.com/online-training-courses.
3. The idea of 'constructive responding' is explained in this article, or you can look online for information about it.
4. Niemiec's [8] as above.
5. Mayerson and Chairman [7] as above.
6. I highly recommend this article. It gives a great overview of the current thinking, with lots of diagrams and explanations of the model plus examples of practice.
7. I came across the idea of the 'enactment principle' in Andy's book.

References

1. Cameron, K. (2008). *Positive Leadership: Strategies for Extraordinary Performance*. San Francisco.: Berrett-Koehler.
2. Kluger, A.N. and Nir, D. (2010). The feedforward interview. *Human Resource Management Review* 20 (3): 235–246.
3. Bouskila-Yam, O. and Kluger, A.N. (2011). Strength-based performance appraisal and goal setting. *Human Resource Management Review* 21 (2): 137–147.
4. Stavros, J. and Hinrichs, G. (2009). *The Thin Book of SOAR: Building Strengths-Based Strategy*. The Thin Book Publishing Company.
5. Gable, S.L., Reis, H.T., Impett, E.A., and Evan, R.A. (2004). What do you do when things go right? The intrapersonal and interpersonal benefits of sharing positive events. *Journal of Personality and Social Psychology* 87 (22): 228–245.
6. Haidt, J. (2000). The positive emotion of elevation. *Prevention and Treatment* 3 (3): https://doi.org/10.1037/1522-3736.3.1.33c.
7. Mayerson, N. and Chairman, V.I.A. (2015). "Characterizing" the workplace: using character strengths to create sustained success. *Kognition Og Paedagogik* 96: 14–27.
8. Niemiec, R. (2018). *Character Strengths Interventions: A Field Guide for Practitioners*. Hogrefe Publishing.
9. Huppert, F. A., and So, T. (2009). What percentage of people in Europe are flourishing and what characterises them? In IX ISQOLS Conference (pp. 1–7). https://citeseerx.ist.psu.edu/document?repid=rep1&type=pdf&doi=1cbb72d9b0da0c61f59035a39737cae02b80827b.

10. Stavros, J. (2020). SOAR 2020 and beyond: strategy, systems innovation and stakeholder engagement. *AI Practitioner* 22 (2): 70–91.
11. Kline, N. (1999). *Time to Think: Listening to Ignite the Human Mind*. London: Ward Lock.
12. Smith, A. (2023). *Practical Appreciative Inquiry: How to Use this Leading-Edge Coaching Method Confidently with Team and Small Groups*. Independently published by Andy Smith under Coaching Leaders.
13. Fialkov, C. et al. (2015). Tukae Tusemesane – Let's sit down and reason together. *AI Practitioner* 17 (3): 27–35.
14. Cooperrider, D. and Godwin, L. (2012). Positive organization development: innovation-inspired change in an economy and ecology of strengths. In: *The Oxford Handbook of Positive Organizational Scholarship* (ed. K.S. Cameron and G.M. Spreitzer), 737–750. New York: Oxford University Press.

6

Appreciative Leadership

As many practitioners have discovered, the impact and effectiveness of an appreciative inquiry intervention can be completely undermined if the leader is not aligned with the philosophy of change that underpins the appreciative inquiry approach. In this chapter we are going to look at how leaders can accidentally sabotage appreciative inquiry efforts and from there consider the importance of the leader's mindset to the success or otherwise of appreciative inquiry interventions. In particular we will be looking at the importance of the leader's understanding and being able to leverage organisational relationships, micro-moments of interaction, the focusing of attention, achieving change through inquiry and sense-making skills. We'll also look at the importance of focusing on what is there rather than what is not, the art of strengths-spotting and of understanding people as people. We'll move on to consider the endemic challenge of leading through uncertainty, and we'll look at that in action by picking up on the case study we looked at in Chapter 5.

First though, let us consider how leaders can accidentally sabotage appreciative inquiry efforts. Early in my career I suffered a few interventions of a 'the operation was successful, but the patient died' nature. In other words, we had a great event, but it had little further impact. Here are some of the situations of which I have fallen afoul.

Practical Appreciative Inquiry: A Toolkit for Applying Appreciative Inquiry to Organisational Challenges, Opportunities, and Aspiration, First Edition. Sarah Lewis.
© 2025 John Wiley & Sons Ltd. Published 2025 by John Wiley & Sons Ltd.

Leadership Actions That Can Undermine an Appreciative Inquiry Event

The leader is all for this exciting and different approach, but unfortunately cannot be available throughout the event. However, they will be there at the beginning and the end. The great danger of this arrangement is that when the group proudly present their plans for action at the end of the day, they will be shot down in flames by the leader who has missed out on the journey, all the thinking, conversation and energy that led to these ideas. If this 'compromise' is stated upfront then it can be pushed back against, and a change of date arranged. However, if they spring this on you at the last moment you just have to do what you can with the people present.

The leader of the group is present for the day but is insistent that the outcomes and ideas from the day need to be referred to some other body to be 'green lit' before people can start to act on them. Two things happen here. Firstly, the energy drains from the ideas as people wait to be told they can go ahead. And secondly, the 'recommendations' have no life or energy for the group to which they are referred, and they are completely divorced from the context in which they were formed. Given this, they are unlikely to be a priority for the decision-making group. It is sometimes possible to reignite the energy once permission is finally given for groups to go ahead, but it's far better to insist that people be able to make decisions at the event.

The leader agrees actions can be decided at the event. Great. But the leader then suggests that the leaders of the various initiatives need some training, usually project leadership training, before they can start their projects. The one time I agreed to this, it sounded like a good suggestion. Trouble was, it took an age for the training to be set up by which time, again, energy had drained from the initiatives.

A final one I would mention is when the leader is present for the day, actions are agreed upon and people are standing around the flipcharts of the projects they wish to be involved in, at which point the leader notices that one group has 5 volunteers, another has 12 and some people do not appear to be volunteering to do anything at all. An inbuilt sense of efficiency kicks in, and before your very eyes he or she starts to rearrange people, so all groups now have equal resources, and to allocate the 'spares' to various projects. Unwittingly he or she has just built in a drag on all of the projects. This project is not a priority for these people, they are not energised by the idea, they have better things to do with their time. They are likely to delay, and then miss, meetings and fail to follow up on their commitments. The situation has changed from being energy-driven to being command-driven, with all the change in motivation and commitment that entails.

There are many other ways leaders can sabotage your appreciative inquiry efforts. I hasten to say that this, of course, is not intentional, as they believe they are improving things. The mismatch between the intent and consequence of their help stems from a basic lack of understanding of, or agreement with, the conceptualisation of the organisation as a social system on which appreciative inquiry is predicated. I share these few specific examples as potential signals that the leader or powerful person has not quite 'got it' when it comes to their role in the process and the understanding of organisations and change on which that process is based. Let us look at this in a little more detail.

The Leadership Mindset Required for Appreciative Inquiry

Appreciative inquiry requires leaders to behave differently if it is to be successful. Traditional leaders are expected to know the answers and to know the way forward; the role of their followers is to follow. However, it is increasingly clear that in our complex, modern world to demand such omnipotence from a leader is unrealistic. It also causes them immense strain as the information available multiplies exponentially: they cannot possibly have the whole picture. Appreciative inquiry is very helpful in this regard as it acts to share the burden of leadership with the whole system or organisation in a structured, manageable way through a clear process. It does not require the leader to give up his or her formal position of leader, but it does require that their perception of their role shift. Let us look at some of the changes required.

Appreciative leaders see leadership as relational. They understand at a fundamental level that people aren't an interruption to the job, they *are* the job. The research shows that 'effective leaders are nurturant and developmental, not forceful, assertive or aggressive, as most would assume' [1]. Relationships are created and sustained through words and deeds. Whitney and colleagues have an interesting model of three different types of leadership conversation: relationship-cancelling, relationship-tolerating and relationship-enhancing [2].

Leadership Conversations that Include or Exclude

Relationship-cancelling conversations are those that exclude others. Such exclusion can be justified on many grounds such as 'they don't care', 'they will be overwhelmed', 'it's above their pay grade', or 'we can't afford to have them off the line'. I experienced this recently when negotiating with a service organisation to bring the client group into the conversation. The anxiety this produced led initially to much concerned discussion about how to protect these people; extensive ground rules, detailed seating plans, facilitated conversations, etc. were suggested and debated. Unable to resolve including clients and working to an appreciative design, the group made the decision to dispense with the appreciative inquiry approach and to revert instead to a standard 'town hall' where experts and clients were safely on different sides of the line, talking at or to each other rather than with each other.

Relationship-tolerating conversations 'allow for the existence of other people and groups as long as they maintain their place' [2]. This was essentially where the project mentioned above ended up. Relationship-tolerating conversations recognise people by role, but not in the full richness of what they can offer. This idea reflects the situation of the note taker who is required to be present at the conversation, a board meeting say, but is not expected to contribute anything beyond their role requirement to the topic under discussion. Let me here confess that many, many years ago when I worked as a leader in an organisation, I was guilty of thinking like this, excluding from the meeting discussion contributions from a bright, concerned and intelligent PA just because her role was to take notes, not to think. I blush now to think of it.

Relationship-enhancing conversations, on the other hand, strengthen the bonds of relatedness, build community and give people a sense of belonging in a meaningful way. Appreciative leaders encourage people to meet and get to know each other. They demonstrate confidence in people. They build and strengthen relationships, which is a foundation for performance, learning and resilience, reflecting Gergen's belief that 'the success of the organization does not reside in the actions of individual actors, but in the relationships among them. It is when these relationships thrive that participants are engaged, inspired and committed' [3]. Creating connections through relationship-enhancing conversations is one way to build social capital and appreciative inquiry, as a co-creative conversational process, it is ideally suited to producing this outcome. An appreciative leader values and nurtures relationships.

Unlike traditional leaders, who tend to think in terms of big set events to change things, appreciative leaders recognise the power of the micro-moment. Since every interaction, every exchange has the power to move the organisation towards or away from its goals, appreciative leaders are aware that how they act in the incidental moments has as much impact, if not more cumulatively, as how they act in the big moments. It is through the judicious use of micro-moments that they ensure the big messages of 'our values', 'our mission' or 'our change' are supported by the small actions of our behaviour. There is no point in expressing a belief in 'the value of our people' if they then blank people in the canteen or on the way out to their car! It is this understanding of how change works that helps leaders see the value of a whole day of structured, purposeful interactions with their whole system. They can see value in all the micro-moments – opportunities to offer affirmation, to discover things, to correct misperceptions, to build relationships and so on – while a more traditional leader, focused solely on achieving outcomes, can easily disregard all this as 'just talk'.

Appreciative leaders use their attention to direct other peoples' attention to the things on which they want them to focus. By consciously and positively directing their attention towards the best of their people and their organisation, by affirming people in their strengths, by recognising and pointing out great practice, they can inspire confidence, self-belief, motivation and achievement. They can use their attention to magnify what other people are doing that points towards the direction of travel the organisation needs to take. Leadership attention is a very valuable resource and is frequently discounted in traditional organisations where the leader's key resources are seen to be their cognitive ability and their structural power. A key factor that influences the success of an appreciative inquiry summit is the leader's awareness of how their continued interest and attentiveness post-event to the ongoing work acts as fuel to those now labouring to produce change in different areas.

As we would expect, appreciative leaders focus on achieving change through inquiry. Asking questions can serve many purposes. They can help with the challenge of sense-making during times of fast change. For example, Kimball [4], while working with a hospital on an initiative to reduce the spread of superbug infections, noticed that while initiatives may be perceived as being very joined up in the leaders' minds, they can be experienced as being very disjointed on the ground. She writes, 'Leaders can ask people appreciative questions helping them make connections'. She gives examples such as 'How does your program complement what people in the other departments are doing?' It also helps to bring people heavily involved in different projects or aspects of the change together to explore and make the connections, perhaps using a world café approach.

I once worked on a large enterprise resource planning project. For the uninitiated this usually refers, as it did in this case, to a large IT implementation. The work involved many project groups. The HR manager, who was key to the project, initiated a series of 'celebration' days, where all the groups came together and shared progress, looked to the priorities of the next phase and so on. This helped enormously in helping the geographically and functionally diverse groups understand how their part of this huge initiative (seven organisations across the world coming from five legacy systems to one common system) fitted with, helped, or was in danger of hindering other people's work. A more efficiency-minded person might have struggled to justify the time and money this involved, but it paid dividends. Not least because it acted as a re-energiser for everyone as they saw the progress being made and appreciated the otherwise 'hidden' hard work and achievements of colleagues. In other words, these occasional events were highly motivating.

Let me give another example. I worked one time as a coach to a leader for whom the power of asking questions was a life-changing revelation. When I first saw him, he was trying really hard to push his answers to the organisational challenges (and they were not bad answers) into the team discussion. They were not taken up. Released, by the adoption of a more appreciative question–focused approach, from the burden of having to supply the answer to every question anyone asked, he changed before my eyes from a highly stressed, anxious, overworked perfectionist, about whom I was truly worried (he looked like a heart attack or stroke waiting to happen), to a still overstretched, but no longer cardiac ward contender, achieving leader. Many other factors contributed to his growth and transformation, but he was very clear that asking questions and being appreciative made a real difference. I quote from an email he sent me. 'As discussed, I talked to everyone before the meeting and set the positive tone at the beginning and used appreciative inquiry (i.e. asked positive or appreciatively oriented questions) in most of the conversations. This is magical, I used the same method for a very difficult conversation with one of our regional managers. The result was unbelievable'.

Appreciative leaders focus on sense-making [5] rather than decision-making. Working from a social constructionist perspective, they appreciate that any reality is only temporary. Loath to make decisions of certainty in conditions of uncertainty they prefer to sense-make. Unlike decision-making, sense-making rests on a temporary understanding rather than a permanent reality. This approach allows leaders to flex and bend as circumstances change. Crucially, as team members are involved in the sense-making, it allows the group to change direction as circumstances change without anyone losing face for having 'got it wrong', or, even worse, sticking with a course they are increasingly aware is untenable but feel unable to change. Appreciative inquiry summits are all about collective sense-making of past, present and future.

They focus on what is there, not what is not, on what people can do, not what they cannot, on drawing out natural strengths rather than relying solely on instilling skills and on leveraging the value of peoples' varied experiences rather than trying to create carbon copies of 'the perfect worker'; this does not come naturally to all of us. Again, back in my early days as a leader, while I could extend endless compassion and individual appreciation to our social services clients, I simultaneously expected my staff to work like clockwork, without needs, as if they were robots, quite unaware that this might be problematic. I would like to think this way of understanding (well, complete lack of, actually) of how to help staff be and give of their best is now completely outdated. Ongoing experience suggests otherwise. See, for example, the post-pandemic push in many organisations to get people back to 9–5 office attendance regardless of any individual circumstances.

As well as having an appreciation of people's different circumstances, appreciative leaders also focus on identifying people's strengths. One of the benefits of working with the idea of strengths in an organisation is that it introduces a new language for talking about difference. One leader reported that 'just taking the strengths assessment changed the way associates interacted with each other and thought about the work that they do' [6]. And this established a foundation for the appreciative inquiry process that followed. Whitney and colleagues identify strengths-spotters as those able 'to hear positive potential through the haze of problems, dilemmas, issues and troubles'. They noted that 'because they seek strengths in people and situations, they readily find them' [7]. Learning to be a strengths-spotter rather than a deficit-identifier can take time and practice.

Finally, and to some extent as a summary, appreciative leaders treat people as people. In other words, as living entities experiencing emotions, passions and disappointments. This means that they recognise that people respond to inspiring stories, are stirred by passion and can be motivated by hope. Appreciative leaders recognise these psychological vulnerabilities and frailties as assets and work effectively with them.

Leading Through Uncertainty

Appreciative leaders are better positioned to embrace some of the key principles of being prepared for uncertainty as identified by Nassim Nicholas Taleb when considering the challenge of a Black Swan event [8]. He suggested that leaders need to accept that they do not know the future and to recognise that they can influence it, but they cannot control it. He suggests they should invest in being prepared for the unexpected, to be ready to respond to it. Leaders that take an appreciative stance are better positioned to work with uncertainty (Table 6.1).

Case Study: Appreciative Leadership in Action

To illustrate something of this in action, let us pick up the case study from the previous chapter. As we saw in the last chapter the story started when the newly appointed divisional leader invited me in and gave a report of his

Table 6.1 Why appreciative leaders are better positioned to work with uncertainty.

- They can be honest with people acknowledging that they do not know for sure what the future holds at the same time as being optimistic about possibilities.
- They can recognise that everything they say and do as a leader has meaning for their followers, and that there is no such thing as a neutral transmission of information or 'doing nothing'.
- They can bring positive psychology to bear, recognising and encouraging the value of positive emotions – laughter, playfulness or passion, while creating stories of hope, possibility and good futures that are accepting of current realities.
- They are well positioned to engage and involve people as much as possible in making the decisions that can be made, trying to ensure that people continue to feel that they have choices about, and impact on, the future.
- They can call on the collective intelligence of the organisation, recognising the wealth of expertise, intelligence, skill and resources in their organisation available to help meet the challenges ahead.
- They can help people find ways to be proactive in dealing with the needs of the business and their concerns, rather than passively waiting to be told.
- They can continue to offer leadership by developing the ability to act 'as if' they knew what to do for the best while at the same time being flexible enough to change tack when new information comes in, and by avoiding feeling that because they are the leader they must have all the answers.
- And they can, of course, be their authentic best self.

initial impressions of the division that emphasised the threat to the division: the dysfunctionality of the senior team and the increasing quality concerns within the context of a widespread blame culture where there seemed to be little accountability and problems were pushed upwards. The initial day I ran with this team is described fully in chapter 5. By the end of that event the group had created an optimistic scenario of the many sources of possible replacement work that existed in the known environment and had recognised the need to galvanise the rest of the workforce.

Over the next nine months the leader and I jointly ran five more days for line managers and frontline staff. During this time the quality issue was spontaneously resolved, the middle managers 'stepped up to the plate', and the senior managers started focusing more on their key challenge of attracting new work to the unit. The future continued to be uncertain. Throughout this time, the leader had to work with an unfolding situation that offered little obvious grounds for hope or optimism. He needed to keep performance and motivation high while being unable to offer the standard carrots and incentives. He had to adapt how he offered leadership as the situation unfolded.

In due course the leader was put in charge of an additional declining division. Within both divisions, given there was no foreseeable future for them, HR was actively encouraging people to apply for other jobs (either within the organisation or externally), although the current work requirements for the two divisions had not yet lessened in quantity or in its need for quality work. These two divisions were possibly going to merge as part of the expected rundown, meaning there would be a duplication of management bodies, and so likely redundancies.

I was asked to work with the uncomfortably combined senior team of the new merged division. Prior to a proposed team day, I interviewed people individually to enquire into the context and need. Various challenges came to light including: a brain drain of the brightest and best and trouble recruiting replacements, motivational challenges, a sense of a loss of direction, a feeling of being abandoned by the organisation and internal team conflicts – partly exacerbated by key skills shortages. A key question facing these managers, it emerged, was 'should I stay, or should I go?' They had not been able to explore this ethical dilemma with anyone and were expected to carry on as if they were personally unaffected by the situation. Meanwhile, they also faced the challenge of both encouraging their staff to seize opportunities as they arose, while also desperately needing them to stay to do the work.

At a point in the event, we gave everyone the questions 'How can I be a good person in this difficult situation? How can we support each other?' to consider.[1] For one of the senior leaders of the two teams, the answer was clear. Looking pale and resolved, he declared that his loyalty to both the product and his staff were such that he had to stay to the bitter end, and he had no alternative. This strong uncompromising statement of 'the right thing to do' made it difficult for any other manager to choose a different path. Despite this, one manager bravely confessed that he had already secured another job on site. This set up a dichotomous discussion rife with metaphors such as rats leaving sinking ships or captains going down with the ship. There was right, and there was wrong, and there was a clear decision to be made. This strong, simple story left very little room for nuance, flexibility or variation. There was only one acceptable choice for anyone who wanted to come out on the side of the angels.

It was at this point that the leader made a great contribution. He made it clear that, much though he cared about the unit, he also cared about his family. This meant that he would have to evaluate how to be a good person almost on a day-to-day basis as the context changed. In this way he modelled ongoing sense-making rather than, as the group had been experiencing, the necessity to make a binding binary decision. Very specifically he said, 'Am I looking for another job right now? No. If a good offer came along would I consider it? Probably'. There was an almost audible shocked intake of breath at this admission of uncertainty and so the possibility that he might leave. This leader was modelling a way of dancing with the unknown, of holding more than one possible position in mind, of sense-making rather than decision-making. The admission had an immediate, liberating effect on the other people in the room.

Following this pivotal moment, and with help, the group co-created more helpful stories of choice, recognised different ways of showing loyalty, developed a concept of provisional (rather than end point) positions and considerations, and acknowledged a shared recognition that there was no right answer in this situation. They developed a more nuanced acceptance of choice, recognising that each person could only do their best by their own lights while attempting to 'do good' in a very challenging situation.

This was an important, leader-led conversation that made it possible for the group to move from a negative downwards spiral of accusation and betrayal in a world of clear-cut choices, to a more nuanced appreciation that opened up the possibility of people making different choices that could all be seen as honourable. Most importantly, from my perspective, it became possible for the person nailed to the mast as a martyr to free himself from

Table 6.2 Seven principles for leading through uncertainty.

- Keep offering leadership.
- Put people first.
- Engender hope and optimism.
- Learn to love emergence and discovery.
- Call on the collective intelligence of your unit.
- Have many review and reflection points.
- Reveal your authenticity and integrity.

that uncomfortable position, and for the person who had secured another post to receive some recognition of the achievement involved in that.

The appreciative leadership was evident in how the divisional leader refused to adjudicate and assert what was the 'right' managerial response in this situation, instead he was authentic and honest about his own situation, offering a more complex picture of what leadership can look like. A while later I was delighted to hear that the deputy determined to go down with the ship had applied for another job. Things were shifting and loosening up.

There was no happy ending to this story, no big 'saving the day' order was secured. However, in the face of a continuing erosion of hope and staff, the division managed to maintain or exceed all its targets until the final product went out. They managed to relocate around 50% of the staff to other areas of the organisation with the other 50% taking voluntary redundancy. The leader noted that the appreciatively focused work, and I would say his appreciative leadership, meant that the unit exceeded all previous targets and set new standards for others to follow. He also mentioned that one part of the business had seen an increase in productivity as opposed to the expected drop off, and that there had been improvements in quality across the units. Table 6.2 outlines some of the practice [9][2] evident in this case study.

Conclusion

In this chapter we have considered the important role leaders play in influencing the outcome of appreciative inquiry interventions. We have noted that successfully engaging with appreciative inquiry requires a very different leadership mindset to that still commonly encountered. We have explored this further through a case study of highly effective leadership in a very difficult situation.

Learning Points

1. Leadership attitudes, beliefs and behaviour affect the effectiveness of appreciative inquiry interventions.
2. Appreciative leadership is a way of being and behaving.
3. Appreciative leadership recognises people as uniquely varied and the organisation as a social system.

Discussion Questions

1. How does being an appreciative leader help with the challenge of leading through uncertainty?
2. When might appreciative leadership not be appropriate?
3. How might an appreciative leader deal with poor performance?

Teaching Exercise

1. Facilitate a class discussion about 'the best leader I ever experienced'. This could be someone participants worked for directly or someone they observed. It can be in small groups or pairs. Include questions like 'What did this leader do that made them so effective?', 'Describe a particular situation in which their strengths as a leader really shone through' and 'How does what you observed of their practice relate to the ideas in this chapter?'

Further Resources

Lewis S., and Moore L. (2011) (eds.) Positive and Appreciative Leadership. https://aipractitioner.com/. Feb. 2011.

Whitney, D., Trosten-Bloom, A., and Rader, K. (2010). *Appreciative Leadership: Focus on What Works to Drive Winning Performance and Build a Thriving Organization*. New York: McGraw-Hill.

Verheijen, L., Tjepkema, S., and Kabalt, J. (2020). *Appreciative Inquiry as a Daily Leadership Practice*. Taos Institute Publications.

Lewis, S. (2016). *Positive Psychology and Change*. Chichester: Wiley-Blackwell Chapter 2.

You might find my Udemy video 'Successfully Leading Through Change and Uncertainty', a useful additional resource. https://www.acukltd.com/online-training-courses.

Strengths cards, available from http://www.theppshop.store, can be a useful way of helping leaders identify their strengths

Notes

1. An account of this powerful moment of leadership can also be found in Lewis [5]. *Positive Psychology and Change* on p. 98 under the heading 'Using micro-moments well'. Apologies to anyone reading who experienced a sense of déja-vu.
2. A fuller version of these principles can be found in Ref [9].

References

1. Greene-Shortridge, T.M. and Britt, T.W. (2013). Leadership. In: *The Encyclopaedia of Positive Psychology* (ed. J.L. Lopez), 571. Wiley Blackwell.
2. Whitney, D., Trosten-Bloom, A., and Rader, K. (2010). *Appreciative Leadership: Focus on What Works to Drive Winning Performance and Build a Thriving Organization*, 160. New York: McGraw-Hill.
3. Gergen, K. (2010). Foreword. In: *Appreciative Leadership: Focus on What Works to Drive Winning Performance and Build a Thriving Organization* (ed. D. Whitney, A. Trosten-Bloom, and K. Rader), ix–xii. New York: McGraw-Hill.
4. Kimball, L. (2011). The leadership 'Sweet Spot'. *AI Practitioner* 13 (1): 36–40.
5. Lewis, S. (2011). *Positive Psychology at Work: How Positive Leadership and Appreciative Inquiry Create Inspiring Organizations*. Chichester: Wiley Blackwell Chapter 4.
6. McCarthy, J. and Polly, S.M. (2011). Applying strengths and AI to Westin hotels. *AI Practitioner* 13 (1): 31–35.
7. Whitney, D., Trosten-Bloom, A., and Rader, K. (2010). *Appreciative Leadership: Focus on What Works to Drive Winning Performance and Build a Thriving Organization*, 68. New York, p: McGraw-Hill.
8. Taleb, N.N. (2008). *The Black Swan: The Impact of the Highly Improbable*. London: Penguin.
9. Lewis, S. (2019). *Positive Psychology in Business: 101 Workplace Ideas and Applications*, 90. West Sussex: Pavilion.

7

Building Resilience for People and Organisations

Resilience, whether personal or organisational is perhaps most simply defined as the 'ability to bounce-back from adversity' [1]. This suggests a return to a previous state after a temporary setback. Much resilience though, can be characterised as the ability to bounce-forward from adversity: to find new ways to navigate a future that has changed forever, perhaps following the loss of a close relationship or a life-changing accident. Similarly in organisations, some events change the environment forever. Indeed, when the two years of Covid-inspired lock-down ended, organisations were faced with the dilemma of whether to attempt to bounce-forward or to bounce-back. In first few years, it seemed that many were attempting to bounce-back to the old full-time office-based model. The possibility of bouncing forward into a working future influenced by the hybrid model that emerged during that time is explored in Chapter 13. Either way, organisations' resilience was much tested by the events of the late 2010s and the early 2020s.

In this chapter we are going to first look at some of the factors that underpin organisational resilience such as learning, processing feedback, knowledge transfer, the ability to rearrange work patterns, ad hoc problem-solving, and effective social capital. We will also look at personal resilience, considering particularly the importance of individual psychological capital, the impact that the organisational ability to embrace diversity has on personal well-being and the role of personal strengths in resilience. Throughout we will consider how appreciative practices can be utilised to support resilience, and finally we will look at two case studies where boosting resilience was a key aspect of the intervention.

Practical Appreciative Inquiry: A Toolkit for Applying Appreciative Inquiry to Organisational Challenges, Opportunities, and Aspiration, First Edition. Sarah Lewis.
© 2025 John Wiley & Sons Ltd. Published 2025 by John Wiley & Sons Ltd.

Appreciative Inquiry and Organisational Resilience

The essential resilience of an organisation resides in its patterns of behaviour. The deeper certain capacities are embedded within, for want of a better expression, the organisation's DNA, the greater the ability to survive and thrive in the face of adversity.

One key capability is that of learning from experience, and this is one area in which appreciative inquiry can really help. Appreciative practice is predicated on learning from the past for the benefit of the future. Discovery interviews facilitate learning from success and illuminate the key resources, actions, behaviours and beliefs that underlie the organisation's most successful moments. It is, of course, also important to learn from mistakes, but rather than being focused *on what went wrong and who is to blame*, appreciative inquiry is interested in learning from the experience in a way that allows us to do something different in the future. Recognising the organisation as a living system, appreciative inquiry helps us recognise that very often things go wrong as the context unfolds. It encourages us to focus on the pattern rather than looking for the clear-cut identification of people at fault. This systemic perspective encourages us to recognise that each decision made by the actors involved at the time was the best they could make, with imperfect knowledge and within the time pressures and stresses of the moment. And that each choice made sets up the possibilities, or not, for further choices. From this perspective our inquiry might focus on asking something like 'How did good intentions result in this unwanted outcome?'

A further key capability that supports organisational resilience is that of being able to process feedback quickly. As a whole-system approach, appreciative inquiry excels at this, allowing information from many sources to come together with varied perspectives and experiences, in conversation with decision-makers. By allowing people from different areas of the organisation to speak to each other directly, the passion and conviction behind the words are part of the conversation. Contrast this with a standard procedure of collecting information, perhaps by questionnaire, and then stripping it of all emotion in a report to be presented to the decision-makers. Unwanted news is much easier to dismiss once muted in this way. It is well known that bad news loses its potency as it ascends the organisation. Hearing directly from those experiencing the changed market conditions, or the complaints from clients, or the frustration with various systems and processes, at an appreciative inquiry summit for instance, creates a much more powerful feedback experience.

Another organisational feature positively associated with resilience is the degree of cognitive diversity in how organisational members think about things and analyse information. This, combined with a culture that cultivates a willingness to question the current situation and the respectful acceptance of these questions by the other members, allows new solutions to emerge. We can see here how appreciative inquiry by creating psychologically safe spaces, valuing diversity of experience and knowledge, and encouraging the involvement of many different perspectives and voices in engaging with organisational challenges, helps to create useful cognitive diversity in organisational life.

And, finally, the connected abilities of being able to transfer knowledge across the system and to quickly rearrange working patterns actively supports the organisation's ability to respond to situations as they arise [2]. Having the whole system involved at once means that organisations can make fast, informed decisions and take immediate actions to address the opportunity or threat.

Organisational resilience is also positively associated with ad hoc problem-solving networks, that is, the ability of people to get together spontaneously as necessary to deal with issues as they arise. I have observed many times the rich side line of low-level but highly impactful problem-solving that takes place when people are provided with an opportunity to have ad hoc conversations with people they do not normally come into contact with, as at an appreciative inquiry summit. 'It was good to put faces to the names', is a regular post-summit feedback comment. Having now had this experience of each other as fully embodied people, with whom they have had positive and productive conversations, they are much more likely to pick up the phone to sort things out there and then if a problem arises.

A quick example would be when, at an event focused on internal stock management, a driver was able to link up with the right person to make a suggestion that reduced the amount of time the lorries spent on the road empty. At another event two engineers from different parts of the organisation based in different countries got together during an open space session to resolve something that neither had been able to get traction on from the organisation. This kind of incidental problem-solving or performance improvement happens all the time at large group events precisely because they offer a unique opportunity to find the right people with whom to have a face-to-face conversation to work together on an issue that affects them at ground level and that, actually, cannot be solved by the usual procedure of running issues up the line of command.

Appreciative inquiry interventions tend to support the development of high-quality connections [3]. In turn, the experience of such quality

> **Positive Effect of Social Capital on Resilience**
> - Allows for ease of co-ordination, facilitating quick responses to change
> - Engenders high levels of employee engagement
> - Facilitates speed of change and adjustment through phenomena of synchronism and self-organisation
> - Facilitates generation of new knowledge through boosted creativity and innovation
> - Boosts speed of information flow
> - Facilitates local level coordination for problem solving, error correction or opportunity-seizing
> - Likely to boost discretionary effort

Figure 7.1 Positive effect of social capital on resilience.

relationships encourages people to exchange more and better information, experience more positive energy, experience a desire to strengthen relationships and to exchange more valued resources, not to mention supporting personal well-being. All of this supports resilience. This network of relationships, encouraged and supported by appreciative practices, creates high levels of social capital [4]. Social capital is an important component of organisational resilience, as shown in the figure below (Figure 7.1).

Another thing to note about resilient organisations is that they do a good job of managing the trade-off between two organisational needs that can pull in different directions. That is, they focus both on growing the organisation, which means enhancing variety, encouraging innovation and tolerating a level of inefficiency, and on building competence within the organisation, which is about developing efficiency. This can be a hard juggling act, but a resilient organisation needs to find its way around it. One way to maintain this dual perspective is to have regular review and reflection points to assess changes, opportunities and threats and to see what adaptations may need to be made. Every now and then the whole system needs to put its head above the parapet and take a look around. The appreciative inquiry summit offers a great process for doing this, whether at the team, division or organisational level.

Appreciative Inquiry and Personal Resilience

Of course, a key part of organisational resilience is also the resilience of individual members. Let us look a little more at individual resilience. One psychological phenomenon that underpins personal resilience is the

Table 7.1 Psychological capital.

Hope	Efficacy
The motivational energy operationalised as planning for goals and the agentic pursuit of goals	The confidence and belief in own abilities to activate the motivation, cognitive resources or courses of action needed to successfully execute a specific task within a specific context
Resilience	**Optimism**
The ability to bounce-back from setbacks or even positive events like increased responsibility	A particular explanatory style about present and future success

amount of psychological capital that is available to us at any particular time. Psychological capital is comprised of four psychological states of emotion and belief: hope, optimism, self-efficacy and resilience itself (see Table 7.1) [5].[1]

The key point about psychological states is that, unlike traits, they can be created and recreated. Appreciative inquiry-based ways of working have positive impacts on all of these elements of psychological capital. Discovery questions which bring resources available to us from both the past and the present into the light can enhance our sense of self-efficacy or the 'yes I can' feeling. Dream questions generate hope and optimism about the future. The way the whole appreciative inquiry process heightens our awareness of our strengths, our resources and our past successes can act to make us more resilient, that is, more able to pick ourselves up after a setback ready to go again.

How an organisation accommodates diversity also has an impact on its resilience. If one of the costs of acceptance by a group is having to downplay difference, this can lead to a psychological withdrawal and a loss of expertise. Recent work on inclusion and diversity and inclusive leadership has also emphasised the importance of an active appreciation of difference rather than a passive tolerance [6, 7].[2] Different people bring different experiences to the challenges the organisation faces. Organisations that have processes and mechanisms, relationships and culture that can access these resources are in a stronger position to respond creatively when the organisation needs to adapt quickly. Creativity is a key strength of resilience.

The Resilience Boosting Effects of Strengths

We've mentioned before how appreciative inquiry can help with the identification of strengths. Just to recap, personal, or character, strengths are the positive traits and capacities that are personally fulfilling, do not diminish others and that are found to be ubiquitous and valued across cultures [8]. See Figure 7.2 below for an outline of how the use of strengths acts to boost resilience.

Research shows that the exercise of our personal psychological strengths is aligned with numerous positive outcomes for ourselves and others. When we are exercising our strengths we are liable to be energised, confident and filled with a sense of well-being. We are likely to find things easy [9]. Our strengths are transferable across situations, always potentially available to us, whatever the situation. To be using our strengths is usually to be having a life-enhancing experience. The effective use of our strengths is connected to optimal performance, well-being, engagement, growth, fulfilment, morale, motivation, authenticity, goal attainment, energy and contribution. Strengths offer the greatest potential for growth and development. And the personal benefits of being aware of strengths are many, see [10] Figure 7.3.[3]

Before we look at this chapter's case studies, we can just note how the case study examined in Chapters 5 and 6, over successive workshops, created and recreated states of psychological capital in the team: hope, optimism, self-efficacy and resilience. We also took time to identify the

Figure 7.2 Relationship of strengths and resilience.

> **Resilience Effects of Specific Strengths**
> - The specific strengths of hope, kindness, social intelligence, self-control and perspective act as a buffer against negative effects of stress and trauma. In this way they aid resilience
> - The specific strength of courage helps to overcome challenges and to ensure active coping skills are developed
> - The specific strengths of love, hope, gratitude and zest are positive correlated with psychological wellbeing

Figure 7.3 Resilience boosting effects of specific strengths.

strengths of the unit. The senior team, and hence the division, displayed remarkable resilience including maintaining high performance in the face of an uncertain future.

Case Study: A Positive Approach to Difficult Issues

The members of a very senior and experienced management team had a problem: a temporary organisational reshuffle had left them with an immediate manager whose management style was at odds with theirs. This was putting considerable strain on the team. Impatient, direct, abrasive, rude even, this manager seemed oblivious to the stress his style of negotiation and decision-making put on others attempting to make their case in difficult negotiations. In addition, he was not above trying to split team loyalties. The team needed to boost their resilience to be able to work well, and not direct all their mental energy and time into dealing with the fallout of this change in their environment.

The team decided they wanted to work on ways to manage this manager that minimised the personal negative effects of stress-inducing contact with him; to support each other in their dealings with him; and to reaffirm and strengthen their core commitments to their team.

I spoke individually to each team member (Figure 7.4).

From this I designed a development day to address the different challenges different team members were experiencing (Figure 7.5).

At the beginning of the event we took baseline measures. We also took time early on to review the team values and to explore how they were being lived by team members at the present time. People talked about when they felt under pressure to compromise the team values and how they coped. In appreciative inquiry terms what we were doing here was strengthening the

> **Outline of Preparation Interview with each Team Member**
> Name
> Thanks
> What do you see as being the key priorities for the day?
> How will you know if the day has been a success? What will be different by the end of the day?
> What do you personally find most challenging about the current situation?
> What are you most optimistic about at present?
> What's been your experience of working with improv actors?
> What do you see as being the strengths of the team?
> If there was one small difference that would make a difference to the abilities of the team to cope with, and thrive, in the present and future, what would it be?
> Is there anything else I need to know to design and run a good day for you?

Figure 7.4 Preparation interview.

positive core of the team, allowing everyone to reconnect with a strong, positive commonality.

As you can see from the day plan, we moved on identifying strengths in a particular situation, that of having a difficult conversation, through the use of discovery conversations. Interestingly we can see here a development of the discovery interview, where we ask the speaker to think of a similar but not quite as effective situation and to identify the differences. I use this particularly when I want to reduce the huge to the manageable. Looking for the small things that we can do that make a positive difference can really boost our sense of self-efficacy. From this we constructed a Resources List. This list, which grew throughout the day, made visible the team resources for dealing with a particular forthcoming conversation that was causing them concern. Its visible presence helped create hope and optimism and boosted the sense of 'we can do this', that is, of confidence and efficacy.

As the plan outlines, a lot of the rest of the day was spent working through scenarios with improv actors. This meant team members got a chance to explore and rehearse different conversations that were coming up that seemed vulnerable to these dynamics. With the actor displaying the characteristics of key people as described to them by those present, team members could concentrate on their own live experience in the conversation.

This was a carefully structured and managed process. Good improv produces the same emotional states as 'the real thing', the difference is that you can

> **Difficult Conversations Team Workshop**
>
> *Overall Objective:* To enhance the ability of the team to have difficult conversations in a way that remains true to their values and produces valuable outcomes
>
> *Specific Aims:* By the end of the workshop participants should
>
>> Have re-affirmed the value and meaning of their team values in this context
>>
>> Have identified, and added to, their existing resources in this area: skills, experience, knowledge
>>
>> Have increased their skill in anticipating and preparing for such conversations
>>
>> Have increased their skill in conducting and managing such conversations
>>
>> Have increased their skill in supporting those involved in such conversation both in the moment and post-event
>>
>> Have a clear list of simple, effective behavioural and verbal tips that help them move a difficult conversational dynamic to a more productive one.
>
> **Workshop format**
>
> 9.15   Welcome, refreshments
>
> 9.30   Getting Ready: Introduction, working together
>
> *Introduce the day and the three of us. Brief context setting of working together today, reference to the 'rules of engagement' – anything else to add. Note change of pace, priorities.*
>
> *Take initial measures against the aims (baseline for evaluation)*
>
> 9.50   The team journey – highlights, values, relevance now
>
> *Story in a word*
> *Looking at the team values – people to each pick the most important or meaningful word in the values (for them) and to tell us a story about how that has helped them in a difficult situation. Expand into discussion of relevance of values to current situation*
>
> 10.30   Team resources – our existing strengths in this area
>
> *Appreciative Inquiry Discovery Interviews*
> *In pairs – each person to share story of a good experience of a difficult conversation that went well, where they changed the course of the conversation, where they got a good outcome. Companion to listen for strengths, skills. Then each to compare that to a situation that was similar but where the outcome wasn't quite so good. Identify some of the things that made the difference.*
>
> *As group collate this learning from experience. Then ask if anything else people remember as good advice from previous courses, reading etc. Add to list. This will be the team resource list that will grow during the day.*

Figure 7.5   Facilitator plan for event.

stop the action, go back and try something different, call a time out if anyone becomes overly emotional and so on. By creating a psychologically safe process to explore the use of different strategies for pro-actively handling the anticipated difficult conversations, you strengthen an individual's resourcefulness.

> 11.15 Specific Challenges – creating the agenda of order of scenarios for rehearsal today
>
> *Construct agenda with group of what scenarios to work on, in what order (in priority order)*
>
> 11.30 Break
>
> 11.45 Working with scenarios
>
> *Working on the scenarios – with consulting teams and observers with clear remits. Debrief after each scenario. Learning points added to resource list. If timing good 2 rounds, otherwise one and eat earlier.*
>
> 1.00 (ish) *Lunch*
>
> 1.30 Working with scenarios.
>
> *2 or 3 scenarios – depending.*
>
> 3.30 Break
>
> 3.45 Working with scenarios
>
> *another 2 scenarios I would imagine here*
>
> 4.45 Gathering the day together – individual bouquets of skill and hope, team agreements
>
> *People to draw a bouquet of approximately 5 key tips, new skills, learning or thoughts that they can gather together that give them hope for the next conversation. To be shared*
>
> *Team to clarify any agreements they want to make amongst themselves that support their ability to live the values in the current context*
>
> 5.15 Finish and evaluation
>
> *Take another round of measures against the aims (evaluation of day)*
> *Agree when next meet and any ideas for that time*
> *Care of resource produced*
> *Thanks and farewells*

Figure 7.5 (Continued)

You'll note that we provided the person in the 'hot seat' for any particular scenario with a team she or he could consult with at any point in the conversation. When they called for a consultation time out, the action would be paused, ready to be picked up again after the consultation.

We also had a separate observation team. This is a very valuable addition to the process, assuming you have sufficient numbers of people. Those in the observing team are not required to come up with suggestions for different ways forward. This means they get to notice things, particularly little linkages of cause and effect that those more actively involved often miss. For example, they might be able to report, 'I noticed when you asked that, a thoughtful look flashed across her face, but you went on to say ... and the

Table 7.2 Outcomes.

Evaluation Criteria		1	2	3	4	5	6	7	8	9	10
Sense of Shared Commitment to Values	Before	—	—	—	—	—	1	—	3	4	—
	After	—	—	—	—	—	—	—	1	7	—
Understanding the Existing Resources	Before	—	—	—	—	3	4	—	1	—	—
	After	—	—	—	—	—	1	3	3	1	—
Skill in Anticipating and Preparing for such Conversations	Before	—	—	—	3	1	1	3	—	—	—
	After	—	—	—	—	—	4	3	1	—	—
Skill in Conducting and Managing such Conversations	Before	—	—	—	1	3	3	1	—	—	—
	After	—	—	—	—	—	3	4	1	—	—
Total	Before	0	0	0	4	7	9	4	4	4	0
Total	After	0	0	0	0	0	8	10	6	8	0

moment passed. I wonder what was going on for … when you said that?' And the actor might be able to give some useful 'in role' feedback on what they were thinking at that point.

Working with good quality improv actors adds expense to the event, but in a situation like this, where rehearsal is an investment in boosting psychological capital and resilience, it is definitely an investment worth considering.

Evaluation of the effect of the day, achieved through before and after measures on four criteria, showed that the team had shifted towards the upper end of the scale on all measures: the intervention was successful against the desired outcomes (10 is high) (Table 7.2).

Case Study: Bringing Appreciative Inquiry to the Disruption of Organisational Change

Let us look at another situation that called for the development of greater resilience. This organisation was going through a restructure. The organisation was picking up some uncertainty from managers at all levels about how to lead their teams through the change transition. They commissioned a two-hour workshop for leaders.

When I have limited time like this with a group who need a quick resilience boost, I tend to focus on creating an atmosphere of positivity, identifying strengths and other resources, and creating a sense of hope and choice about the future. Initially we spent some time covering some theory, as requested by the commissioner, on what happens to people during change, and identified the priorities of leadership during change and uncertainty. Interestingly, the feedback strongly suggested that this was seen as the least useful part of the session and that it was the interactive element that was by far the more powerful experience.

We moved on to work in groups to hold discovery interviews exploring and sharing people's stories of leadership moments or experiences of which they were proud, for example, asking when they felt they had been at their best as a leader. People then used these stories, plus any other knowledge they might have of the person, to identify their leadership strengths, using sets of strengths cards. People were gratified and interested to hear others' observations of their strengths, and many recorded them. These two exercises are designed to create positivity and to boost confidence in their strengths and abilities, so increasing self-efficacy. As the session progressed, the level of laughter and smiling in the room noticeably increased, suggesting increasing positivity.

One of the participants was leading a team that were facing closure. They described a horrible situation where the team felt they were failing, people wanted to leave, and they felt increasingly ignored by and isolated from the rest of the organisation. The team leader described a sense of just sort of dribbling towards an end where the team would disappear without even a whimper. She did not look forward to coming into work and did not think her team did either.

The question we asked was, 'Now that circumstances have changed, what does success look like?' As we discussed this, the leader realised that they needed to change the existing service-level ideas of success, which were no longer deliverable, into some that matched the current task, that of closing down their unit. In other words, I encouraged that particular leader to think about what a really great closing down process would look and feel like and what the team would need to be focusing on to make that happen. Essentially, we identified an appreciative topic for an appreciative inquiry: 'What does it mean to have a successful close down?' This reframing facilitated a positive and productive shift in the leader's psychological capital.

This 'redefining of success' exercise is one that I have found to be immensely helpful in different situations. Without being aware of it, people are frequently caught up in an old paradigm of success where they carry on measuring themselves and their team against that old standard which is, by definition, no longer achievable. This often reveals itself in a general feeling of failure or incompetence, which they do not really understand. Feeling like this threatens resilience. Once it is recognised that the group's task has fundamentally changed, then all else follows. Leaders now have something positive to work towards rather than something to avoid. They can identify a whole new set of 'signs of success' and redirect their own and their team members' attention towards those things.

We also talked about the importance of 'doing it for yourself', particularly when senior management time and attention is very scarce, as it often is when a change project is being pushed through. How could they celebrate the achievements of the team over its lifetime? How could they share that story with others in a joyful, celebratory way? How could they create an atmosphere where people could own their strengths and maintain their morale, putting them in a better position to go for new jobs? How could they support each other to boost each other's skill set and CV? Could they ask the other teams they had worked with what they had most valued about their service and what they would miss? Could they devise a closing ritual that would allow them to mourn a little for the past, while also looking forward to a different future.

This workshop had effects in the moment on both mood (positivity) and self-efficacy (strengths and successes) and opened the idea of proactive choice of how to engage with change. They also left with ideas about how to help their teams maintain morale and proactivity in the face of the changes. I have included this case study to demonstrate that even a very short session, run with appreciative inquiry principles, can be effective in boosting resilience in the face of perceived adversity.

Conclusion

In this chapter we have considered the nature of resilience. We have identified factors that research suggests influences organisational resilience such as learning, processing feedback, knowledge transfer, rearranging work patterns, ad hoc problem solving and social capital. We have also looked at personal resilience and considered the role played by psychological capital and personal strengths. In both cases we looked at how appreciative inquiry summits and approaches can generate and support these factors. We also looked at a couple of case study examples of how appreciative inquiry was used to help a team enhance their resilience.

Learning Points

1. Resilience is a state as well as a trait, and it can be boosted both at the organisational and the individual level.
2. Appreciative inquiry boosts psychology capital and social capital, both of which support resilience.
3. Appreciative inquiry supports the identification of strengths and resources, which also boosts resilience.

Discussion Questions

1. How might you design an appreciative inquiry intervention directly focused on boosting the resilience of an individual or a team?
2. How does the idea of bouncing-forward help us think about resilience?
3. What other factors, beyond those mentioned in the chapter, might affect an organisation's resilience and how might appreciative inquiry work with those factors, if at all?

Teaching Exercise

1. In pairs, share stories of yourselves at your most resilient. Use these as a springboard to identify each other's strengths or to identify the context issues that supported your resilience at that particular time

Helpful Resources

I have a couple of blog articles that outline exercises with groups that might be useful: https://www.thepositivepsychologyshop.com/blogs/news/use-appreciative-inquiry-and-strengths-cards-to-boost-mood-self-awareness-and-confidence

And on boosting resilience:

https://www.thepositivepsychologyshop.com/blogs/making-changes-easy-and-engaging-exercises-for-change/creating-a-resilience-plan-in-testing-times
Resilience cards and strengths cards are available at www.theppshop.store.

McArthur-Blair, J. and Cockell, J. (2018). *Building Resilience with Appreciative Inquiry: A Leadership Journey Through Hope, Despair, and Forgiveness.* Berrett Koehler.
Sukhvinder, P. (2023). *The Resilience Handbook: A Practical Understanding of Resilience.* Published by Pabial Sukhvinder A great practical resource.

Notes

1. The table in Table 7.1 is sourced from Ref. [5].
2. While this is the direct reference: Ref. [6], I sourced it from this chapter: Ref. [7].
3. The research that supports this table can be found in Ref. [10].

References

1. Masten, S.A. and Reed, M.J. (2005). Resilience in development. In: *Handbook of Positive Psychology* (ed. C.R. Synder and S.J. Lopez), 74–88. Oxford University Press.
2. Sutcliffe, K.M. and Vogus, T.J. (2003). Organizing for resilience. In: *Positive Organizational Scholarship* (ed. K. Cameron, J.E. Dutton, and R.E. Quinn), 207–224. Berrett Koehler.
3. Dutton, J. and Heaphy, E. (2003). The power of high-quality connections. In: *Positive Organizational Scholarship: Foundations of a New Discipline* (ed. K. Cameron, J. Dutton, and R. Quinn), 263–279. Berrett Koehler.
4. Baker, W. and Dutton, J. (2009). Enabling positive social capital in organizations. In: *Exploring Positive Relationships at Work: Building a Theoretical and Research Foundation* (ed. J. Dutton and B. Ragins), 325–346. Psychology Press.
5. Warren, M.A., Donaldson, S.I., and Luthans, F. (2017). Taking positive psychology to the workplace: positive organizational psychology, positive organizational behavior, and positive organizational scholarship. In: *Scientific Advances in Positive Psychology* (ed. M.A. Warren and S.I. Donaldson), 195–227. Praeger.
6. Moss, G.S., Dodds, C.I., and David, A. (2016). Inclusive leadership: boosting engagement, productivity and organisational diversity. *Equal Opportunities Review* 268.

7. Boniwell, I. and Smith, W.A. (2018). Positive psychology coaching for positive leadership. In: *Positive Psychology Coaching in Practice* (ed. S. Green and S. Palmer), 159–178. Routledge.
8. Peterson, C. and Seligman, M.E.P. (2004). *Character Strengths and Virtues: A Handbook and Classification*. New York: OUP.
9. Niemiec, R.M. (2017). *Character Strengths Interventions: A Field Guide for Practitioners*, 2. Hogrefe Publishing.
10. Lewis, S. (2014). How positive psychology and appreciative inquiry can help leaders create healthy workplaces. In: *Creating Healthy Workplaces* (ed. C. Biron, R. Burke, and C. Cooper), 223–238. Gower.

8

Engaging with the Particular Challenges of Project Management

Project teams have some particular distinguishing characteristics which create a unique team-building context. For example, there is often a demand for instant performance while the team itself has a limited life. They often bring together people from different areas of the organisation, which possibly have different local work cultures. They may also come from different professional disciplines, each with its own understanding of priorities and ways of viewing and understanding the world. And there is likely to be allegiance to many leaders, as well as, or instead of, the project leader. These characteristics create some particular challenges to team formation and performance.

In this chapter we look at some of the existing tools for project management and then move on to consider the approach advocated by Charles Smith [1]. Working from this perspective, we consider how appreciative inquiry can be incorporated into, and can add value to, project management at the start and throughout the life of the project. We conclude by examining the commencement of a large organisational project, looking at how an appreciative inquiry approach was brought into a project set up as a Prince2 implementation process.

The Psychology of Project-Craft

The complex demands of project-working are well recognised, and a host of processes and systems have been devised to support project-working. These in turn are supported by a plethora of online project management tools that are aligned to different approaches to change. So, for example, the Prince2 approach is very much a planned approach to change, while the more recent Agile methodology takes a more iterative, flexible approach. Even so, projects can sometimes appear as the archetypal bureaucratic approach to change, with their emphasis on tracking and monitoring progress against milestones and targets. Of course, this is important, but what is often overlooked is the psychology of project teams.

Charles Smith, an experienced project manager turned organisational psychologist, undertook some research into how successful project managers *actually d*o project management compared to how they tell us they do it. He found that the best, while making good use of the tools available, take a very psychological approach to getting project teams to work well together. In particular, he found that successful project managers have an unrecognised project-craft that they call on to aid the delivery of the 'formal plan'. Let's look at some of his findings and consider how they can be viewed from an appreciative inquiry perspective.

Smith noted that project managers need to help the organisation develop a local language for talking about change. They need a language that resonates with their particular organisational culture and context, and that speaks to all the different disciplines involved in the project. Many of the popular project management approaches have engaged with this challenge, creating their own specific language of swim-lanes or scrum working in an attempt to enable shared, precise communication. But in my experience, this imposed 'common' language often doesn't cut it with people who aren't project managers. Instead of acting as a language that resonates with the organisation and that brings commonality, it serves instead to mystify the process and can undermine leadership confidence, as in the case study at the end of the chapter. Besides, there are many different project management languages, all in competition with each other: one website offers a guide to 600 definitions for 'common' project management terms![1]

Instead of adapting to an imposed language, it helps if the words used to talk about the desired change have meaning for all those taking part in the conversation. Appreciative inquiry can help organisations and project teams work together to find their own way to talk about the challenge or opportunity. With its emphasis on co-creating meaning, understanding and aspiration, appreciative inquiry can help organisations discover metaphors of change that are home-grown and that resonate with those present. It can help organisations develop their own organisational shorthand for talking to themselves about themselves in the context of change.

Project teams create change plans, Smith notes, in an attempt to keep uncertainty and complexity at bay, to reduce ambiguity and to make change manageable. In this light, project plans featuring accounts of action, certainty and predictability can be recast as stories of order designed to help keep chaos at bay, rather like fairy tales are supposed to help children manage the terror of the world by making it containable and predictable. This is an important function of the whole project management methodology, and undoubtedly people do benefit from the sense of control, proactivity and predictability that plans create. The danger comes when important people forget that the plan is a story of hope about the future rather than a prediction of future certainty; that is, it is a social construction, not a preordained path to salvation.

Leaders at least need to be able to remember that, in essence, the story of the future life of the project is not real; it is a social construction, that all is conditional and that, as the situation develops, different possibilities and ways forward may emerge. Maintaining this awareness can be hard when the plan takes on a life of its own. As an inherently iterative constructionist process, appreciative inquiry can help manage this paradoxical need to provide enough of a sense of certainty about what is happening that people can keep moving forward, while also allowing for regular 'revisits' to the basic processes of scanning the environment and making sense together to inform the next move. In this way, the awareness of social realities that appreciative inquiry brings can help the team navigate between the project reality and the ever-changing organisational, or larger, context.

Smith also suggested that, when thinking about the project team members, it is useful to think of them as each belonging to separate tribes. Therefore, when trying to get them to work as a team, the leader is negotiating amongst tribal loyalties. This metaphor is helpful in highlighting that their other team membership identities are strong and permanent while project identities are weak and temporary. People aren't stupid; however much the project is paraded as their great opportunity, they know to whence they are returning. When the tribe calls, even during their project team stint, the urge to respond will be strong.

This recognition of team members' relational context highlights the morass of divergent agendas, cultures, identities, priorities, power-plays and affiliations amongst which the project manager is trying to create commitment and conjoint action. The way forward is through dialogue. It has to be possible to safely name and explore conflicts of loyalty or interest as they come up, as explored in the case study below. Appreciative inquiry, as a dialogic process, is very well suited to the challenge and is particularly well suited to working with, and negotiating between, many voices and many different organisational realities.

Overall, says Smith, project action and talk is all about sense-making. Sense-making, we might say, is to social systems as cartography is to map-makers, which means there are numerous ways of making plausible sense of any particular situation, just as there is an indefinite number of plausible maps that can be constructed of a particular terrain. As with cartography, the actual map drawn is decided by the need and the use of imagination. With sense-making, however, the challenge of creating accurate maps is compounded by the ever-changing social world. Members are pulled off the team and others join. Goal posts move unexpectedly. Nothing stays the same. Their task is to carve out moments of stability in this continuous flow of change to enable the team to take stock and reconfigure as necessary. An appreciative inquiry summit is a perfect sense-making and reorienting process for this.

The sense made at any particular time is reflected in project artefacts. The various diagrams, maps and risk registers any particular methodology demands are physical enactments of sequential sense-making and plans for the future and are important for this purpose. What is also important to note though is that they are *records* of changed thinking, understanding and ambition rather than *drivers* of the same. This point is frequently missed as people often fondly believe that to have drawn up the plan is to have made the change. We are wise to remember the appreciative inquiry process of co-creative sense-making first, record-making second.

Taking an Appreciative Approach to Team Member Diversity

The quality of relationships within a working group is a key indicator of its health and performance potential, and this applies as much to project teams as any other. Team members benefit from knowing each other in a meaningful way so they can understand how other people are making sense of the situation and so why they say what they say. As a relational, dialogue-based process, appreciative inquiry creates lots of opportunities for relationship enhancement.

One relational factor that can enhance or derail a team is how it engages with team diversity. Within project teams, in addition to protected characteristics, there is likely to be diversity in cognitive schema, professional jargon, professional worldview differences and so on. For example, typically scientists can be reluctant to present information or ideas unless supported by a degree of evidence, while creatives are renowned for their ability to fly free from present realities. Such differences in how ideas, facts, possibilities and probabilities are regarded can cause confusion and conflict. The degree of diversity of this nature in a mixed project group is not always immediately apparent and if not attended to can greatly reduce the efficacy of the team. MacPhail and colleagues' research has revealed a U-shaped relationship between performance and group diversity [2] (Figure 8.1).

Effectively, when there is very little diversity in a group, members understand each other very well and indeed can often rely on what one might think of as a kind of organisational shorthand when discussing things; that is, lots of assumptions don't have to be spelt out, they can just be taken as read. We might say the group members' mental maps are very similar, and in this situation team performance, all other factors being equal, tends to be high. At the other end of the scale, when the team contains a large amount of diversity, team members are likely to quickly realise they can't rely on a shared understanding of the world, and instead they have to co-create or jointly negotiate this. They realise they will get nowhere if they don't put in the work to understand the many different perspectives in the group, and this work is likely, all else being equal, to result in high team performance.

But performance drops right off in the middle of the curve where the group is neither extremely diverse nor extremely homogeneous, but somewhat in

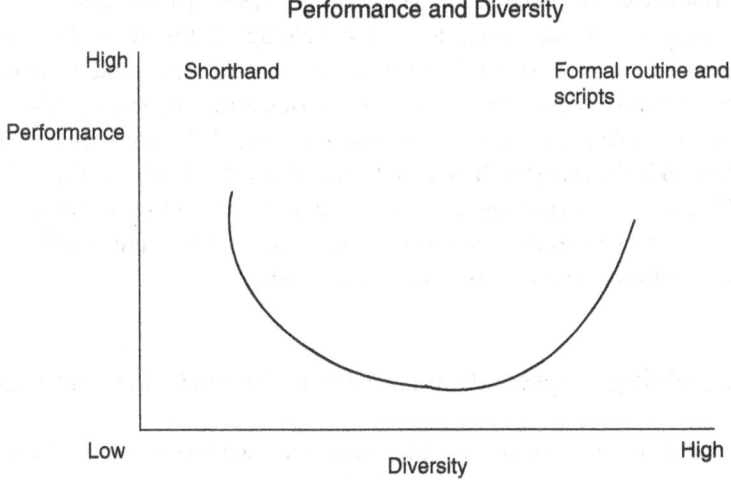

Figure 8.1 Relationship between diversity and performance.

between. This, interestingly, is the danger spot for poor performance. The researchers identify how this lack of a common organisational grammar, that is, ways of talking about the organisation, change and so on, can lead to destructive rather than creative differences. This in turn can lead to a loss of expertise as people minimise difference rather than risk conflict or being misunderstood. Feeling misunderstood, especially amongst an unfamiliar group, can increase feelings of exposure and vulnerability, contributing to a lack of psychological safety.

When people don't feel safe in a group they behave in risk-adverse ways, often by carefully minding the quality or content of their contributions, or indeed by withdrawing their contribution or otherwise disengaging. It is this psychological process, amongst others, that contributes to the phenomena of apparent group agreement in the room splintering the moment the group is out of the room. People haven't dared risk pushing back against a suggestion or decision proposed, instead giving a compliant response. This 'agreement' has no strength in the face of, for example, a strong disagreement about the decision back in their 'home' team. This weak compliance is revealed in team patterns of behaviour where decisions get made but aren't enacted, don't stick or keep getting reversed: there is no real group commitment to them.

The challenge is how to preserve people's professional expert identity which is a core part of their sense of self, and to integrate that with their new, grafted on and only temporary remember, project member role. Part of the answer is that the team needs to make a positive effort to incorporate the professional identities, to create a shared 'we'. The authors suggest that the conscious, overt and explicit naming, recognition and valuing of the strengths, talents, knowledge and skills associated with the functional background is important to helping forge these two identities in a productive way. The ambition is to create reciprocal expertise affirmation meaning that each team member understands the expertise-based contribution of other team members. A lack of this is one of the challenges I've observed that HR experts can face in senior teams where their areas of expertise and so ability to contribute to strategy and finance conversations are not always clear to others.

Applying Appreciative Inquiry to Project Management

Discovery interviews around past successes, achievements and sources of pride can be an engaging, enjoyable way of helping people gain an insight into each other's professional worlds, learn something of what is

Engaging with the Particular Challenges of Project Management   121

> **How To Use Appreciative Inquiry to Aid Project Team Development**
> - **Create Positivity** by identifying sources of pride, celebrating success, encouraging mutual appreciation and recognition, and judicious use of humour
> - **Build Commonality** by taking the time for and invest in group dynamics using discovery and dream.
> - **Capitalize on difference** by reframing conflict as an expression of difference. Difference is a valuable team resource.
> - **Create an economy of strengths** by thinking trading strengths within the team to create value
> - **Enhance Relationships** by creating genuine acceptance of the uniqueness of each member

Figure 8.2   How to use appreciative inquiry to aid project development.

important to that person and gaining a sense of their core values, while also strengthening personal relationships.

Overall, then, appreciative inquiry approaches can be assimilated into successful project management, starting with a good discovery conversation at the beginning about the best project-team experiences people have previously had and learning from those. Then the team can move on to a dreaming session focused on imagining this project as the best project experience ever. This future possibly is developed into a pull motivation by exploring how such an experience would it be, what it can achieve, how it will feel to be part of the team. Then by turning to the design stage, the team can think about how they need to be doing things now, from the very beginning, that will give them the greatest chance of working well together to a fruitful conclusion. Elements of this process, or the whole process, can be repeated as needed throughout the life of the project (Figure 8.2).

Case Study: A Project Team-Based Large-System Change

A holding company decided that its seven small- to medium-sized UK companies all needed to be on the same IT system. I referred to this assignment briefly in Chapter 6. Across the seven companies there were five different legacy IT systems, some working extremely well, some not so well. Interestingly, there was no overall UK director, rather these seven organisations reported to four different international managers.

To support the UK organisations with this large change project, an external project manager was appointed, and an initial strategy meeting of the lead project team was scheduled to kick things off. At short notice I was invited to facilitate this initial event which was to take place on two days separated by a few weeks.

Attempting to prepare, I had a preliminary chat with the project manager and, although it was clear he had a whole system of project management in his head and in written form, I struggled to understand what he was proposing for the event. Although we both used the word 'process' its use didn't produce a shared understanding. I was asking about 'how' he proposed to run the meeting, when in small groups, questions to be posed, exercises and so on. He saw the event process as the agenda for the two days. The agenda he had already prepared was full of technical terms. It was evident we did not have a common change language. He assured me that the managing directors were all fully au fait with the project and on board with it.

This prompted me to ring round the seven company leaders who I knew had all had contact with the project manager. I found they had been bedazzled by the project manager's technical talk, diagrams and weighty project folder, and had felt unable to reveal their lack of comprehension of what he was saying. This is no reflection of the project manager, who was good at his job; it was more a reflection of the very danger exemplified by MacPhail and colleagues [2]. Reciprocal expertise affirmation was not possible between me and him, and possibly between the directors and him: we just didn't understand enough of each other's professional worlds.

In addition, the leaders reported feeling very uncertain of their ability to lead through this project, both individually in their own companies and collectively. Many wanted a UK managing director-type person to be appointed who could 'knock our heads together'. I couldn't pick up any sense of a shared vision of what this huge and hugely disruptive initiative could achieve or what the business benefit was, only a sense of being pushed into it. Some were predicting that the push towards uniformity meant they would lose some specifications, which meant they were likely to be worse off afterwards. And all directors were unable to see how they could provide the bodies for the various joint project teams that were proposed without their own production suffering.

It was clear that without addressing some of these psychological aspects of the change project, the project manager's aspiration to use the two days to push on with making decisions and allocating resources to project teams would flounder. With the human resources manager's support, it was agreed that the initial day event could be redesigned to address these fundamental project team formation and identity issues.

At this initial event were the seven managing directors, the project manager, the HR manager and a few other senior staff who would be leading various areas of the overall project, about 14 people in all. One of the managing directors had been nominated to be overall project lead. His reluctance to step into that space was evidenced by his refusal of an invitation to make opening remarks, backed up by where he chose to sit, close in with his peers, and his body language. The leadership vacuum in the room was palpable, as was the level of tension and general anxiety.

We invested time in creating psychological safety. In the introductory round people introduced themselves firstly by their business-as-usual role, then by their assignment project role at which point they were asked to complete the sentence, 'I'm here to…' This meant everyone knew who was in the room and how they fitted into the future of the project. Time was then spent negotiating and elaborating 'how we want to work together'. I offered some initial suggestions, for example, that we think about how we make sense together, that we look to find commonality over difference, that we keep it simple by avoiding technical jargon, that we be brave in saying what needed saying while also being disciplined in choosing what to say and what not to say, and that we be forgiving (by which I meant not point-scoring). People discussed elaborated, and added to, these suggestions.

A base-line round of self-assessment against five objectives for the two days was highly revealing. Against questions such as 'How happy am I with the way things are going?' and 'How prepared, ready and able am I to lead on this project?' scores ranged from 2 to 10. The 10 scores were consistently the project manager's. I find this exercise very effective in bringing difference to light. Faced with the range of scores, it was hard for the project manager to maintain his belief, based on his interactions with people that had given him no reason to suspect otherwise, that all was on track and going well.

Asking the group to look at what they had produced and to comment on what it told us allowed people to open up about why they had given the score they had. In this way the managing directors were able to bring into the room much of what they had shared in our confidential conversations. This conversation allowed each of them to see that they weren't alone in their confusion. The other leads could also express their uncertainty about what the role they had been given meant. In this way the emphasis in these opening stages was on building trust and psychological safety and establishing room for a diversity of opinions, experiences and feelings about the change project.

After the break, the project manager gave an overview of the project, its scope, ambition, and general plan of execution. Given what had gone before, the group was now able to actively question any aspect that they didn't understand.

By now the group had a shared understanding of where they were as a group with the task of leading the project, a shared understanding of the broad scope and ambition of the project and an idea of the role they would each play in the project. The focus moved to the question of, 'How are we going to do this? How are we going to jointly lead this project?'

There was a discussion about how decisions would be made: which would have to be made by consensus and which people could make in their own context. This was an extremely useful discussion that brought out into the open some people's fears that the proposed changes the project would bring were not to their benefit, while others described their current IT as 'two yoghurt pots and some string' and were clearly delighted at the prospect of an upgraded system. Somehow this differential impact was going to have to be managed by them all. All this can be seen as the airing of tribal loyalties, as outlined by Charles Smith.

Those who were being taken out of their current roles to be brought in as special group leads expressed their frustration at not being able to devote time to their existing 'home' teams; they were grappling with a sense of letting others down. From an appreciative inquiry perspective, it is good to understand the client's starting position and their concerns, but not to amplify them unless it will be helpful. Instead, the emphasis was on ensuring that they felt they had been heard, in all their diversity, before we moved on.

The atmosphere in the room had shifted considerably from the beginning. It now felt possible to shift the conversation around to identifying what resources they could bring to the challenge. This was an appreciative discovery interview. In mixed groups they shared stories of previous experiences of joint project working, of working with the particular IT system, their experience of programme implementation and other highlights of leadership experiences. From this we identified personal resources of leadership, wisdom and judgement and success factors for project-working. We plastered these over the walls on flip charts. This exercise helped the group recognise the resources it had to bring to this unwanted and rather overwhelming challenge. Collectively, of course, there was a wealth of relevant resources available. This helped create some group resilience in the face of the task and the potential disruption.

Next, we moved to creating a dream aspiration of the future. If this project delivered on its promise, and the change experience was as good as could be, under their leadership, how might things be in two years' time? For a group still coming to terms with an imposed change, this was a hard stretch of the imagination. It was hard, even for the most optimistic, to see beyond the initial demands of time, energy and expertise, the likely frustration, the abandonment of other cherished projects and the general extra workload. Appreciative inquiry is an iterative process, and this first dream exercise was an initial attempt to try to create some pull motivation for the project. At this early stage, this exercise might not have revealed particularly inspiring dreams, but it did at least raise the question 'What might be beneficial about this?' and also made it clear both that little thought had been given to this and that the view beyond getting through the implementation phase was very murky at best. This ambition to create a pull motivation was revisited, more than once, with this group, as the project progressed.

I hope you can see, from this detailed account of the very early stages of the project, how beginnings are so important to project life. In the activities outlined above we addressed the issue of creating a common language. In particular from one of the dream exercise pictures came a name for the project: the 721 project. This stuck for the length of the project and, while it might seem simple, is a great example of a metaphor that encapsulates a lot and works for the organisation as an organising image or metaphor [3].[2]

We acknowledged the 'tribes' challenge and engaged in collective sense-making. We also worked on building relationships. We used discovery interviews to bring into the light the collective resources of the group to face this challenge and we used dream exercises to start to create a pull motivation for the project. We did more work over the next planned day. At the end of the two days the range of scores on all the baseline questions had shrunk, particularly on the 'How ready and able do I feel to lead on this project?' question, where the lowest self-score was now 7, suggesting a major shift in the group's sense of confidence about engaging with the task.

I continued to be involved with the group over the two years of the project. I just want to mention one other session, which was with one of the teams that had been pulled half-time off their business-as-usual role to work on a project team. During their team-building event we used Lego to help them express how they were making sense of their situation. The image that remains with me is a Lego boat with people facing in both directions, rowing against each other. As eloquent an expression of divided loyalties as you could hope to see. The question, working within the metaphor presented was, of course, 'So what needs to be different so these people can face and pull in the same direction?' The participant soon worked out that he needed to have a conversation with his business-as-usual boss that allowed him to feel he had that boss's permission and blessing to devote half of his time to this other project, which was for the good of the organisation as a whole.

Conclusion

In this chapter we have looked at how appreciative inquiry can help project teams work together by creating a shared language, navigating areas of difference, managing tribal loyalties and creating grounded aspirations for the future. The case study illuminated how the appreciative interviewing and paying attention to the psychological aspects of working together using appreciative inquiry approaches created a necessary basis for engaging with a more traditional project management approach.

Learning Points

1. Project teams face particular challenges.
2. Particular attention needs to be paid to co-creating a common change language, navigating 'tribal' loyalties and supporting sense-making amongst the team.
3. Hidden diversity in professional orientation and cognitive styles needs to be navigated and negotiated in an atmosphere of psychological safety.
4. As much attention needs to be paid to the psychology of project teams as to the work process.

Discussion Questions

1. How are project teams different from usual work teams? What challenges and opportunities do those differences present?
2. What do you think of the idea of 'project-craft' as exercised by effective project leaders? What does it mean to you and how have you experienced it?
3. What are the particular diversity challenges of project teams and how can appreciative inquiry help with them?

Teaching Exercise

1. Hold discovery interviews: What has been your best experience of working in a multidisciplinary project team? What made that possible?

Further Resources

Whitney, W., Trosten-Bloom, A., Cherney, J., and Fry, R. (2004). *Appreciative Team Building: Positive Questions to Bring Out the Best of Your Team*. Lincoln: iUniverse.

Smith, C. (2007). *Making Sense of Project Realities: Theory, Practice and the Pursuit of Performance*. Hampshire: Gower.

Notes

1. https://www.smartsheet.com/complete-glossary-project-management-terminology.
2. This idea comes from Gervase Bushe. I believe in Ref. [3].

References

1. Smith, C. (2007). *Making Sense of Project Realities: Theory, Practice and the Pursuit of Performance*. Hampshire: Gower.
2. MacPhail, L., Roloff, K., and Edmondson, A. (2009). Collaboration across knowledge boundaries within diverse teams: reciprocal expertise affirmation as an enabling condition. In: *Exploring Positive Identities and Organizations* (ed. L. Roberts and J. Dutton), 319–340. Routledge.
3. Bushe. G.R. (2013). Generative process, generative outcome: The transformational potential of appreciative inquiry. In: *Organizational Generativity: The Appreciative Inquiry Summit and a Scholarship of Transformation (Advances in Appreciative Inquiry)* (ed. D.L. Cooperrider, D.P. Zandee, L.N. Godwin, M. Avital and B. Boland), Volume 4, 89–113. Bingley: Emerald Group Publishing Limited.

9

Boosting Innovation and Creativity

Innovation and creativity are the secret sauce of thriving organisations. The ability to adapt to changing environments, to reconfigure to seize opportunities, to build on successes and to try new initiatives are the abilities that enable organisations to adapt faster to changes and threats, to stay in the 'fitness zone'.[1] But many organisational processes place a priority on efficiency which, by foregrounding repeatability and consistency, inadvertently deters such innovation and creativity. Repeatable, consistent and efficient processes often act to actively drive creativity and innovation out of the organisational culture.

In this chapter we establish the need for creativity and innovation and then look at these ideas in more detail. To do this we reframe innovation as generativity and then consider the relationship of this to the 'resistance to change' challenge. We consider the importance of participation and positivity. Next, we examine in detail how each of the phases of appreciative inquiry contributes to the generation of new ideas, focusing particularly on the power of stories and storytelling. To conclude we consider how appreciative inquiry can focus on innovation and creativity as its topic of inquiry, and then we take a brief look at a couple of examples from the literature of using appreciative inquiry to boost creativity.

Understanding Innovation and Creativity as Generativity

When I'm asked to help organisations, a frequent request is 'we need people to think, be proactive, to take responsibility, to be creative'. When an organisation is facing change or desires to change, it needs everyone to have

---

Practical Appreciative Inquiry: A Toolkit for Applying Appreciative Inquiry to Organisational Challenges, Opportunities, and Aspiration, First Edition. Sarah Lewis.
© 2025 John Wiley & Sons Ltd. Published 2025 by John Wiley & Sons Ltd.

their thinking caps on and producing an abundance of ideas of how to be different. It needs to boost people's ability to be creative. But what do we mean by this?

One way of understanding creativity and innovation is to think of it as the generative capacity of a person, group or organisation. Generative capacity, or generativity, refers to the ability of the system to create something new in the discourse, context, future vision or imagination, an exciting new possibility or reconfiguration that pulls the system forward. We might say that generativity creates something new in the system's resources.

Such resources include what can be envisioned by the imagination: things need to be imagined before they can be realised. According to Bushe [1], generativity occurs when a person or group of people discover and create ideas that are compelling to themselves and to others, and that provoke further new ideas. A generative idea is defined as one that causes people who hear it to shift how they think about things and that opens up new possibilities. The evidence that the person or system has hit upon a generative idea is that it keeps being talked about, the discourse shifts, and there is a new turn in sense-making which releases the potential for new actions.

How the Appreciative Inquiry Process Generates Ideas and Energy

Understanding generativity as the phenomena or capability at the root of innovation, we can now explore how the practice of appreciative inquiry encourages this. I find this is one of the hardest ideas for people to grasp in advance of experiencing an appreciative inquiry. Presented with a 'content-free' design they wonder, 'Where will the ideas come from?' The answer, of course, is that it is the questions we ask that stimulate new accounts and that allow those new accounts and previously unheard voices to connect in hitherto unrealized forms. From these discussions new ideas emerge, or even leap suddenly into life.

When facilitating an appreciative inquiry it is fascinating to watch how, as some ideas gain traction, others, to which people may previously have been quite wedded, lose ground; their former adherents are now willing to relinquish them for more newly attractive propositions. With appreciative inquiry we aren't pushing new ideas into people, but we are creating conditions for them to occur; we are drawing them out. In this way we can see that appreciative inquiry is just as concerned with the elimination of problems as any other change process, but it moves the organisation on through generativity rather than problem-solving.

Another benefit of appreciative inquiry in terms of its generative impact is that it is a participative process, and the ideas that emerge have the weight of the group behind them. This active 'co-creation' means that resistance to change and to the need to achieve buy-in at some later stage are much reduced if not completely eliminated. The action ideas that are generated and agreed upon are implemented by the very same people who created them. This means the energy travels with the idea. The reduction of the need for persuasion means more of the event energy can be put to tackling the 'how' of implementation, for each idea has been assessed as being of benefit.

Given this, we might ask why organisations use suggestion boxes instead. From the leader's point of view their attractiveness is their ease and efficiency, and, like a lottery, they occasionally throw up something that does catch the decision-makers' attention. On the whole though, the savings of time and money are pointless if the process is ineffective in achieving change, as frequently proves to be the case, in large part, because the energy and passion, the personal investment behind the idea, gets lost in translation to printer ink.

Bushe [2][2] also points out that the reciprocal and contagious experience of positive affect while working together is a necessary condition for generative connections. In other words, you cannot bypass the early stages of an appreciative inquiry, which builds connection and positivity, to get straight to the 'creative' part. Accommodating this can produce a sense of frustration at 'time-wasting' in efficiency-minded commissioners and leaders' who want to get straight to the 'action and ideas' part. However, the creation of positivity amongst the group, usually fostered very adequately by a fire-lighter exercise and the early discovery conversations, must be preserved to the get the benefit of the process. As we examined in Chapter 2, positive affect has a big impact on creativity and the ability to work well with others.

1. The generative process of the 5D appreciative inquiry cycle

Let us look now at how the different stages of an appreciative inquiry cycle contribute to the generativity of the event. In the discovery phase we ask questions intended to produce new or 'generative' talk rather than 'rehearsed talk'. This increases the likelihood of the conversation producing the sensations of novelty and surprise as people both say, and hear, things they have not said or heard before, and positive things at that. This means that heart and spirit become involved as well as cognition, which helps to build relationships. Together, as awareness of the resources, resourcefulness, strengths and a general positive core of the group are brought to the fore, these factors work to effect a reframing of reality: they help the group to experience their world slightly differently. Things begin to change.

Working Generatively with Discovery Stories

What the discovery phase produces is stories, often previously untold or not so widely shared, of the positive. There are lots of ways of working with stories. I like to mix groups who have all shared a story in their initial group with other groups for the next round. If we started with groups of six, this process should ensure that each new group of six now has 36 stories available to it. Then, when I ask them to identify what seem to be some of the common or shared features of what made these special moments possible, they have 36 positive stories available to them as evidential resources. Working this way can lead to the identification of the small differences, crucial factors or setting conditions necessary for great moments to occur. Ideas begin to develop of what is needed to create the new, desired condition.

Bushe offers a further way of working with stories, which he labels synergenesis.[3] This involves using the stories from the discovery interviews as a springboard for brainstorming. In this process the stories from the discovery conversations about great, peak or exceptional moments are recorded in some way. Then, groups are assembled and the people in them are asked to read or view the stories one at a time. After the stimulation of each story, the group is asked to brainstorm possible ideas for action or the way forward. The idea is to keep going until the group have shared all the stories and have run out of ideas. They can then look at and reflect on what they have produced. It's important to note that this process is not deductive reasoning; it's stimulated leaps of imagination and creativity: a much more exciting, brain-activating creativity-stimulating process for most people.

The synergenesis process can be particularly useful when it proves impossible to gather everyone in the system together at one time in one place. In such a situation one way forward is to encourage pairs of people to

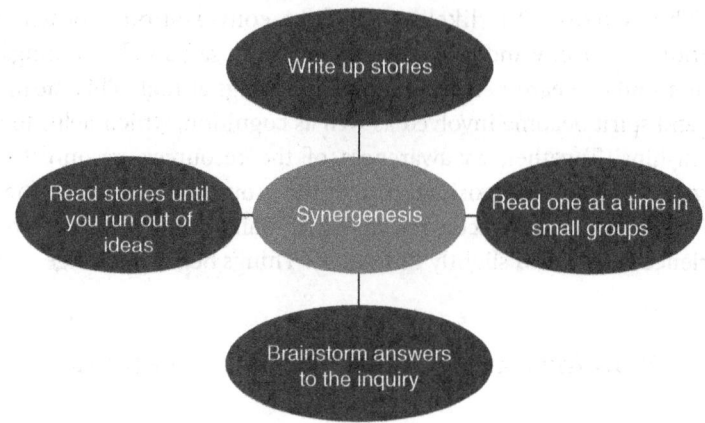

Figure 9.1 Synergenesis: Using appreciative stories to generate new ideas.

hold discovery interviews when possible and to ensure the stories so produced are written up or recorded on video. At a later date, the inquiry can hold synergenesis brainstorming groups as the next phase in the process (Figure 9.1).

The dream phase is the heart of the creativity of appreciative inquiry as people propel themselves into a best possible future (and remember, this is always one grounded in 'the best of now' – what is known to be possible in exceptional or peak moments – not blue-sky thinking) and use their imagination to create a lived reality. This is where we get people to fire up their imagination using the discovery conversations as a springboard. It's a kind of reality rooted daydreaming, or wondering 'what if', which is recognised as an important part of the creative process.

Such relaxed mental roaming allows our imagination to leap over the many current obvious problems and barriers to a time in the future when we have achieved our aspirations and our goals. A good dreaming process acts to fire up the imagination and creates motivation to do something now to make the dream come true.

The ideas generated by these dream sessions can be expressed in many creative ways, often to the surprise of the commissioners. I have worked with groups of sober civil servants who have expressed their dreams of inspiring futures through poetry and song; academics telling of their aspirations using balloons; council workers creating dramatic playlets to show the best of all possible futures; and engineers creating collages of their journey forward.

Do not be shy about encouraging ways of expression that are organizationally 'countercultural'. I often suggest, that having conjured up an attractive possible future in conversation, the next task is to present it in a way that is different and will excite other people, attract them to the vision and make them want to be part of the future described. These exciting and dramatic presentations of the future tap into human emotions in a way that a bald bullet list of statements or ideas rarely does. Without much prompting, people start connecting the various future-pictures presented, finding commonality and identifying the most attractive, exciting or meaningful ideas expressed.

By the end of discussion or inquiry the group as a whole should have a shared sense of where they want to be heading and the kind of futures they want to be creating. With this shared sense acting as the roadmap, people can be to be given permission to get on with making it happen, to be enabled to take voluntary and visible action, to be creative. While the leader's role becomes that of creating coherence and connection. Creativity is rarely a linear process; rather experimentation, hypotheses, prototypes and iteration are key features of creatively exploring possibilities.

In the design phase the creativity lies in identifying the small but important things that will make it more likely the hopeful and attractive future will come about. This often includes things like identifying people to influence and processes to renew.

Then, of course, the real power of change lies in the nature of destiny. With the whole group having a shared sense of 'we know where we want to go' and having identified and agreed upon the best ideas from the event, people sign up to take voluntary, visible action to make things happen, and I can tell you they do. It's important that the event has been negotiated and set up so that, at this point, our fired-up volunteers do not feel they need permission to act, rather they can get on with things immediately, while leaders create coherence and connection.

Inquiring into Creativity

It is also possible, of course, to do a specific appreciative inquiry into creativity. In this case the process might start with discovery interviews inquiring into when people have been at their most creative. In this way, the group can learn about the environment, relationships or resources that make it more likely they will feel inspired and creative. From this, people can dream together about how life could be, how creative they and the organisation could be, if these conditions prevailed more of the time. Next, they can be helped to identify things they can be doing in the present to make that future more likely, and then, finally, they can work out how they are going to make those changes.

As well as using the whole 5D cycle, or an appreciative inquiry summit to stimulate creativity, it is possible to use appreciative practices in a more incidental way to stimulate ideas.

The simplest appreciative inquiry-based skill to apply in different situations is that of asking generative questions. In essence, these are questions that are likely to produce new conversational contributions and patterns. Such questions tend to have certain characteristics. For example, they have an element of novelty, they are questions that people have not considered before and that they may well be surprised to be asked. Many positively framed questions are of this nature. However, imagination-based questions, or questions that ask people to combine two seemingly opposed ideas can also have this effect of producing new thought.

Effective generative questions connect to things that are deeply meaningful to the participants. These are questions about important things such as their work, values and experiences. By asking about what matters and giving express permission to answer with reference to feelings, such questions act to ensure that people are engaged psychologically, not just rationally. Good generative questions act to reframe reality, often by focusing on aspects of the context that are normally overlooked or ignored. In the simplest terms this means asking about positive things when the 'reality' is perceived to be wholly negative. The answers reveal many more positive things going on than people believed was the case. A new perception of the situation is created, and innovation becomes possible.

Another 'use anywhere, anytime' technique from appreciative inquiry that can help shift a conversation into a more generative place is that of doing the flip, or inquiring into the dream. This moves the conversation into a generative space where people have to start using their imagination rather than their memory. In the same way that good science fiction introduces impossible ideas that inspire scientists to create what they saw on *Star Trek* as a child, so good dreaming sessions conjure up exciting ideas that enlarge the sense of the possible. The creative horizon expands.

On a final note, encouraging people to risk using their initiative and to be innovative or creative requires that we recognise and reward very early and tentative attempts to offer something new. This is something managers and leaders, in the enthusiasm to find instant solutions, can sometimes overlook.

When we want to encourage creativity amongst a group then we need initially to welcome any idea put forward with open arms. By initially rewarding the act of contributing an idea, and resisting the temptation to immediately evaluate that idea, we grow people's willingness to put ideas forward. In this way we can develop sufficient robustness that people are confident enough to be able to take the of risk an idea being rejected and to continue contributing ideas even when they are. Only when people truly believe that the *act* of creative contribution is genuinely welcomed and appreciated can the risk of applying some critical evaluation be taken.

The Relationship Between Appreciative Inquiry and Improvisational Theatre

On an interesting note, Alexandra Arnold [3] talks about the similarities between appreciative inquiry and improv, coining the term Appreciative Improv. She discovered the relationship when assisting an appreciative inquiry student who had previous trained in improvisation with his assigned discovery interview. During this process, they discussed the similarities between improv and appreciative inquiry. She notes that using appreciative inquiry, in itself, is like getting permission to do things differently, to play, to have fun. Just like improv, appreciative inquiry offers a new perspective on our whole world. As with improv, the essence of appreciative inquiry is that nothing is rehearsed or prepared, and the effect is instantaneous. Her partner in the experience described appreciative inquiry thinking as a 'connective tissue' between the many roles we play in life. When, doing appreciative inquiry, she suggests, we are inspired by creativity, playfulness and an ability to be in the moment. This idea of improv, which requires a partner to bounce with, brings home the idea that in appreciative inquiry creativity is essentially co-creativity. Let us now consider a couple of case studies.

Case Study: An Organisation Adapting to Market Changes

An insurance company [4], already a 'best place to work' needed to respond to market changes. It was decided to use appreciative inquiry to create an organisational culture that could adapt, innovate and grow at the pace the market demanded. A series of events was held that involved everyone in the inquiry. Then, a carefully designed programme used trained internal facilitators to lead a two-day conference of leaders and champions to discuss what had emerged from the series of events. Five compelling futures emerged, which were explored through creative enactments. The group identified the key cultural elements that underpinned these futures. One they encapsulated as 'Be original. Use your creativity to anticipate what your customers – internal or external – need before they know they need it'. Further reflection on work to that point identified innovative new areas for the strategic direction of the company.

A small group of innovation champions was formed. This group launched an Ideas Site. Here people could post an idea, vote on an idea or help build on an idea. Notice how their prior work involving the whole organisation made it more likely that this 'suggestions box' idea would become a 'live' part of the process, as it did. Some ideas became the focus of an 'innovation jam' – a structured gathering to guide all those who chose to participate in determining how to best bring the idea to fruition. Note again the co-creative element of this process. Many of these ideas were taken up and implemented.

They also formed a group of ideas helpers, made up of subject matter experts in all areas who could mentor new ideas to fruition. Their role was to help the team members expand and explore their ideas, helping them understand who they needed to work with and what they needed to consider to move the idea forward. It was not their role to evaluate the worth of the idea. Every idea submitted to the ideas site was supported by two ideas helpers.

Progress was evaluated nine months into the programme, by bringing the culture champions together into a 90-minute process. The changes they described seeing or experiencing included 'increased creativity across the workforce'. They reported that people were speaking up, contributing new ideas and doing things differently. The champions went on to identify how they could creatively apply appreciative inquiry to future challenges. There were many other positive impacts from this extensive programme which I have not documented here, but which can be found in the original article.

Case Study: Creativity for Business Growth

Our second case study concerns a banking organisation [5] in Hong Kong that needed help with business growth, team collaboration, achieving growth in market share and professional development. One of the objectives of the intervention was to help team members think creatively.

While business had been good, the impact of the pandemic meant the company had to think of new ways to keep going. Collaboration, cooperation and creativity were key. A breakthrough moment for the facilitator occurred when, during the module on innovative and creative thinking, she realised they were working in their functional subgroups. She challenged them to work and think as the larger group, bringing the different perspectives together. This had a positive effect. The author identifies that asking three questions when someone puts forward an idea – namely, What do I appreciate? What can I amplify? And only then What can I add? – means ideas have more room to breathe before being evaluated

Conclusion

In this chapter we have considered the inherently generative nature of appreciative inquiry, noting how generativity is the basis for the innovation and creativity so sought by organisations. We have looked particularly at the power of working with stories as a source for imaginative leaps into possibilities for the future and also noted that much creativity is really co-creativity. We also looked briefly at a couple of examples of inquiries designed to boost creativity.

Learning Points

1. Creativity can be stimulated in an organisation by a creativity- and innovation-focused appreciative inquiry summit, and by applying appreciative inquiry practices as micro-interventions.
2. Generative questions are key to creating new images, aspirations and ideas.
3. Each phase of appreciative inquiry contributes to its creative potential.
4. Positivity is an important aspect of creativity in appreciative inquiry.

Discussion Questions

1. What is meant by the term 'generativity'? And how does it differ from creativity?
2. What questions might you centre an appreciative inquiry into creativity around?

3. How can you work with discovery interviews and stories to generate creativity when it's not possible to bring the whole system together?
4. How is appreciative inquiry similar to improv?

Teaching Exercises

1. Pair up for discovery interviews about moments of the greatest sense of creativity. Share the stories to identify features of the organisation or environment or other factors that seem to increase the likelihood of creativity occurring.
2. Design an appreciative inquiry process to address the challenge of 'Being creative within boundaries' or 'If innovation were a lived value, what would be different around here?'

Helpful Resources

The reader is referred in general to Gervase Bushe's work in this area. http://AIPractitioner.com is another source of inspiration.

Lewis, S., Passmore, J., and Cantore, S. (2016). *Appreciative Inquiry for Change Management: using ai to facilitate organizational development.* Kogan Page.

In addition, these chapters from Appreciative Inquiry for Change Management are particularly relevant to this chapter.

Chapter 3: The development of conversational approaches to organisational change
Chapter 5: The power of the question
Chapter 6: The power of conversation
Chapter 7: Extending practice, working with story in organizations
Chapter 10: Developing your conversational practice
Chapter 11: Becoming an appreciative conversational practitioner

Notes

1. This phrase comes from complex adaptive system modelling. For more on this see Chapter 2 of Lewis (2011). *Positive Psychology at Work.*

2. Ibid. and see also Ref. [2].
3. Shared in a presentation at the World Appreciative Inquiry Conference in 2013. A video of this presentation is available here: https://player.vimeo.com/video/178085772. The idea is also present in other of his writings such as the reference above.

References

1. Bushe, G.R. (2013). Generative process, generative outcome: the transformational potential of appreciative inquiry. In: *Organizational Generativity: The Appreciative Inquiry Summit and a Scholarship of Transformation*, vol. 4, 89–113. Emerald Group Publishing Limited.
2. Bushe, G.R. (2007). Appreciative inquiry is not (just) about the positive. *Organization Development Practitioner* 39 (4): 30–35.
3. Arnold, A. (2022). Nourish to flourish: appreciative resources. *AI Practitioner* 24 (3): 50–54.
4. Trosten-Bloom, A., Wilson, S., and Real, K. (2015). From best to 'even better' rapid relational results at ARAG North America. *AI Practitioner* 17 (3): 57–68.
5. Raman, L. (2021). Using appreciative inquiry for team collaboration, creativity and innovation. *AI Practitioner* 23 (2): 24–30.

10

Challenging the Silo Mentality

A perennial challenge for organisations is how to manage a number of design tensions. Organisations often struggle to work out how to create sufficient commonality (a tendency towards centralization) while also being responsive to local conditions (a tendency towards decentralisation). Or they struggle to ensure individuals develop areas of expertise (a tendency towards specialisation) while also maintaining an adaptable workforce (a tendency towards multiskilling). Another frequently encountered challenge is how to ensure a consistent product or outcome (a tendency towards standardisation) while also ensuring innovation and creativity (a tendency towards variety). Maybe the key challenge is how to maximise the use of resources (a tendency towards efficiency) while also being able to target resources to the greatest effect (a tendency towards effectiveness).

In this chapter we look further at these challenges and how their irresolvable nature tends to manifest in organisational behaviour and actions, often stabilising into a highly siloed organisation. We identify some of the disbenefits to this organisational form that can accrue over time, particularly rising levels of cynicism and dysfunction, and how organisations typically respond as the dysfunction becomes clear. The chapter then moves to consider how appreciative inquiry can offer a way of quickly bringing siloed organisations to a state of wholeness so that organisation-wide issues can be productively addressed. We consider this particularly through the effects of accumulating dysfunction on organisational energy and with reference to the wholeness principle. An extended, dissected case study is offered to show how to put theory into practice.

Practical Appreciative Inquiry: A Toolkit for Applying Appreciative Inquiry to Organisational Challenges, Opportunities, and Aspiration, First Edition. Sarah Lewis.
© 2025 John Wiley & Sons Ltd. Published 2025 by John Wiley & Sons Ltd.

Why the Siloed Organisation Is Popular and How It Becomes Dysfunctional

Commonly, the inability to successfully manage the both/and nature of the tensions outlined above is that an organisation develops a way of doing things that works for them until it does not. By this I mean that as time goes on the downsides of the chosen configuration begin to loom larger and larger as the original benefits retreat. Eventually the current configuration is recognised as unsustainable and the organisation lurches into a new shape. This is usually labelled a 'reorganization'. Such reorganisations tend to occur periodically in the life of an organisation.

A time-honoured configuration that organisations frequently adopt to achieve at least some of the above desires is that of a bureaucratic, standardised, organised by function, command-and-control structure. Make no mistake, this highly siloed structure can and does deliver in many contexts for some length of time. It is how Henry Ford reduced the cost of cars such that they became affordable by the masses. Vast empires have been run along these lines. It is a successful formula until it is not. What are the downsides that tend to accrue over time?

The downsides of silo-working

Working in narrow silos of specialism, with clear lines of reporting up into the organisation, people can lose sight of the big picture. This can lead to a loss of meaningfulness and so also of motivation. Obsessed with the minutiae of the forms they have to process, or the particular widget they tool, they lose sight of the overall ambition of their part in getting, let us say, people timely help or of making the final product, both of which can, when strongly connected to the particular task, be highly motivating. By contrast, pushing paper or working on an assembly line is rarely motivating in itself. When people become disconnected from these motivators, organisational energy is lost.

The adverse effects of silo-working on the potential for change

When people beaver away (or not) in their clearly defined specialist areas, it is as if they were independent of other departments, free to concentrate solely on the work of their own silo. But, of course, the definition of a system is that the parts are interdependent. In siloed organisations the small acts of communication, problem-solving and human interaction that help things run smoothly – what is sometimes known as its social capital [1][1] – are steadily eroded as all communication about issues is instead sent up the line. Meanwhile those at the top of the organisation rarely have the capacity, knowledge or motivation to resolve what appear to them to be at best minor issues or, more frequently, examples of unhelpful carping between departments.

In this way small misalignments or misunderstandings between departments can build up into big frustrations and inefficiencies, leading to the unhelpful disparaging of one department by another who just cannot understand why their colleagues are behaving in such unhelpful or positively obstructive ways. Those involved have no means by which to address and resolve these issues directly. It becomes hard to change things.

Strangely, communication challenges also occur in the opposite direction when carefully crafted leadership messages completely misfire. The view of, and feel about, the health and shape of the organisation experienced by those at the top can be very different to the view and feel of those situated elsewhere. Sometimes, the messages sent from the top leadership down the organisation about how things are and what needs to be done seem so at odds with the local experience that those receiving the message have little choice but to reject it. At this point, both the top and the bottom of the organisation may well view each other's messages through the lens of 'they would say that wouldn't they', each believing that the others do nothing but moan or that they wear rosy-tinted glasses and have no idea how things really are. In this way cynicism, an energy-corroding state, becomes a part of organisational life.

Organisational responses to silo-working dysfunction

There are various ways organisations respond to these challenges. They might introduce a new process designed to solve some specific issue. Or they might try different ways of putting the top of the organisation directly in touch with the bottom. Alternatively, the organisation might roll out a programme of communication skills training. For example, I was party to a whole series of these that took place in the UK Civil Service at the end of the 1990s. Groups of 100 people at the time, working exclusively in their training group of 10, were 'run' through the training. As I'm sure you can guess, the shape of the training delivery exactly modelled the shape of the departmentalised siloed system, even if the 'training' silos were of a temporary nature.

Or there might be a big reorganisation to 'shake things up' and to 'get rid of some dead wood'. In this process, departments might be moved around to sit next to each other or rejigged in some other way. However, unless the established patterns of communication and relationship are fundamentally affected, these cosmetic changes often achieve very little as former mental models and patterns of behaviour persist. The lack of fundamental change is frequently echoed in the language where reference is commonly made to previous organisational forms. For example, when a newly designated allegedly 'joined-up' 'customer journey' team continue to refer to themselves internally as the sales team, the marketing team and the customer complaints person. The connection and rejuvenating energy boost that was the intention of these changes has not come to pass; the organisational energy has been dissipated on surface forms and little has changed at the system level. A shift in the system energy is key to effective organisational change.

The Nature of Organisational Energy

A great paper by Vogel [2] helps us understand the nature of organisational energy. Both Vogel and appreciative inquiry recognise energy as a transforming resource. In appreciative inquiry sessions as people become 'energized' they are transformed before our eyes. Increased animation is evident, and people seem more dynamic; quiet wallflowers are suddenly able to hold a room's attention because they are talking about something that really matters to them. The generation of such energy transforms potential futures; while un-energised people are disinclined to 'spend' any energy to get something done, energised people are a force for movement.

Organisational energy, while clearly related to individual energy, can also be thought of separately as a resource of a collective unit. Four different collective or organisational energy states have been identified by Vogel and his colleagues: productive energy, comfortable energy, resigned inertia, and corrosive energy.

These four states can be seen as lying across two dimensions, intensity and quality, as in Figure 10.1. Intensity ranges from high (activated energy) to low (non-activated energy). Quality ranges from positive to negative reflecting how the energy is constructive or destructive of the organisation's goals. During the kind of planned change interventions often initiated in siloed organisations, people frequently either try to ignore the change process and to continue in their same old ways (comfortable), or they become

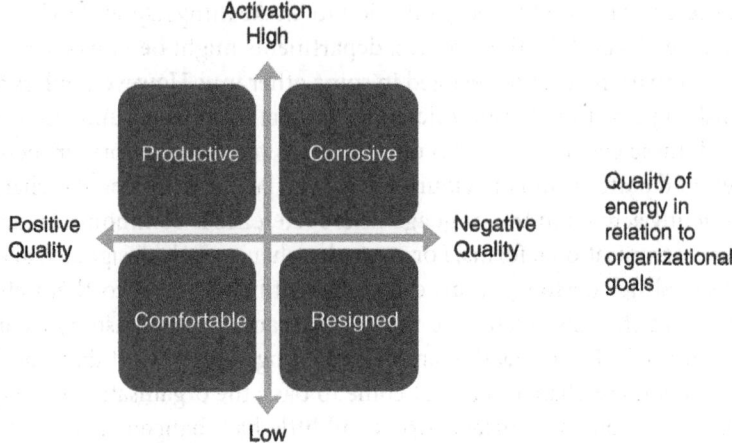

Figure 10.1 Organisational energy.

passive (resigned) or at worst they work against the changes (corrosive). The challenge is to move people into the productive zone during the change process and to help them remain productive as the future unfolds.

The desired state of productive organisational energy can be thought of as a collective, temporary, emergent state, a natural contender for dialogic organisational development. Appreciative inquiry works to transform resigned inertia or corrosive energy into productive energy to move things forward by bringing the whole system together, creating a degree of commonality and generating energising positive emotions. It is this that is so often missing in the efforts to counteract the disbenefits of silo-working through silo-based change attempts.

What Does Appreciative Inquiry Bring to the Challenge?

The appreciative inquiry summit might have been specifically designed to tackle the siloed organization challenge. This is particularly true when, in addition to working to create productive energy, we focus on the wholeness principle. This principle recognises that wholeness brings out the best in people and organisations, and that bringing people, particularly all stakeholders, together in large group forums stimulates creativity and builds collective capacity [3].[2] It encourages us to acknowledge that every person has value and that every voice belongs. Addicott, exploring this principle, specifically writes that 'Embracing wholeness opens up possibilities of transcending silos and silo mentalities. Creating a unified vision that the entire workforce understands means that everyone can work with that vision in mind, this enhances trust between teams and departments. Embracing the wholeness principle highlights the interconnectedness' [4].

In practice, the principle means ideally bringing the whole system together in one space. For heavily siloed organisations where individuals from one department rarely see anyone from other departments, this in itself can be revelatory. But the real magic of appreciative inquiry is the way that conversation groups can be continually remixed so that people have interactions with others from all over. And, given that appreciative inquiry conversations are typically positive and bonding, people are likely to find the experience life-affirming and energising. In this way, as well as getting the work of answering the challenge done, relationships are created and strengthened. People's mental maps of the organisation and of their role or place in it are also reconfigured. People begin to understand other people's perspectives and actions in a different light. Different conceptions of the organisation allow different actions to emerge. Relationships are built across the organisational divides. This is an investment for the future, and it builds social capacity thereby enhancing the probability of low-level problem-solving taking place. The events themselves generate productive organisational energy and frequently produce immediate benefit as well as long-term change.

Case Study: A Merged Organisation

The case study I want to share here does not concern a huge organisation, but one that suffered from silo-type challenges, as merged organisations or teams often do. Siloed organisations are divided by mental 'departmental' barriers as well as physical location. This means that, in the merged organisation, although the organisational structure chart may have been redrawn, the previous division between 'us and them' frequently remains in place. Drawing on this commonality, I hope the example below will illuminate the general principles of working to create ideas and experiences of wholeness when assisting divided organisations. By walking through the event design in detail, I hope to make clear the purpose, activity and outcome of each element of the design.

The organisation had been created by a larger body that bought two small businesses and hoped that combining them under one leader would produce advantages. The two previous organisations remained located in two different countries, and the core functions of engineering and production straddled the two sites. Although the group was now nominally under one head of organisation, reaping the hoped-for benefits of bringing two excellent small organisations together was proving challenging. This event was focused on the joint management team.

The objective for the event was 'to align the group towards delivering success in the future', and many of the specific aims included the word 'shared', as can be seen in the facilitator's event agenda in Figure 10.2.

Creating such documents is useful both for me, in making me think things through, but also very useful to share with clients to help them gain a tangible sense of what is actually going to be happening at the event. The guide clearly lays out the purpose of each activity, and how it will be achieved, as a basis for conversation and discussion. It also offers a sense of security to clients concerned with the strange, emergent nature of an unfamiliar process.

This is part of the psychological contracting[3] about a particular event, which helps keep expectations aligned. Of course, a plan is only a plan, that is, it is an aspiration for how a future will unfold, not a determination. Appreciative inquiry events are systemic (note, not systematic) meaning they respond in real time to what is going on in the room, so may deviate widely from the 'plan'.

When I'm creating a document like this, I attempt to create an elegance of design and a sense of flow as one activity feeds into another. Here I have had to weave in some work around the Boston Map[4] that the client specifically requested. I tried to find a place for it in the flow of the event. Many of the aims for this event are typical of a 'silo-work busting' event, while others are very clearly related to the appreciative approach taken.

Let us look through the design for a few other points of interest. Under 'Getting Started' the outline refers to 'working together'. This is a term I prefer to 'ground rules' or 'rules of engagement' and, while I give a few starters-for-ten ideas for guidance, the agreement about how we will work together is co-created in conversation. I always include this section in any group work, even a training event. It is crucial for surfacing hesitations or barriers to engagement in the event. Essentially, I speak about how this is a learning or discovery space rather than a performance space, and a little about what that difference means, and suggest that we agree just to speak for ourselves, making space for others to have different views and so on. Having also run over the housekeeping, I then ask people to discuss,

> **Company Event: Complex Organization: Simple Principles**
>
> *Overall Objective*: To align group towards delivering success in the future
>
> *Specific Aims*: By the end of the day the group should:
>
> > Have a shared sense of the evolution of the organisation
> > Have identified changes for the better over last 15 months
> > Have identified key success factors
> > Have a shared understanding of the current situation and the strategic priorities
> > Have a shared map of accountabilities and dependencies
> > Have identified the Cash Cows, Stars, Dogs and Question Marks in the product portfolio
> > Have created shared visions of the future in terms of profitability, performance, product and people
> > Have identified areas that need attention to achieve these future visions
> > Have begun working on some of these areas
> > Know each other better and understand each other's work situation, challenges and aspirations better
>
> *Workshop format*
>
> 8.30 Getting Started
>
> > Welcome, general introduction and context setting **(General Manager)**
> > Housekeeping, working together, introduction to event process (Sarah (SL)) (Altogether 30 mins)
>
> > Continuum of change
>
> > > Length of service exercise (Line up by length of service with organization. SL to divide into cohort clusters. Ask cluster two questions – Tell us about the organization you joined, what was it like? What seemed to be the strategic priorities at that time? Clusters to share)
> > >
> > > (Purpose – history, introductions, connections and continuity, resources, mood boost)
> > >
> > > (SL - 60 minutes)
>
> *Break*
>
> > Changes for the better
> >
> > > Mixed groups (newbies spread amongst groups). Identify changes for the better since Oct 2021 – both direct consequences of event and other things since. As many as can identify. List on flips. Reflect.
> > >
> > > (Purpose. To note progress. To identify successes and improvements. Mood boost, group cohesion)
> > >
> > > (SL 60 minutes)

Figure 10.2 Company event: Complex organisation, simple principles.

Building on the best of this year

> UK has had a great year on deliveries and orders. Team Leader One to identify the best of the Nordic Experience this year, or signs of growth/improvement to build on. **(Team Leader One)**
>
> In different mixed groups (esp mixed UK/Nordic) – What are we doing right? Strengths and positive psychology cards to aid discussion. Groups to identify 5 top things they think are contributing to the success. (Purpose- identifying root causes of success. Introduce ideas of other potential success factors (by looking at cards). Mood and celebration) (SL 60 mins)

12.30　Lunch

13.15　Where are we now, looking forward?

> **Update from General Manager and Team Leaders Team One and Two** on strategic priorities, business plan, bigger context etc. Also, clarity re recent changes – current structure etc.
> (Purpose – present common ground re big picture/context)
>
> **(General Manager and Team Leaders Team One and Two** – 30 minutes)

Accountabilities and dependencies

> Thread exercise. Part 1 Everyone given a thread – to hand other end to their formal manager. All look at picture/pattern created. Part 2 - Given different colour thread – everyone asked to connect other end to the person on whom they are most dependent to get their job done (could do iterations of this).
> (Purpose – to vividly illuminate the difference between the formal map of the organization and the 'making it work' map of the organization. Also reveals 'hotspots' of dependency (call it bottle necks) in a visceral way.)
> (SL 60)

Boston Map: Understanding our product portfolio

> Place products in sections of Boston Map. Cut-out pictures of the products to stick up could be nice.
> (Purpose – shared understanding of product portfolio in strategic terms, beginning to identify ideas for question marks)
> **(Marketing Manager?** 45 minutes)

15.30 Break

16.00　Our aspirations for the future

> Building up from data identified so far today: Strategic Priorities; Business Plan; Success Factors, Boston Model. To imagine how it might be to be in the organization in three (?) years time (calling on the four pillars – profitable growth, improved performance, product portfolio, people – What are we working on? What is our most profitable

Figure 10.2　(Continued)

	line, customer? How are we recruiting, inducting and managing people? What are some of the great things happening? etc. Share images. *(Purpose: Use of imagination to create motivation – and creativity. To create potential ideas, possibilities. To be winnowed in next exercise)* *(SL 60)* What do we need to attend to, to achieve these aspirations? *Group discussion - First identification of areas to grow and build on, or for correction. Also, can think about this overnight* *(SL 30)*
17.30	Conclusion of day – achievement, thanks, looking forward to tomorrow **General Manager?**
Day 2	
8.30	Regroup *Chance for anyone to comment on yesterday. Introduce plan for morning. Might need something energizing to get people going before we ask them to use their brains.* To Action! Open Space *As at last event, people nominate topics from the 'areas that need attention' to ensure future success, then go to discussions. Marketing Manager can suggest the creation of a timeline, identification key milestones as one of the things that needs attention and can be started here. Two rounds* *Sharing of (and building on) outcomes of the rounds of discussion.* Going Forward *Concluding discussion around what happens following the event. Insights gained; aspirations created.* Thank you and goodbyes!
12.30	Finish

Figure 10.2 (Continued)

in pairs or small groups, what they think about what I've suggested about how we might want to work together today, and what else they need to discuss, share, raise or ask about to be able to be fully present and be able to contribute meaningfully to the event.

In some cases, the ensuing discussion is done and dusted in 10 minutes; in others it can trigger a long discussion in its own right. It is likely to be the first emergent conversation of the day. Taking the time that is needed here will pay dividends later in the process. It is, in my opinion, a crucial activity and should not be skimmed over, however warmly the commissioner assures you that they are all used to working together and are one big happy family. Perhaps even more so then! In this instance it did not take long.

Let us walk through the activities of the day, seeing how they work to reduce the silo effects. The 'Continuum of Change' length of service exercise is a favourite of mine. It achieves the outcomes as noted in the plan and also frequently produces lots of positive emotions of laughter and fond reminiscences, as it did in this case. In this case the many recent joiners were clearly puzzled by the way some aspects of the organisation didn't make any sense. Much of the way the organization ran seemed a bit random rather than being coherent or logical.

As the groups described the organization they joined and the challenges they encountered, the sequence of decision-making that resulted in the current structure became clearer. In this way, I find, it becomes very apparent that many current 'problems' were initially solutions implemented to solve an earlier problem. The chain of solution-focused decision-making that led to the current structure becomes clear. As we might say, many aspects of organisational life that struck the newcomers as strange 'seemed like a good idea at the time'. And probably were, but maybe they had now outlived their usefulness.

It also helped members of both previous organisations understand each other better now that they had 'lived' some of each other's history. It exposed the very different development history and culture of the two organisations, which, in turn, illuminated some of the current sources of conflict.

Using a process like this to explore the context and circumstance of past decision-making also means that people have their past efforts recognised and honoured. It becomes clear that it truly was a good idea at the time! This being the case, people are then more able to let ideas go rather than feel the need to defend them as the decreasing utility of some prior initiative or change becomes ever more apparent. The strategic priorities question that is incorporated into this exercise works to create a history of strategic priorities onto which present considerations need to be built or aligned. This context-embedded approach to developing strategy stands in opposition to the idea that strategy development starts with a blank piece of paper. In this instance it really helped clarify the different history and nature of the organisations, one a highly dynamic, fleet of foot entrepreneurial small entity, the other part of a huge organisation, used to doing things in a much more bureaucratic, slow, considered way.

In the 'Changes for the Better' section I wanted to connect them back to the last time they were able to get together, which was over a year before,

Challenging the Silo Mentality   151

and I directed their attention very deliberately towards identifying positive changes. This exercise meant they co-created a positively oriented story of the recent past. Note the instruction to spread new joiners amongst the group. This allowed them to hear about, become impressed by, and identify with, the organisation's sources of pride. This redirecting of attention to the usually untold, or lesser told, story of positive progress acts as a necessary corrective, especially when people are likely to arrive at the session with their heads full of current problems and challenges. The story of positive changes over the last year that we created was, of course, not the whole story, but it was an important and probably underaccounted part of the story.

Having unearthed and shared stories of success from the last year, and having had some input on those from a management perspective, the group moved into 'Building on the Best of This Year'. In mixed groups they were asked, what are we doing right? Then, using strengths cards and positive organisation cards[5] they worked to identify the root causes of success. The groups were then brought together to identify the top five factors and invited to consider other potential success factors. This was an engineering organisation, and using the term 'root causes of success' in the document was designed to resonant with the language of the organisation in terms of the common engineering approach of seeking out the root causes of failure. I trust you can see this is a way of holding discovery conversations with the language moderated to better fit this particular organisation.

This was followed by an executive-led aspiration-sharing session. Generally, I try to keep these 'talking at' sessions as short as I can, but they do serve to create some commonality, at least about how the most senior people see things. At their best these inputs can be very motivating. At other times they can send the event in an undesired direction. In any particular session we will work with what is going on in front of us, all grist to the mill of creating sufficient commonality and positive forward purpose to help the group. In this instance the session was essentially a recap of information that had previously been communicated. People were able to comment and question and so begin to co-own this account. This reduces the barriers between the executive group and the senior managers.

I deliberately followed this post-lunch fairly passive session with a very active 'get up and move' exercise, 'Accountabilities and Dependencies'. This exercise is designed to illuminate different patterns that exist within the organisation. In this instance I wanted to illuminate the formal 'command and control' pattern, supported by the silo structure, and then the informal 'getting things done' pattern. As it says in the notes, this basic exercise can be used to illuminate other patterns such as 'To whom do you turn to find out what is really going on?' or 'Who has the most motivating, energising effect on you?' and so on.

Generally speaking, the formal pattern is the public story the organisation holds about how it works. Other patterns of communication and behaviour are rarely the same as the formal pattern and can be very revealing. It is these hidden patterns of relationship and communication that can be inadvertently squashed by silos and hierarchies and accidentally destroyed in restructurings. In this instance it was fascinating to see how people from both locations were in fact using each other quite effectively at the lower levels. Exposing this pattern in such a visual way enabled it to be acknowledged, valued and potentially built upon.

The final element that needed addressing before everything was brought together was creating their product portfolio. The Boston Map with its classifications of cash cows, stars, dogs and question marks offers high face validity and is simple to use. In this instance I suggested we could make this Boston Map exercise fun and engaging by doing collage work. The exercise is designed to create a shared sense in the group of their product portfolio in strategic terms, as indeed it did.

Having addressed the past and the present, towards the end of the day we moved to 'Our aspirations for the future' that is, into the dream phase of appreciative inquiry. I introduced this session using phases such as those in the plan. Note the use of the present tense in these prompt questions. Ideally in the dream phase people imagine themselves into, and briefly live in, a future state. Language use makes a huge difference to how successful this is. Saying 'I am', rather than 'I will be' connects to self-image, self-concept and the emotional self in a very different, more meaningful and more resonant way. In this instance they worked in mixed groups to create images of the future, which were then creatively presented for sharing.

Towards the end of the first day of this event by asking, 'What do we need to attend to, to achieve these aspirations?' I invited them to share initial thoughts about what needed attention. These thoughts were left to marinate over night.

Refreshed by sleep and the evening's informal conversations, they came with lots to discuss for the following morning. After regrouping, we moved in an open space session which effectively merges the design and destiny phases. I frequently use the open space methodology in this way, finding it an excellent way to create groups of people with the energy and aspiration to have a positive impact in a specific area. In this instance six practical problem-solving or initiative-developing conversations covering the areas of financial management, product development, strategic alignment, strategic/business planning and communication processes were held. One of these groups was two people, one from each location, who were finally able to give enough focused, collaborative time and attention to find a way forward on an issue that had been an irritant for some time. They were thrilled. Ideas for projects to be taken forward followed on from these discussions and were taken up by volunteer groups who just had time to formulate the first or next steps before the event drew to an end.

In addition, the event produced the outcomes hoped for in the plan as well supporting people to know each other better and understand each other's work situation, challenges and aspirations better. They laughed and had fun together, which builds social bonds; worked together in positive and supportive ways, modelling future ways of working; showed a maturity in owning areas of less-than-perfect achievements in the collective performance; developed further appreciation of the similarities and differences in the areas of operations; increased the social capital of the leadership and management group, and so the organisation; and created a potential 'positive proposition' [3][6] for the organisation: 'We win it – We build it – Our customers feel loved'. This last of course is a 'generative image' that emerged during the event. A generative image is one that acts to hold the many insights and ideas generated together in a simple image or phrase, which encapsulates a vision or aspiration.

I hope you can see that by working together in this way, much productive energy was generated and effective silo-busting was achieved.

Conclusion

In this chapter we have considered how, in an attempt to create stability in a context of dynamic, unaligned needs, organisations tend to fall into the relatively fixed pattern that seems to best fit their situation. Over time, this pattern can move from delivering benefit to delivering disbenefit. The sense of disbenefit can grow as the organisation becomes increasingly 'siloed'. We have looked at how appreciative inquiry events offer an opportunity to 'silo-bust', allowing new patterns of organising, and productive energy, to emerge. Working this way can avoid some of the organisational trauma often associated with drastic organisational restructuring. Finally, we worked through a case study illuminating how appreciative inquiry builds connection and relationships and allows disjointed parts of an organisation to work together more smoothly.

Learning Points

1. There is no perfect form for an organisation as the tensions within organisations are contradictory and unresolvable except temporarily.
2. Appreciative inquiry offers a way to create sufficient, temporary wholeness in a siloed system to allow for fundamental shifts in mental maps, enhanced relationships and the emergence of informed, co-created aspirations.
3. Appreciative inquiry is a robust process that can be used in a modified form when the principles are clearly understood and support the design.

Discussion Questions and Practical Exercise

1. What are the benefits of highly siloed organisations?
2. What were the benefits and drawbacks of this event only being for management?
3. What other ways could the Boston Map work have been accommodated in an appreciative inquiry design?

Teaching Exercises

1. Think of a siloed organisation you know. How might you design a one- or two-day event to create a sense of organisational 'wholeness'?
2. Interview a manager about what they see as the benefits and drawbacks of the way their organisation or team is structured. What would they like to be different, and why? Then think about how potentially, using appreciative inquiry, you could help them achieve some of their desires for the future.

Helpful Resources On and Offline

Joanna Wilde's bookWilde, J. (2016). *The Social Psychology of Organizations: Diagnosing Toxicity and Intervening in the Workplace*. London: Routledge Includes the word 'silo' in its index and is written with an awareness of the issue of the siloed organisation.

Notes

1. This is another term from positive psychology. More can be found about it in either of my books, *Positive Psychology at Work* and *Positive Psychology and Change*. Or the original paper: Ref. [1].
2. For more see Ref. [3].
3. Psychological contracting refers to the, often unspoken, expectations around a formal agreement. If you haven't come across this idea before I recommend it to you.
4. This is a well-known strategy model from the Boston Consulting Group. It is easy to explain, and I find it occasionally useful.
5. Card sets like this help by both giving groups a language with which to engage with the question or exercise, and also a way of tangibly organising their thoughts. The handing back and forth and general handling of the cards is interactive: it's relational action. The specific card sets referred to here are Positran Strengths Cards and Positive Organisational Development Cards. Both are available from theppshop.store.
6. Provocative propositions are a way of working with the dream stage. For more see Ref. [3].

References

1. Baker, W. and Dutton, J. (2009). Enabling positive social capital in organizations. In: *Exploring Positive Relationships at Work: Building a Theoretical and Research Foundation* (ed. J. Dutton and B. Ragins). Psychology Press.
2. Vogel, B. (2017). Experiencing human energy as a catalyst for developing leadership capacity. In: *Developing Leaders for Positive Organizing: A 21st Century Repertoire for Leading in Extraordinary Times* (ed. B. Vogel, R. Koonce, and P. Robinson), 275–306. Emerald Publishing Limited.
3. Whitney, D. and Trosten-Bloom, A. (2003). *The Power of Appreciative Inquiry: A Practical Guide to Positive Change*. San Francisco: Berrett-Koehler.
4. Addicott, F. (2022). Nourish to flourish: awareness of wholeness: two principles in balance. *AI Practitioner* 24 (4): 94–95.

11

Motivating Performance with PRISMM Coaching

It is an interesting paradox that so often in organisations performance conversations have the precise opposite effect to that intended. Held with the ambition of motivating people to greater performance, they often leave people feeling demoralised and demotivated. There are a number of reasons this happens; for example very often the performance appraisal conversation becomes a bureaucratic routine, and the focus shifts from having a stimulating and motivating career and ambition-oriented conversation to meeting the time demands of an annual process and completing the paperwork. In other cases, the process is tainted by an overemphasis on corrective feedback. Very quickly people's increasing reluctance to attend dovetails with time-pressed managers' desire to save time, and, if it happens at all, it becomes a perfunctory 'box-ticking' exercise.

And yet, people have a right to know how to succeed at work; to know what is expected of them; to feel that someone is interested in their progress, is noticing their achievements; to have a sense of how they can progress in the organisation and in their career; and to be helped if they make mistakes or are underperforming. In this chapter we will look at an approach to performance improvement that has been developed from an appreciative inquiry perspective and is based on the appreciative inquiry principles: the PRISMM Coaching model. We will also consider the importance of creating an organisation or team-wide performance culture which is further explored in a case study.

Practical Appreciative Inquiry: A Toolkit for Applying Appreciative Inquiry to Organisational Challenges, Opportunities, and Aspiration, First Edition. Sarah Lewis.
© 2025 John Wiley & Sons Ltd. Published 2025 by John Wiley & Sons Ltd.

The Importance of a Performance Culture

Before we look at a specific performance coaching approach, it is worth emphasising that the best designed performance appraisal process is unlikely to deliver great performance if it is not embedded in a performance culture. A performance culture is one where a shared understanding of the desired future, a few key principles to inform practice and decision-making and consistent further improvement-oriented evaluation is embedded in the way people and groups work together. It is the habitual sharing of moments of achievement or performance, the quick conversations after key meetings of what went well and what could have been done better, the noticing and praising of good performance, the quick correction of errors or mistakes on a day-by-day basis that produce both clarity about the desired performance and an ambition to achieve it. In such a culture the giving and receiving of performance feedback, both amplifying and corrective, is part of everyday life.

In an organisation with a performance culture, the performance appraisal round becomes a pulling together of all that has been going on in the previous period and a springboard to the future. I see the annual appraisal rounds as punctuation points in what is ideally an ongoing conversation about what people are doing well and what they can do better, along with what's gone wrong, how can they put it right and how can we make it less likely to happen in the future.

Feedback can be very beneficial to people's performance when done well. Because organisations are full of broken or non-existent feedback loops, people aren't always aware of the impact of their actions. Good feedback can close the loop. Essentially there are two forms of feedback: amplifying and corrective.

1. Amplifying feedback

Amplifying feedback illuminates what is wanted and how to achieve it more of the time. It is given to help people understand what they are doing right. It is often undervalued as a form of feedback. One reason for this is that managers sometimes assume that people know when they are doing well or doing things right. This is not always the case, and a lack of confirmatory feedback can lead to a slow erosion of confidence. Another reason is that managers' sometimes feel as if it is an unnecessary incentive: that salary alone should do the job of inspiring good work. Yet survey after survey shows that while people do indeed need and appreciate the money, they also work for appreciation, or recognition, or to feel helpful, or to make a difference, or to feel they are doing something valuable with their time or to feel they are contributing to something worthwhile. Amplifying feedback helps meet some of these needs.

Another difficulty is that some managers seem to feel that amplifying or positive feedback is a valuable resource that will become a base metal if thrown around too liberally. Thinking this way, they withhold any praise unless the performance is exceptional. This means they miss the opportunity to shape, grow and build performance through the thoughtful use of targeted and timely positive feedback. There are a number of processes that support the giving of amplifying feedback, specifically the feedforward interview, the enthusiasm story and diamond feedback [1, 2].[1]

2. Corrective feedback

The other main form of feedback is corrective. We give corrective feedback when we do not want people to do something, or we want them to do it differently. While we might have an emphasis on giving amplifying feedback, sometimes we owe it to people to give corrective feedback. There are two key situations where corrective feedback can be helpful.

One is where some procedure, rule or process has not been correctly followed or applied, in other words, a situation where there is this one right way to do the job. The other is the exercise of poor judgement. I am excluding situations that constitution criminal misbehaviour or gross misconduct from this discussion. The first situation, on the face of it, is an informational or communicational challenge. However, if giving the person the correct information does not produce the required change then other factors for non-compliance will need to be considered.

The second is a learning situation. The person needs help and support to better evaluate situations. They need to be offered a review, and possible improvement, of their own resources or other resources available to them, and an opportunity to create and consider alternative courses of action. From an appreciative inquiry perspective, some points to bear in mind when addressing corrective feedback are outlined in Figure 11.1. By preparing in this way, the likelihood of having a productive, relationship-building conversation rather than a resentful, relationship-harming one is enhanced.

A final word of warning: whatever else you do, keep the two types of feedback separate. Regardless of what you may have heard, combining them in a

> 1. Where was the good intent in this situation?
> 2. Could it be a strength in overdrive that has caused this issue or problem?
> 3. What am I working to achieve in this conversation?
> 4. How will I know if the conversation has been successful?
> 5. How can I develop sufficient trust or psychological safety between us to enable the person to hear the information I need to give them?
> 6. How can I frame this, for myself, as an honest and helpful conversation?
> 7. What is the minimal acceptable change I need to see, and what is my dream of how this conversation could transform the situation?

Figure 11.1 An appreciative approach to giving corrective feedback.

good news/bad news configuration does not produce balanced feedback; it produces a sandwich where the bread is contaminated by the filling.

Appreciative PRISMM Coaching

A key tool in performance management is coaching. This might be of an ad hoc nature, making use of micro-moments, or of a more formal nature. Appreciative inquiry is a natural coaching process [3].[2] Here I want to introduce an expanded appreciative coaching model, The PRISMM[3] model, which, while being based on appreciative inquiry, also pulls on positive psychology and systemic consulting to create a powerful positive approach to coaching.

Appreciative inquiry emphasises the power of asking different questions to generate different accounts and stories. Systemic consulting, like appreciative inquiry, is interested in the social construction of reality and encourages us to recognise that all accounts are only ever partial, that the story is never complete and that there is always another perspective, voice or question that might throw a different light on the challenge, however 'stuck' the situation might feel. Meanwhile from both positive psychology and appreciative inquiry we can take the transformative power of positivity. We know that by inducing positive affect we increase people's problem-solving abilities. By helping people remember some of their best moments we are also supporting the development of a positive identity from which they will be better able to act with confidence, integrity and conviction.

Appreciative discovery interviews also, as we discussed, reveal past resources and resourcefulness, bringing them into the fore and into the conversation. This, along with the shift in mood, starts to create potentialities and possibilities for change. We also need to create motivation for change: there is a big difference between knowing what you ought to do, feeling that you should do something, or even recognising a course of action as a good idea, and actually wanting to do it. The heliotropic nature of the attractive images of the future created in appreciative inquiry practice pulls people forwards. Attractive images of the future create the energy necessary for an active commitment to a course of action. And of course, it's easier to do something, as we know, when it aligns with our strengths, and while strengths identification is not a spelt-out stage in the model, it is certainly something I would include as an early part of the coaching process.

The coaching relationship itself is of key importance in any coaching model, so we are looking to build high-quality connections [4][4] with our coachee as part of working with the PRISMM model. And finally, both systemic consulting and appreciative inquiry have a great interest in the power of story to sustain, or change, situations. Part of what we are attempting to do during coaching is to help people change their story to one that is more helpful to them.

Pulling on these sources of theory and action, the model ensures that the ideas generated are powered by the motivation to achieve a better future: that they are concordant with the person's values and that they take into account the specific context of that person. Let us move on to explaining the model (Figure 11.2).

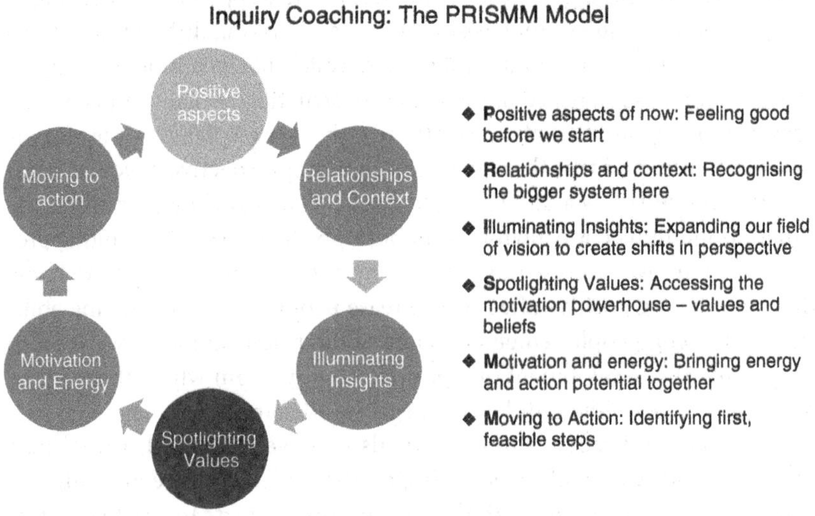
Inquiry Coaching: The PRISMM Model
Positive aspects
Relationships and Context
Illuminating Insights
Spotlighting Values
Motivation and Energy
Moving to action
Positive aspects of now: Feeling good before we start
Relationships and context: Recognising the bigger system here
Illuminating Insights: Expanding our field of vision to create shifts in perspective
Spotlighting Values: Accessing the motivation powerhouse – values and beliefs
Motivation and energy: Bringing energy and action potential together
Moving to Action: Identifying first, feasible steps

Figure 11.2 PRISMM model.

The first phase of the model, *positive aspects of now*, has a focus on inducing a state of positivity before engagement with the specific challenge. The ambition is to help the person shift into a good mood before they engage with the topic of the session. We know that when people feel good, they are likely to be more sociable, more open to new ideas, more able to deal with complex information, more resilient and more tenacious [5]. Spending time brightening someone's mood by encouraging them to talk about things that make them feel good will help the session be persistent, creative and imaginative. We use good appreciative questions here that inquire into the positive and what is currently going well, aiming, by bringing such memories or moments alive, to create positive affect in the moment. This is an equivalent to the discovery phase of appreciative inquiry.

The next element of the model is *relationships and context* which identifies relevant features of the bigger context. Here the ambition is to move on to identifying the other people important to the topic or situation under discussion and exploring their relationship or attitude towards the coachee and the topic. This is a necessary antidote to the prevalent belief in some cultures, particularly most Western cultures, that people have endless agency. They do not. They are frequently constrained by the relational context around them. The questions we ask here help us get the picture of the person we are coaching 'in the round'. We might ask questions like, 'If I asked the other people on the team the significance of this to the future, what might they say?' or 'Who else thinks this is an issue worth engaging with?'

This phase is followed by *illuminating insights*, which aims to expand the field of vision and to enhance the sense of possibility by creating shifts in perspective that throw new light on the topic, reveal new insights and possibilities for action and that expand the story about what is going on and what is possible. Such insights are created by asking questions that encourage a jump in time from the present to somewhere else, usually the future. For example, we might ask questions like, 'If by some miracle when you came to work tomorrow the problem had disappeared, or had been resolved, how would you know?' or 'Imagine it's two years' time and you are looking back. What advice would you want to give yourself right now?' These unusual, unexpected questions have the effect of expanding the person's thinking. Exploring other perspectives encourages the generation of other interpretations. In this way other possible understandings of what is going on and what is possible begin to emerge without us having to furrow our brows to find them. This phase is designed to have a similar effect as the dream phase of appreciative inquiry by opening up possibilities.

It is usually somewhere around this point that people become more aware of the sources of hope and possibility that exist within their context. They might realise they need to approach their challenge or opportunity differently or to rethink how they understand it. Maybe they need to alter their stance towards, or have a conversation with, someone. As these insights develop, so do new possibilities for action.

However, ideas go nowhere unless there is energy behind them. So the next step, *spotlighting values*, is designed to create an alignment between the idea of action and the person's own values. The person needs to feel 'I want to do this' not 'I guess I should do this'. Questions like, 'What is the heart of the matter, here, for you?' or 'What one change would free your energy for this?' can help identify an individual's core values. Essentially this phase helps access the motivational powerhouse of values and beliefs.

Then *motivation and energy* acts to bring these two powerful factors together and to build momentum towards action. Questions such as, 'How brave can you let yourself be here?' or 'What could you do that would move things along 1%?' allow an exploration of possible action steps and help identify those with real energy and motivation behind them. At this point, the coach and coachee are likely to have co-created context-specific ideas for action, aligned with values and energy and supported by momentum.

And so finally the *moving to action* focuses on identifying first, feasible steps. Usually, the hardest step to take to change something is the first. To help with that first step, in this final stage of the model, questions like 'What first step will take five minutes?' Or 'What is the most important thing for you here?' are used to start to create a plan of action that aligns with their values and has a positive energy charge.

This positive appreciative coaching process is designed to encourage an increase in self-awareness, develop a better understanding of the wider context, produce self-directed action, empowerment and personal growth, as well as enhancing performance.

Case Study: An Inquiry into Creating a Great Performance Management Culture

The ambition was to revitalise, refresh and enhance the organisation's performance management culture using an appreciative inquiry to discover what created great performance management in the organisation. The commissioners wanted to call on appreciative inquiry and strengths-based approaches, but, as we shall see, their understanding of how knowledge is translated into action remained in the diagnostic mode. This impacted the whole process in various ways. For example, the event was, effectively, made up of representatives rather than the whole system. In addition, they wanted a two-event design. The first effectively to 'gather data' in the form of positive stories and the enabling factors, and the second, a much smaller group, to turn these into action ideas.

In this way, this case study is a prime example of working with what you can negotiate. In this instance I was able to persuade them to make an attempt to video-capture some of the storytelling. The rationale behind this is that it's the nearest you are going to get to people hearing directly, to hearing the passion, engagement, positive energy etc. with which the story was originally related. It is these factors that can make a story motivating and inspiring to others, which is much weakened, if not completely removed, when the story is transcribed. They also decided to pull in a graphic artist to create an image of the event.

An invitation was sent out in the hope of recruiting 50 volunteers for the event. Given that appreciative inquiry was a very new approach, the invitation included particular suggestions and information as shown in Figure 11.3. You can see in this invitation that there would be a call for volunteers to make up the second group, the learning from which would then be disseminated more widely in the organisation.

Let us take a look at the facilitator's agenda for the session (Figure 11.4).

Given there was expected to be 50 people, and only a limited amount of time, I suggest here that we ask people to introduce themselves to others as they work together rather than doing a preliminary round of introductions. As usual we had a 'working together' session to establish the mood for the morning. I notice I did not include a fire-lighter but rather asked them to go straight into sharing their stories. This is poor practice. I would always suggest at least a five-minute energising positivity-oriented fire-lighter warm-up in the 'getting started' section.

Usually, I give people fairly short instructions for the discovery interviews, and it works fine. These instructions, on a slide, would be the first two paragraphs in the guidance notes below, and then I would speak to paragraph three. But on this occasion a set of instructions was wanted by the commissioners. I read this as an expression of anxiety about how people would cope with this unexpected request to talk about good things. The guidance notes for this initial conversation are shown in Figure 11.5.

> The workshop will be conversation-based and you will get lots of opportunity to hear about your colleagues' positive experiences in this area. There is no specific need to prepare, but if you would like to, you could give a few moments thought to these questions:
>
> - When I have most felt able to really do good work at xxxx, and what made that possible?
> - What specific incidents can I identify where something someone said, or did, inspired me forward or got me back on track after a disappointment?
> - When do I believe, feel, or know, that I really made a difference to someone else's understanding of the task or objective and how they could achieve it?
> - How have other people helped me succeed at work?
> - How have other people given me confidence in myself, and how have I done this for others?
> - When have I received truly helpful corrective feedback? What was different about that experience from other corrective conversations I found less helpful?
> - Who have I observed who seems to have a real knack of constantly steering people along the right path in a positive and inspiring way? How do they do it?
>
> While this workshop will be based on collecting great stories and discovering what makes such moments possible, we will be holding a second workshop to work on turning our discoveries into a lived experience for everyone in the organization. If you would like to be part of the ongoing journey, you will be able to volunteer at the end of this workshop.
>
> We would love to capture some of the most inspiring, illuminating, informative or just plain awesome stories to be shared more widely to show others what is possible, inspiring everyone to raise their game. We will have a video-camera and camera person at the ready to capture the best on tape immediately after the event. We hope you will be willing to share your wisdom, insights and experience when your colleagues identify your story as a great exemplar that illuminates what 'a positive performance culture' looks like in action!

Figure 11.3 Event invitation.

I chose a pyramid structure of story-sharing so we could identify some great stories to share as a wider group, which we did before we went into the break and the first opportunity to speak to camera.

When we came back from the break, we moved into identifying the common themes. Notice how I have mixed the groups again to keep 'cross-pollinating' across the experience so reducing the need for time-expensive feed-out sessions. I asked for the output to be recorded on flipcharts. This means we can all gather around them all for a large group reflection. I generally ask people something like 'When you look at this, what do you see?'

Motivating Performance with PRISMM Coaching

Growing our positive performance culture

Overall Objective: To understand what really helps people work better and to imagine a positive performance culture at xxxx.

Workshop format

9.30 Getting Started

This will include articulating (and on a flipchart) our quest **'To discover and understand what really helps people to understand what is expected of them and how to succeed. What really helps people face challenge, overcome setbacks and find energy and enthusiasm to achieve things important to them and to the xxxx community.'** *To understand what a positive performance culture looks like in action.*

It will also include an outline of the process of the morning
Introduction to graphic artist, introduction of video option
Awareness that we will be looking for volunteers to take process forward
Suggest introduce selves as they go

Housekeeping and working together

10.00 Discovering what helps people work better

Participants invited into groups of four to share experiences that helped them work better (guidance sheet provided).

10.20 *Ask to form groups of eight to share stories and stimulate more.*

10.40 *Groups asked to identify one or two great stories for wider sharing*

10.45 Sharing our inspiring stories

Top stories shared with whole room. People asked to consider recording to camera in break

11.00 Break

11.15 What makes these moments possible?

In new groups (6 people), to consider stories heard and bringing all the stories participants have heard to mind, to identify some of the common themes that made these moments possible from multiple possible domains (behaviour, attitude, emotions, context, relationship, knowledge, organisational process etc.)

To record on flipcharts. To share and discuss

People reminded to record to camera both stories and any inspiration or insights they have had about what makes a great positive performance culture, in break

---

Figure 11.4 Growing our positive performance culture.

12.00	Lunch Break
12.30	So let's imagine: How could it be if we had a truly great positive performance culture here?
	In groups to imagine it is 2020 and xxxx has taken the learning from today and really and truly embedded it in the organization (not to worry about how that happened!). To describe how work is performed, what conversations are taking place, what support is in place, how relationships support great work, how people get both corrective and amplifying feedback... and how the difference shows itself
	13.00 Sharing the visions
13.20	What next?
	Thanking people for being part of this. Next part of process is to take the inspiration of today and turn it into some statements of principle that capture the essence of what makes the difference, with HR and IT colleagues, so that it can inform work being done in this area. Ask for volunteers to be part of the next part of the process
	Remind people can still make a video
	Thank you and goodbye!

Figure 11.4 (Continued)

or 'What reflections, comments, observations or suggestions would you like to share about what you've created here?' This gives people the opportunity to inquire into words or ideas on their colleagues' sheets. This exercise often produces comments along the lines of how much commonality there is across the outputs and on occasion, an observation that reflects the simplicity of the things that make a difference. More than once I've heard, 'It's not rocket science', offered in a surprised sounding voice.

Observations like this start to make the aspiration seem achievable. It's a case of we do know how to do this, we have the tools, that is not the issue. It locates change very clearly in the domain of behaviour and relationships, which are things people can affect. It makes the desired state less an unobtainable, unconnected future nirvana, and more something glinting in the present, hidden in unexplored corners, that needs to be brought into the light to flourish. The question then becomes, how do we nurture this way of behaving in our organisation?

This enabled us to move to the dream phase. After that, in the event, I also asked for a word reflecting their experience and something those present could take and use from today.

Motivating Performance with PRISMM Coaching 167

> Guidance notes for your conversations
>
> Take turns to share experiences of when you did really well at work, when you really achieved something and succeeded, one of your peak moments. A time when you had a positive impact, when you know you were performing at your best and something good for you, your team or the organization was happening.
>
> Tell the others about that experience, expand on it, create a rich picture of that experience: relive the experience.
>
> Once you are right back there, start to think about what helped that moment happen, anything and everything that contributed to that experience being possible. Talk about anything specific you can put your finger on that really nudged or moved you in the right direction and contributed to that moment of great performance – it can be something great or small, something that is continually present, or something unique to that experience.
>
> For instance, you might feel that it was, either in the moment or at some unrelated time...
>
> > Something someone said
> >
> > A specific conversation
> >
> > Something someone took the time to show you
> >
> > Some feedback that was really useful and made a difference
> >
> > Something you learnt from a course or a book
> >
> > Something you tried off your own bat that worked – so what gave you the courage to do that?
> >
> > An exceptional experience or moment
> >
> > Something from the PDR process
> >
> > Or something less tangible that is just present in the xxxxx culture or way of working that contributed to that moment of excellence
>
> Just keep taking turns until time is called

Figure 11.5 Guidance notes for the discovery conversation.

Following the event, the organiser prepared Table 11.1 as a record of the outcome. We can see how this document reflects the usual working and language of the organisation. For example, the very title, 'What makes us perform well', from a more appreciative perspective might have read 'What enables us to perform at our best'.

For me, while this document does faithfully reflect the flipchart content, using phrases directly from them, the life is lost. It does not speak to me. I do not find it inspiring or motivating, it's just a lot of captured words or random phrases in a table. The last column is an attempt to tie the outcomes back to the four organisational values. The whole document is reflective of the reductionist, systematic, efficiency-oriented nature of

Table 11.1 What makes us perform well?

Condition for success	Enables	How	Key principle(s)
Safe environment/ non-judgement	• Change • Innovation • Creativity • Ownership	• Go out of comfort zone • Ideas are supported • Fail 'small' and learn • Feel able to ask for help when needed • Take accountability for actions	• We act boldly • We stretch ourselves
Manager/leader capability Motivation	• Willingness of team to grow/space to step up and take a risk • Engagement • Focus • Passion and enthusiasm	• Right amount of autonomy/stretch/ support given to team • Connection with greater purpose • Knowing ourselves • Enjoying what we do • Electing to be here	• We act boldly • We make it count
Recognition and appreciation	• Engagement • Employee satisfaction • Motivation • Energising	• Celebrating milestones and successes • Encouragement • Demonstrating that you are on the right track • Knowing where you stand	• We make it count

Diversity and inclusion	• More effective performance • Authenticity	• Different perspectives and skills • Collaboration • Energy focused on work and not on trying to conform to an ideal	• We act boldly • We pull together
Self-awareness	• Growth & learning • Openness • Adaptability • Resilience	• Honest conversations • Constructive feedback culture • Understanding strengths & development areas	• We stretch ourselves
Sense of values and principles	• Fairness • Respect • Trust • Making time for each other • Removing pain/inefficiency • Adding value	• Creating consistency • Positive intent and action	• All

many large organisations. Fortunately, the organisation also had the excellent graphic representation, suitably messy and full of life, and a few video recordings that brought some of this sterile document back to life.

The facilitators agenda for part two of the process is in Figure 11.6.

Let us start at the market square. While the description here is messy, essentially this is an exercise to reconnect with the previous session for some and to catch up on the previous work for others. Notice I am using the raw documents from the previous session. These act as a visual prompt to the memory, to the feelings present when they were created and are much more powerful at doing this than, for example, Table 11.1.

Having jogged people's memories, I then asked for a large group sharing of highlight moments from the first session. This is all an attempt to recreate the thoughts, feelings, energy and ideas present back then, to bring the life of that session into this one. I'm trying to bring the discovery and dream work alive in the present.

We then moved into the design phase using a brainstorm and sort process. I then used Covey's [6] circles to help them realise what they could actually control themselves. There is often a danger at this point in the process that, since the group is representative rather than a whole system, they default to identifying things that other people need to do, changes that other people need to make. I see my role in this exercise as to challenge them to identify things they themselves can do and to think about the first steps that are within their control that might enable them to exert influence elsewhere in the system. What is an absolutely pointless outcome is a long list of things that 'they' (usually people higher in the hierarchy) need to do and nothing that we can do.

As you can see, in 'Next Steps' I built on this by asking for volunteers to take influencing ideas forward and for everyone present to commit to doing something in their own area of control to move things forward.

This, to my knowledge, was not a particularly successful or impactful piece of work, and it's not hard to see why. There was insufficient understanding by the commissioners of the whole world view of organisational life on which appreciative inquiry is predicated, so instead it was seen as a useful tool for a particular exercise. Poor mobilisation of the organisation for the event meant we got a lot fewer people signed up than was hoped for. Instead of dialogic action in various forums to motivate people about this possibility to influence the organisational future there was a reliance on 'the usual' communication channels, emails and the occasional management announcement. As we saw in Chapter 4, this is something a preparation team can mitigate against.

\multicolumn{2}{l}{**Growing our positive performance culture at xxxx: Part Two**}
10.00	*Context setting and introduction to event*
	X to outline context, quick reminder by Sarah of 'working together' ideas. (All this necessary as we have new people in the group.)
	Group Introductions
	Quick round of introductions just so everyone knows who is in the room
	Market Square Connection and Catch-up
	The outputs from the last sessions up on the walls. Also Y's art work. Those present last time to cluster by their dream poster and a theme poster (with a volunteer to go by the artwork – Z?). Newbies to distribute themselves amongst the three existing groups and the artwork group.
	One person from each group to remain by the posters, the others to travel around to the others. The 'host' to outline what the poster is all about and answer any questions about it.
	Group Debrief
	As a large group – Most inspiring things that have stayed with you/or you have just been reminded of since the last session, or (for newbies) that you are struck by from your market square tour.
10.40	*What do we need to be doing now to make these futures more likely?*
	In small groups – use post-its (one idea or system one post-it) to discuss and write down any system, process, meeting etc. that could be modified, changed, introduced that would support these ambitions (including if possible idea of 'how' it could be modified, changed, created etc.).
	Post-its to be collated on a wall by theme re system, process identified. Create a 'collective heading' post-it (different colour)
11.20	*What can we do immediately, and for what do we need the help or support of others?*
	Circles of Influence and Control
	Flip paper with circles of Control and Influence. Group to identify which 'themes' go in which circle – 'collective heading' post-its put in appropriate circle
11. 45	*Next Steps*
	For the items in the influence circle- call for volunteers to create process to influence as needed. (no volunteer, no action)
	Individuals to identify what they can do to move the items in the control circle forward
12.00	*Thank you and Goodbye*
	X to close workshop

Figure 11.6 Growing our positive performance culture at xxxx: part two.

It was a split event meaning that lost energy had to be regenerated, and which also put pressure on time. The first event I had designed for 50 people, although in the event the number present was nearer 20–24, from memory. And some people had to leave before the end. These factors also had an unhelpful impact on the event. From memory, not very many videos were made. There were many reasons for this, not least distance of the camera and cameraperson from where the food and refreshments were situated. Throughout, we can see an uneasy marriage of emergent and bureaucratic ways of functioning which only became apparent as the intervention progressed. I do not hold this up as my finest hour.

Rather, I present this case study as an example of what an appreciative inquiry into a great performance culture could look like. It is an example of working with what you can negotiate, of bringing an appreciative approach to a piece of work fairly solidly situated in a command-and-control, bureaucratic culture and way of working. It also offers material for a debate about when a degree of compromise becomes too much.

Meanwhile, I fondly believe that the events had some value for the people present. For the organisation as a whole though, I suspect not so much.

Conclusion

In this chapter we have considered the importance of organisational culture to performance. We also looked at two forms of feedback: amplifying and corrective. We introduced the PRISMM coaching model that pulls appreciative inquiry together with positive psychology and systemic consulting. And finally, we presented a case study as a stimulation to discussion.

Learning Points

1. The development of a performance culture is important to support performance enhancement activities.
2. Feedback can be amplifying or corrective. Each is important and should be given separately.
3. Appreciative inquiry can be used in many ways to support performance and the development of a performance culture.

Discussion Questions

1. Why is the well-known 'feedback sandwich' a bad idea?
2. What causes performance appraisals to become demotivating, and how can this be corrected?
3. What is the most powerful thing anyone has said to you, or asked you, that's had a positive impact on your performance? Why was that?

Teaching Exercise

1. In groups, discuss the compromises made in the case study. Using the facilitator's agendas as a starting point, how would you ideally have planned and executed this intervention?

Helpful Resources

You might find my Udemy videos 'Seven Steps to Effective Performance Conversations', 'How to Have Successful Courageous Conversation at Work' and 'Coaching Skills for Managers' useful additional resources. They are available here: https://www.acukltd.com/online-training-courses.

Meanwhile, http://www.theppshop.store stocks a variety of strengths cards, suitable for different client groups, and the PRISMM Coaching Cubes.

While for online or virtual work, http://Deckhive.com has a great range of products to support performance. More information can be found here: https://www.acukltd.com/deckhive.

See also Lewis, S. (2016). *Positive Psychology and Change*. Chichester: Wiley-Blackwell. Chapter 5.

Lewis, S. et al. (2016). *Appreciative Inquiry and Change Management*. London: Kogan Page. Chapter 8: Extending practice, working with appreciative coaching.

Lewis, S. (2021). Appreciative Inquiry Coaching in the Workplace. In: *Positive Psychology Coaching in the Workplace* (ed. W.A. Smith, I. Boniwell, and S. Green), 515–528. Springer.

Notes

1. These are all explained Chapter 5 of Ref. [1]. For the original work visit Ref. [2]. Clive Hutchinson of Cougar Automation introduced me to the diamond feedback model, and he credits Pete Taylor of Brilliance Training of introducing it to him. I don't know if credit goes any further back.
2. See the excellent text Ref. [3].
3. This is a model of appreciative coaching that I have developed. There is no further reference for it.
4. This is another term from positive psychology. I recommend Ref. [4].

References

1. Lewis, S. (2016). *Positive Psychology and Change: How Leadership, Collaboration and Appreciative Inquiry Create Transformational Results*. Wiley-Blackwell.
2. Bouskila-Yam, O. and Kluger, A.N. (2011). Strength-based performance appraisal and goal setting. *Human Resource Management Review* 21 (2): 137–147.
3. Orem, S.L., Binkert, J., and Clancy, A.L. (2007). *Appreciative Coaching: A Positive Process for Change*. San Francisco: Jossey-Bass.
4. Dutton, J. and Heaphy, E. (2003). The power of high-quality connections. In: *Positive Organizational Scholarship: Foundations of a New Discipline* (ed. K. Cameron, J. Dutton, and R. Quinn), 263–279. Berrett Koehler.
5. Fredrickson, B. (2010). *Positivity: Groundbreaking Research to Release Your Inner Optimist and Thrive*. Simon and Schuster.
6. Covey, S.R. (1991). *The Seven Habits of Highly Effective People*. Provo, UT: Covey Leadership Center.

12

Releasing the Synergy of Teams

Teams are the building blocks of much of organisational life. When they work well they provide a structure that facilitates effective communication and co-ordination throughout the organisation, they give everyone an organisational home, they allow for co-operative working and can be the basis for the formation of strong relationships. At their best they add value by combining effort in such a way that the whole is greater than the sum of the parts. However, as most of us know from experience, they can also be a source of misery, conflict, isolation. They can act to hide social loafing and lead to underperformance. A lot of the difference rests with the team configuration, the leadership on offer and the nature of the team task.

In this chapter we will first clarify the difference between a team and a group, identify the well-known factors that support team success and then move on to consider the contribution from positive psychology to this discussion. In particular we will look at the role positive emotional experiences and the ability to identify and use strengths make to successful team working, noting how appreciative practices can help bring these features into team life. We'll look at how teams get stuck or become dysfunctional and, using a case study, examine how appreciative inquiry can help a team heal relationships, improve working practices and move forward.

Practical Appreciative Inquiry: A Toolkit for Applying Appreciative Inquiry to Organisational Challenges, Opportunities, and Aspiration, First Edition. Sarah Lewis.
© 2025 John Wiley & Sons Ltd. Published 2025 by John Wiley & Sons Ltd.

What Is a Team?

The idea of a team is based on the concept of interdependence: everyone needs everyone else to get the job done. However, this basic requirement is sometimes overlooked, and it is not uncommon for a group to be mistaken for a team. To be clear, a group is a collection of people who may well work in close proximity, even under the same leader, but who are not dependent on each other to achieve the task. Beware of being drawn into doing team building for a group.

What Makes a Successful Team?

Finding the key to successful teamwork has been something of a holy grail for years, and much research time and effort has gone into seeking answers. As a result, we know the core factors that help teams be effective and productive. They need an inspiring team task. Member roles and responsibilities need to be clear and, importantly, they need to be expandable. That is, the team and the people in it need to be able to evolve their roles; there needs to be room for growth and development. Within the team, relationships are important, as readily becomes apparent when asked to help dysfunctional teams. Whether or not team relations caused a dysfunction, they are very likely to be a casualty as people seek to make sense of the painful situation they find themselves in. All in all, it tends to help if team members at least basically trust and respect each other even if they aren't best buddies. And while there are successful leaderless teams, there is little doubt that effective leadership helps in most situations.

Adding in what we have learnt from positive psychology, we might extend the list to cover the experience of positivity in the team, an awareness and use of team members' strengths and the development of a team micro-culture oriented towards well-being and flourishing, all of which are part of the appreciative approach. We have covered positivity extensively elsewhere, showing that when people feel good they are more sociable, creative and open to new ideas. They are also likely to be more forgiving and more willing to express gratitude, appreciation and admiration, all of which encourage team flourishing and help build good relationships. A team that creates a positive work culture is likely to experience better quality relationships, which in turn feeds into more attentiveness and alignment, creating the self-ordered synchronicity that feeds into high performance, see Figure 12.1.

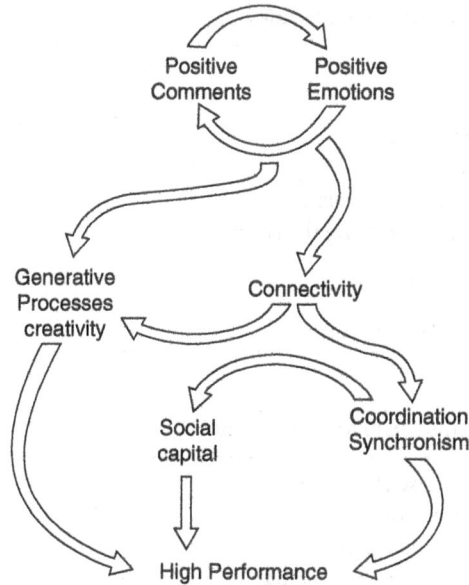

Figure 12.1 Social dynamics of high performing teams.

Creating Team Positivity

So how might a team leader create and recreate those moments of positivity? The table below shows how various appreciative inquiry tools can be used to create such moments. One is explored in more depth at the chapter end. We can use these effective tools with our teams to create positive moments as opportunities arise in normal team life, such as coaching, meetings, performance management conversations, delegation or task allocation (Table 12.1).

The final suggestions in Table 12.1 are strengths-spotting and task allocation. This brings us to the role of strengths in team success. Successful teams find ways to help people understand their strengths, use their strengths and to play to their strengths as much as possible at work. To help people identify their strengths we can use one of the many psychometrics now available. Or in a more informal way, we can ask questions that help people identify when they are likely to be using their strengths (Table 12.2).

Once the existing pattern of strengths in the team is known, we can recruit for the strengths needed both by the role and by the team. We can allocate roles by strengths, and when that isn't possible, we can recraft [1][1]

Table 12.1 Positivity-creating activities.

Appreciative questions
Discovery interviews
Flipping stuck conversations
Exploring success stories
Expressing gratitude and appreciation
Spotting, naming and amplifying the good
Root causes of success analysis
Strengths-spotting
Allocating tasks to fit strengths

Table 12.2 Strengths-identifying questions.

When am I most energised?
When do I experience flow?
What do I do purely for pleasure?
What do I experience as life-enhancing?
What activity do I use to reward or treat myself for doing something I don't like to do?
What am I doing when I feel self-motivated?
What do positive skills do I bring to everything I do?
What do I find almost impossible not to do when the opportunity presents itself?

the role to fit the particular individual's strengths profile. We can further complement that by developing role fluidity, meaning that people can swap or trade parts of their roles that don't play to their strengths but do play to someone else's. Or perhaps we can create complementary strengths pairings: leader and deputy; salesperson and administrator; presenter and researcher. Very importantly, we can consciously share out the things that don't play to anyone's strengths amongst team members.

When Teams Get Stuck

Despite everyone's best efforts, it's not uncommon for a team to get stuck or disaffected and to underperform. Teams in such a situation tend to display some particular characteristics. Members are confused and upset by lack of fit, asking themselves, how can I be working this hard and feeling this bad?

They seek to find the cause of the unhappy situation they find themselves in and start casting blame. Everyone expresses strong negative emotions or apathy. There is a history of repeated ineffectual attempts to move things forward, usually by 'making a decision'. Patterns of oscillation can be observed: problems are solved and re-solved, but somehow things don't move on. Decisions made don't stick. And because people have put a lot of time and energy into trying to make sense of their situation, maybe talking it out in little cliques or with their friends or partners, there is a lot of rehearsed speech on offer, which, self-evidently, isn't moving things forward.

It's worth taking a moment to notice what happens when a rational problem-solving approach is taken to this situation. Firstly, usually the team have already tried solving the problem through analysis and the application of brainpower, but doing more of the same only leads to experiencing more of the same. The diagnostic phase of the intervention, usually inquiring into the past seeking explanation, only encourages repetition of the ineffective rehearsed talk, as it is heard as a question of what happened and who is to blame. The lack of progress, and the continued rehearsal of the difficulties, leads to a downward spiral of despair at irresolvability of the issues. Negative emotions continue to be very present, if suppressed.

Appreciative inquiry offers a different approach to working with this kind of challenge. The case study below illuminates approaching such a situation from an appreciative practice base.

Case Study: Working with a Stuck Team

The commission in this case study was to help improve the work performance of a small team within a professional not-for-profit institute. Initially I interviewed all team members to gather an understanding of existing accounts of the situation (Figure 12.2).

The whole interview was structured from the appreciative simultaneity principle (the question is the intervention), and so the questions were chosen with a mind to the accounts they would produce. The positive principle informed the appreciative section of the interview. The anticipatory principle was gently present in the future section where people were asked to talk about what they would like to happen in the future. Similarly, the poetic principle was inherent in the suggestion that they could have an impact on the future. And the whole interview was based in a social constructionist

> Name
>
> Timing, process, confidentiality/anonymous, questions
>
> **Appreciation**
>
> When is the events team at its best?
>
> When are you at your best, in the context of the team and its work?
>
> Who or what else affects how well the team can do its work?
>
> How does the team know when it has been successful? And who else knows?
>
> **Changes**
>
> In your view, what have been the significant changes for the team over the last however long?
>
> What changes would you like to see?
>
> Who else might like to see changes and what changes?
>
> **Future**
>
> What do you think is going to happen in the future?
>
> What, in your opinion, does the team need to do differently to ensure the best possible future?
>
> **Current times**
>
> What do you consider to be the most significant issues for the team at the moment?
>
> How would you like the team to view you?
>
> **Other things**
>
> What else do I need to know to be able to effectively help this team work together more effectively?

Figure 12.2 Case study interview format.

understanding that there are many accounts of a situation that are equally valid and that no one holds a monopoly on the truth. In this way the interviews were constructed to very clearly serve three functions: they were an appreciative process intervention in themselves; they produced data about how the situation was currently perceived, experienced, understood and accounted for; and they produced qualitative data for a later evaluation.

Notice that at no point in the interview were team members asked directly for their account of what was wrong and who was to blame. However, the last section invited people to say anything they had come prepared to say, were driven to say, and would have felt cheated if they hadn't been able to say. Including this question at this point in the first part of the process has many benefits. Firstly, their story is heard but not broadcast or amplified. Secondly, they are relieved of their duty to tell you how 'things really are'. And thirdly the process positions you as a repository for the stories of frustration, disappointment, blame and so on. And very often, having safely deposited their story with you, their need to share it at the event is greatly reduced.

Broadly speaking it was clear that the staff group were frustrated and disaffected, with many considering leaving. They had experienced relatively high turnover during the last few years, and there appeared to be a lack of a clear induction programme for new staff. It was felt that work was not distributed fairly. Staff members had many ideas for how things could be improved yet felt that nothing actually changed. It seemed that the team had difficulty in making and implementing decisions and moving forward in its development. From these interviews, it was clear that emotions were running very high with members reporting shouting matches in team meetings, tears, blaming and social isolation and that this team could hardly bear to be in the same room together. This was not a fun place to work.

Notice that I learnt all this despite asking positively oriented questions. Yet there were also grounds for hope. No conflict, I always feel, without commitment. If people didn't care, they wouldn't bother to have the argument. And although they were thinking of leaving, they hadn't as yet. Something was holding them. Some dream, either from how things had been in the past or a sense of how things could be, was still engaging them. Following discussion with the team and the commissioner, the agenda of work was agreed upon as follows: We would work to establish proactive and positive leadership and management – of people, process, boundaries, customers and work. We would develop a sharper and empowering sense of purpose, aspiration and value. Issues of autonomy, group co-ordination and teamwork would be clarified and resolved. And, ways of recognising, registering and broadcasting success would be devised.

It was not possible to negotiate a suitable time period together; instead one full day and two half days separated by time, were made available. The first full day aimed to create a shared account of the current context and core activity of the team and to develop a shared understanding of when the team was working at its best and how they all contributed to that (Figure 12.3).

The process for this day was built around the appreciation, poetic and construction principles, while the discovery element was the core focus. Within this there was an ambition to move beyond the strong story the team held that the team problems were all about a 'clash of personalities in the team'. This understanding of their situation clearly wasn't creating positive change.

> *Objective*
> To create a shared account of current context and core activity
>
> *Aims*
> By the end of the day, team members should:
>> Have a shared understanding of when the team is working at its best and how they all contribute to that
>>
>> Have developed a shared account of the context within which they are expected to perform
>>
>> Have identified how the team, through its context and strengths, adds value to the process of organising events (or could do so)
>>
>> Have begun to work on a form of words that addresses why they exist and what they aim to become
>>
>> Have identified team and/or individual actions to take the process forward
>
> *Process of the Day*
>
> Introducing the day
>
> How we are going to work together today
>
> The team at its best
>
> The web of expectations
>> *Lunch break*
>
> What's so special about us?
>
> Purpose and vision
>
> Starting to do it differently
>
> *Workshop Participation*
> For this event to be most effective, it needs everyone present to be willing and able to contribute their understanding, knowledge, experience, hope, enthusiasm, concerns, hesitations and energy. The day will be a series of structured activities, with periods of reflection. It will be very participative with much small and large group activity and discussion.

Figure 12.3 Agenda for first team event.

The first two activities took some time as people were very nervous about what might happen during the day. Although very much not my usual practice, on this occasion it was appropriate to encourage fears to be aired so that we could agree how they could be mitigated against. Essentially the fear was that the hurtful and harmful behaviour that had occurred in team meetings would reoccur here. This is the point of having the 'working together' phase of the day. I was able to explain how the process, and I, would hold the day to a different pattern, and that, while we would be addressing the team challenges, we would be doing it very differently to their usual conversations. No one left and we reached a point of agreement to keep going with the event.

I had also noticed, as I was talking through the plan for the day, that some people were looking interested, that a light was coming on in their eyes about talking about some of these things, and it looked as if some people had had a thought when I'd suggested we'd be sharing good experiences. All of this encouraged me to judge that I had sufficient readiness to move onto the rest of the event. Essentially, I had compliance, but I would have to rely on the process to create commitment.

After a break, team members paired off and, as a discovery interview process, shared a highlight moment of teamwork. The feedback from this exercise revealed that the team had discovered new things about itself. For instance, two people who had paired up chose, by accident, the same episode as their example. They had had no idea that the other had felt so positively about the particular episode they were both involved in. The change of emotional tone in the room as these stories emerged was palpable. For the team, the idea that any one of them, never mind all of them, could identify a good team experience was a revelation. As a bigger picture is revealed and a different account of how the team is working emerges, so different possibilities for action are created. The team were both astonished and delighted by this evidence of good feeling within their group. This was an example of transformational discovery. Simultaneously, the mood in the room in the moment changed, and so did the narrative the team held about itself.

They then worked together to identify what made the particular events or moments they had shared so effective in teamwork terms compared to other similar but not so good episodes. It soon became apparent that these 'good times' tended to share the theme of being offsite and involving only a few members of the team. However, it was also clear that the different nature of the work and the feedback loops available also played a big part in creating the difference. An important point about an appreciative approach is that the process doesn't then immediately move on to 'solve' the 'problem' of how to replicate those features in other environments. Rather, the information is left to do its process work through people's changed understanding and is held in abeyance to be used to inform later parts of the process, as appropriate.

The team then moved on to identify the different parties (stakeholders) who had an interest in what they did and to start to think about their expectations of the team and their criteria of success. This exercise can be seen as a reference to the wholeness principle of appreciative inquiry. This team was part of a bigger system. It wasn't possible to work with this larger system in the room, but exploring it in this way created an awareness of the larger context within which the team were attempting to work.

Again, a wealth of data was elicited by the exercise. When asked to consider what they had produced the team noted the sense of relief gained by getting it all 'out there'. Some of the tensions and paradoxes evident within the system were identified. This gave me the chance to point out that such 'system' tensions often got played out within a group that held an awareness of all these agendas. This observation was not explored further at this time, although some members of the group nodded in agreement.

The team moved on to identify how they each added value to their collective process; the view was again expressed that it was very useful to have this knowledge made explicit and 'out there'. Even when people work together as a team, their daily work and activities are often opaque to, or hidden from, each other. Finding interesting and engaging ways for people to share the best of their contribution helps build team connection and appreciation and in this case, to start shifting their stories about each other.

They then moved on to create a statement of purpose and vision. This happened remarkably smoothly, reflecting the progress the group had made in working together and developing a shared understanding. Finally, each individual member committed to doing something different as they returned to the work environment, and some team activities to move things forward were identified.

Approximately a month later the team met for an afternoon with the aim of creating a shared vision for the future and a shared understanding of how to make it happen. The session started with identification in pairs of how things were changing for the better since they had last met. While this initially seemed challenging, they were soon able to come up with many examples, demonstrating once again that we see what we look for and the power of directing attention to shift the perception of, and story about, reality. The artefacts produced in the last session were also reintroduced, and people were asked to recall how they had first felt on seeing all this. This is the positive principle in action. The group are moving on to think about change, and so this first exercise was designed to help them reconnect with the positive energy they had generated last time we were together.

People were then asked to pair up and interview each other 'in the future', the essential organising question being 'How would things be if more of these good things were happening more of the time?' Here we are moving onto the dream phase of appreciative inquiry. The kind of questions they asked each other included: What are they doing? Where are they? Who is around? What are their achievements, aspirations, hopes etc.? What are people saying about the department? This exercise generated terrific energy.

Each pair then fed back these pictures of the future. It soon became clear that this list of future features formed aspirations for change and could be mined for items to form a template for the measurement of change, as well as ideas about the direction of change. A beginning was made on identifying those that easily lent themselves to measurement. Note this is an example of how to create context-specific evaluation processes.

The pairs then returned to interviewing each other, this time inquiring into how the transition had been made from the past to this future. In this way they were creating a ladder of change, asking questions like, 'How did some of these things start to change? Who did what?' This is one way of engaging in the design stage of appreciative inquiry; looking back from an imagined future can create a clarity about what will help and hinder the realisation of that future. People then worked as individuals or in pairs on how some of these future outcomes could be achieved, creating ladders of change.

The last session was a more production-orientated morning, focused on delivery. The essential question of the morning was: What are we going to do? Once again, the session started by asking team members to identify changes for the better since they had last met. People found this exercise harder than the previous time, which was put down to the pressure of a forthcoming big project which was in danger of sending the team back into old ways of relating. It was noted that highlighting this was useful in itself. From a positive psychology perspective, we can identify it as the effect of negative emotional states on perception. This serves to illustrate that positivity and positive energy are states that need to be, and can be, recreated and renewed throughout, well, life really!

We then brought everything that had been done over the last two sessions, that is, all the flipcharts and data generated, into the room and people looked at what they had done over last two sessions. The general tenor of the observations and comments was about how much they had done and the progress they had made. People particularly remembered how they had felt doing the future-oriented exercises.

The team then interviewed each other one by one, with the others acting as a listening and reflecting team, about what they thought should be done, not worrying for the moment about who might do it. Everyone got 10–15 minutes to explain their views. The many ideas were captured on flipcharts. The team looked at all the information they had produced. They then held a discussion about what they would do and how they would organise themselves to do it. This discussion was facilitated and recorded by the team leader. Essentially an action plan was drawn up with names and dates against events. This is a conflation of design and destiny asking both what could we do, and what will we do?

I got together again with the team seven months after the last intervention to assess progress. Initially each remaining team member (two had moved on during the process) and the commissioner were interviewed, after which the team got together as a group to assess the progress so far. In addition, I re-asked the questions I had asked in the initial interviews, so we could assess progress against those baseline measures. For all of these, the mode had moved by several increments in the right direction, and the range had narrowed, indicating an increase in the team's knowledge of itself. For example, against the question of how well as a team we share knowledge and skill, the dial had moved from a range of answers of 3–8, to a new range of 7–9 with a clear mode score of 8. The interviews and discussions noted many other positive changes including an increased sense of empowerment amongst team members, that team meetings were becoming more learning spaces, that there was less frustration in the team, and that the team generally were working better together. Needless to say, there was plenty more that could have been done to improve things further.

Conclusion

In this chapter we have considered the known factors that are the bedrock of high-performing teams, and we have identified the insights offered by positive psychology. We then considered the nature of stuck or dysfunctional teams and explored how an appreciative inquiry approach can have a transformational effect on such situations by walking through a case study.

Learning Points

1. A group is not a team.
2. The factors that support high team performance and successful team working are well known, just not always easy to create or maintain.
3. Appreciative inquiry is an ideal process for working with stuck or dysfunctional teams due to its emphasis on creating positive team states and

pull motivations, identifying strengths and creating new team stories about the past, the present and the future that allow for different actions and behaviours.

Discussion Questions

1. What are some of the best teams you have worked in, and what made them special?
2. How do teams become dysfunctional, and how does appreciative inquiry help move things forward?

Teaching Exercises

1. In pairs or groups, ask people to identify opportunities, in their own context, to create little blips of positivity for their team or team members.
2. In pairs or groups, ask people to select one of the strengths-identifying exercises to identify each other's strengths. Use a set of strengths cards to help. Encourage them to think how these strengths might be beneficial to their team.

Helpful Resources

Theppshop.store stocks both strengths and emotion cards.

Whitney, W., Trosten-Bloom, A., Cherney, J., and Fry, R. (2004). *Appreciative Team Building: Positive Questions to Bring Out the Best of Your Team*. Lincoln: iUnivers.

Smith, A. (2023). *Practical Appreciative Inquiry: How to Use This Leading-Edge Coaching Method Confidently with Team and Small Groups*. Independently published by the author and available through Amazon.

Lewis, S. (2011). *Positive Psychology at Work*. Chapter 7: Positive relationships at work. Wiley-Blackwell.

Note

1. See more on job recrafting and team performance here: Ref. [1].

Reference

1. Mäkikangas, A., Aunola, K., Seppälä, P., and Hakanen, J. (2016). Work engagement-team performance relationship: shared job crafting as a moderator. *Journal of Occupational and Organizational Psychology* 89: 772–790.

13

Virtual, Remote and Hybrid Working

The Industrial Revolution model of work, gathering people together in a specified place for set hours each week, was thought of by many as the 'normal' working mode through most of the twentieth, and into the twenty-first century, even though there was always a large contingent of people and trades that did not fit the model. Various economic downturns towards the end of the twentieth century added an army of freelancers to artisans and others, such as farmers, who already worked outside the corporate model. International connection and the advent of the internet continued to boost numbers working outside the 'normal' frame. However, it was only when great swathes of the Western world went into 'lockdown' in the attempt to combat the spread of the initially highly deadly corona virus that the corporate 9–5, five days a week model of work was really challenged.

Offices and factories stood empty as people and organisations struggled to adapt to what was known as the working from home model of remote working. This 'working at home while still being part of a larger organisation' model raised a number of challenges both for the individuals suddenly working in their cramped, unsuitable apartments attempting to communicate with colleagues over the internet, and for organisations struggling to maintain their culture, sense of identity and productivity under these different working conditions. While many organisations have returned, or at least have attempted to return, to the old model, many others have incorporated an element of remote working into their normal way of running. How can an understanding of appreciative inquiry help with these challenges?

This chapter explores some of the challenges posed to individuals working remotely from their organisational colleagues and illustrates how the

---

Practical Appreciative Inquiry: A Toolkit for Applying Appreciative Inquiry to Organisational Challenges, Opportunities, and Aspiration, First Edition. Sarah Lewis.
© 2025 John Wiley & Sons Ltd. Published 2025 by John Wiley & Sons Ltd.

effective use of appreciative inquiry processes can help with these. It goes on to consider the challenge of holding virtual appreciative inquiry summits. It then looks at recent research suggesting how hybrid working can best be managed and the part appreciative inquiry can play to support this strongly emerging organisational trend. The chapter concludes with a case study.

Some of the Challenges of Remote Working for the Individual

There is no doubt that remote working can be a challenge to well-being. This can be caused by the stress of unsuitable working conditions, the conflicting role demands of work and home, social isolation, and the changed nature of the work. How much any individual is adversely affected depends, obviously, on their personal situation.

Even so, the strong pushback against demands, post-lockdown, that people return to the office for a fixed number of days each week suggests a lot of people have come to appreciate the various benefits of working from home, including a sense of greater autonomy, greater productivity and a huge reduction in low-quality commuting time. It is also worth noting some research that suggests that remote working, with limited online contact, can be beneficial to the mental health of neurodiverse individuals by limiting social interactions and by providing greater control over the environment [1].[1] However, despite the apparent time-saving benefit, diminished social contact can erode people's sense of well-being over time. Applying appreciative inquiry thinking to interactions online can bring well-being benefits to remote workers. These interventions support workplace cohesion and identity, and can boost performance, benefiting both the individual and the organisation (Table 13.1).

Applying Appreciative Inquiry to the Challenges of Remote Working

1. Creating and recreating positive emotional states with discovery interviews

Appreciative inquiry as a process creates positive emotional states that are now clearly recognised as boosting mental and physical health. Table 13.2 introduces 30 positive emotions and key identified benefits each emotional state can bring.[2]

Table 13.1 Working from home challenges and possible appreciative inquiry responses.

Challenges	Appreciative responses
Low mood	Creating and recreating positive emotional states with discovery interviews and celebrations of achievement. Fun, laughter, physical activity
Loss of sense of connection and purpose	Creating positive, aspirational images of the future, reidentifying positive core. Short, more frequent team or buddy contact. Strengthened feedback loops of positive consequences of work or activity
Loss of motivation and energy for work	Identifying and working with strengths. Buddy system. Good positive feedback loops. Enthusiasm conversations (see Chapter 11)
Work stress, overworking	Recrafting work to better suit remote working, capitalising on flexibility of remote working patterns and individual strengths
Sense of isolation, weakening relationships	Virtual social contact, not all exclusively work focused

Discovery interviews are a great way to shift mood in the moment. Asking people about a good experience, for example a recent success or achievement in which they can take pride, a recent sparkle moment or what energises them in their life right now, enables them to re-access good feelings. This is because memory and emotions are highly linked. When someone actively remembers a peak or highlight moment, when they were full of confidence and doing something they loved, when they are encouraged to talk about that and to expand on it, the memory comes to life emotionally. Their mood begins to change as they relive how they felt at the time. I have found this to be a very powerful, highly reliable way of helping people shift their mood to a more positive place in the moment.

2. Creating positive, aspirational images of the future

Appreciative inquiry also focuses on creating positive images of the future. This acts to boost mood and can be encouraged by asking questions that help connect people's day-to-day work to the bigger picture, such as, 'How is what you are doing now going to make a difference to the future?' 'Who is going to benefit by what you are doing?' 'How can you set things up so

Table 13.2 Some of the mental and physical health benefits of positive emotional states.

Emotional state	Mental and physical health benefits
Activating Emotions	
Curiosity	Enhances emotional wellbeing, vitality and emotional intelligence
Energy	Reduces stress and anxiety, strengthens the immune system
Hopeful	Improves resilience, self-care and sociability
Inspired	Boosts happiness and helps with the management of stress
Interested	Helps us feel positive and active
Zestful	Increases motivation, courage and life satisfaction
Relational Emotions	
Affinity	Boosts our immune system
Compassion	Associated with well-being, relieving depression and anxiety
Humility	Promotes good self-esteem, satisfaction with life
Intimacy	Associated with high self-disclosure, which can help mental health
Love	Boosts the immune system, reduces stress and improves resilience
Trust	Increases feeling of relaxation and lessens anxiety and muscle tension
Restorative Emotions	
Forgiving	Improves mental health
Fulfilled	Lowers stress levels and increases optimism
Grateful	Associated with lower levels of depression and stress
Optimism	Associated with better coping and with better health
Playful	Increases in self-care, reduced anxiety, relaxed state of mind
Pride	Contributes to self-esteem, self-worth, resilience and well-being
Soothing Emotions	
Contentment	Contributes to happiness and reduces effects of negative emotions
Happy	Associated with longevity, physical health, resilience and confidence
Peaceful	Benefits our physical health and boosts our resilience
Relaxed	Associated with lower stress levels
Safe	Supports feelings of self-assurance and confidence
Serene	Increases clear-mindedness, creates and embeds positive memories

Table 13.2 (Continued)

Emotional state	Mental and physical health benefits
Transformative Emotions	
Admiration	Inspires a desire for self-improvement
Awestruck	Increases feelings of calmness, reduces anxiety, increases well-being
Generous	Combats depression, strengthens the immune system and lessens stress
Joyful	Undoes the harmful effect of difficult or damaging emotions
Transcendence	Associated with feelings of peace, joy, good for mental health
Uplifted	Increases generosity and kindness

that you get feedback on that?', or 'What is the most inspiring thing for you about what we do as an organization?'

It is a mistake to think of these mood-boosting activities as just things to do before the meeting really starts. Instead, they can be an integrated way of ensuring the meeting is energised and connected, that problem-solving capabilities are enhanced, that the group can cope with and hold ambiguity or disagreement in productive ways. It's a double win; there is a mood-boost benefit for the people involved, and there is a boost to the effectiveness of the meeting.

3. Identifying and working with strengths

We know that working to strengths helps boost mood. Strengths can be revealed through appreciative interviews and by working with strengths cards. A personal favourite exercise of mine is to hold a strengths-identifying conversation off the back of a discovery interview. Working online, this can be achieved by equipping team members each with their own pack of cards[3] which they can refer to in their own workspace to help them identify and name another's strengths. Alternatively, packs of strengths cards are now available in virtual workspaces.[4]

Spending time helping people identify each other's strengths and thinking about how they can be applied to help alleviate some of the risks of remote working is a good investment in performance, tends to be morale boosting and aids self-development. For example, someone with a nurturing strength might be willing to ensure daily chats with a more isolated team member.

While someone with a strength of creativity might be happy to help someone else develop ideas. Using team strengths to the benefit of all helps everyone.

4. Recrafting work to better suit remote working

One benefit of people understanding their strengths is that they can then recraft how they exercise their role so that how they work is adjusted as best as possible to the remote work environment and requirements, and to utilising their strengths. This is likely to make work more engaging for them and to boost their well-being. Strangely, the uninterrupted nature of work that remote working makes possible for some often comes at an increased risk of becoming burnt out [3].

5. Achieving high productivity without burnout

Many people are astonished at how much more productive they are away from the distractions of an office and may not notice that it comes at the expense of working consistently harder or concentrating for longer periods, both of which are tiring. They need to be given permission to 'work differently' to recognise that in these changed circumstances energy is the key determinant of productivity, not time spent 'at the desk', for instance. Appreciative-style questions can help people discover what works best for them.

6. Capitalise on the flexibility of remote working

There are other ways we can use appreciative inquiry to help people best manage this new working environment, recognising that the work and life pattern is going to be different for different people. Appreciative inquiry's recognition of the value of diversity can help managers here. Rather than wanting to force everyone into the same mode, they can act to gain the benefits of emerging work patterns. A meeting to explore this might ask questions such as, 'When in the day do you find you do your best work?', 'What do you need from others to make it possible to work at your best from home?', or, 'Describe your best day combining your work and life activities. What do you dream it could be?'

7. Maintaining motivation

Even when people are able to organise their home-working schedule to suit both the organisation and themselves, remote working can produce the challenge of staying motivated. Without the regular blips of pleasure experienced joshing with colleagues or chatting inconsequentially about nothing much, the day can begin to seem all work and no play. In this situation mood can quickly drop, and then it can be hard for people to motivate themselves to get on with things, especially things they were not looking forward to, do not enjoy or find hard to do. As we have explored above, appreciative inquiry interventions can act to boost mood and motivation. There are also some helpful motivation-maintaining techniques from 'regular' work management advice, as in Table 13.3.

8. Supporting work relationships

For many people a key relationship network is their work colleagues. Unfortunately, working from home can have an adverse effect on these relationships. Sustained for years by daily incidental contact and fuelled by interest in the ongoing mini-sagas of others, work-a-day positive relationships tootle along without anyone needing to give them much thought. When these opportunities for lots of micro-moments of connection are suddenly lost, the friendships, which seemed so solid, can whither on the vine. Ensuring online working includes opportunities for connection by including small-group fire-lighter sessions or appreciatively oriented paired conversations can help revitalise these connections.

One way to boost mood, relationships and motivation while working virtually is to hold an appreciative inquiry online.

Table 13.3 Techniques to help maintain motivation.

Break big projects down into small tasks.
Set clear targets for the next hour, day, week.
Make a list, prioritise it, and tick things off as you achieve them (for most people 'ticking things off the list' gives them that little positivity boost).
Take a break.
Decide at the end of the previous day what the first task is for tomorrow.
Use a task that you are looking forward to as a reward to yourself for doing the less pleasant one first.
Tackle hard tasks in small bursts, followed by a reward of some kind such as having a sweet treat with your cup of tea, or taking five minutes exercise going to post that letter.

Hosting an Appreciative Inquiry Online

Holding appreciative inquiry events online is different to holding them face-to-face. Fortunately, a lot has been learnt about how to create and host such events online over the last few years.[5]

One key point is the need to use time differently. Face-to-face events are typically run in a concentrated timeframe, with the whole system in one physical place, over a day or longer. With a virtual inquiry, it is better to go for much shorter sessions spread out over a number of days. Keeping any online session to less than two hours at any one time is recommended to preserve engagement and energy levels. And should there be a second session the same day, then there should be at least a 30-minute break between them.

It is always important to encourage active participation in an appreciative inquiry event, and this is even more important when working in a virtual mode, which tends to facilitate greater passivity. Conscious attention needs to be paid to maximising everyone's participation and contribution while online. It's good practice to ensure that there is a mix of the whole group working for collective meaning-making, time spent in smaller groups for more intense discussion and time for individual reflection. This combination helps maintain attention and participation. In addition, it can help to push all preparation activity into a prework phrase, so people arrive expecting to be active and are already engaged with the process. Table 13.4 outlines some principles to inform practice.

There is also a need to carefully plan how to connect up different group conversations. The benefits of some of the connective practices used face-to-face can be created online. For example, the marketplace sharing process (whereby people visit each other's stands) can be replicated online through

Table 13.4 Principles for designing virtual appreciative inquiry from Stirling-Wilkie.

Connection before content
Short focused sessions
Limited use of presentation and talking heads – push this into pre-work
Agree on ground rules
Design for inclusivity
Wide variety of interactive processes
Design around context, required business outcomes, human experience, relational dynamics

---

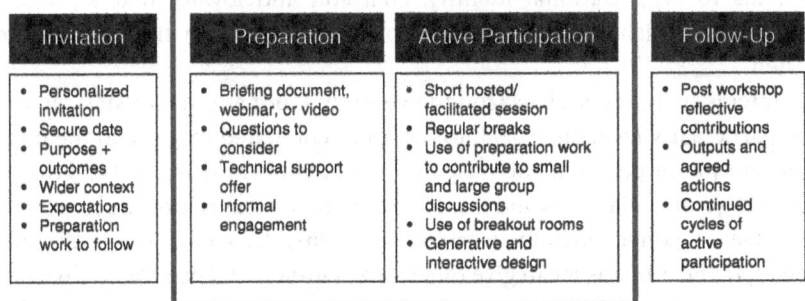

Figure 13.1 Process for online appreciative inquiry from Gwen Stirling-Wilkie, by permission of author and publisher.

a process whereby the document (the virtual flipchart) moves around each group, rather than the groups moving to each virtual whiteboard.

To support the energy and interactivity of the event, group reactions and thoughts can be captured and connected using the virtual programme functions. For example, the chat function of Zoom or Teams can be used as the 'connector' of the small-group outputs, so that there is no need to do feed-outs in the main Zoom room. Using chat this way also works to create a record of event output, as does using the whiteboard function.

The 'walk and talk' activity often included in face-to-face sessions can be accommodated by asking participants to pair up on a phone chat. Released from the big screen, they are free to move and chat even if they aren't physically in the same space. This adds a different dynamic to the event.

It's also a good idea to create small presession breakout rooms in which people can meet and mingle before the session begins, maybe over coffee. In this way the various elements of a great appreciative inquiry process can be achieved in an online environment, as suggested in Figure 13.1.

Effects of Remote Working on the Workplace

The effects of remote working are felt by the organisation as well as by individuals. Research has shown[6] that remote working can lead to weaker workplace ties and can lower staff engagement and loyalty. It can be hard to establish or maintain a strong organisational culture. Weak cultures are associated with conflict and mistrust. It is the growing realisation of these threats to organisational identity, cohesion and loyalty that are likely behind the push towards getting more people back in the office more often.

Interestingly, research has found that both junior and senior staff tend to be particularly keen on visits into the office compared to those in the middle. For junior people it's because they tend to benefit from on-the-ground learning from colleagues and from general office socialisation and are likely to have less congenial home working arrangements. Senior people also like being in the office as it can give them a cross-functional overview of what is going on between different roles and teams. Assuming the workforce is also present of course! And for some, who tend to manage and evaluate effort by staff's devotion to being present, the loss of this proxy for actual performance is sorely missed. This pressure to get people where they can be seen, combined with a concern about the waste of an expensive resource, acts to support the compromise position of hybrid working.

Hybrid Working

Hybrid working attempts to mandate a specified number of days a week when 'the workforce' by and large must be physically present in the same space. In some cases, the outcome of this is that people, coerced into commuting into the office, then act while there as if they were working from home, remaining isolated and disconnected. This is a particularly likely outcome when attendance is poorly coordinated, and the people who would find it useful to see each other aren't present on the same day. To work effectively, the hybrid model needs to be more carefully designed.

1. Getting the best from hybrid working

There seems to be considerable resistance from a lot of people to returning to the old model of five-day-a-week attendance; it looks as if hybrid working is going to be around for a while yet. There has been much interest in this emerging model of work, indeed a new term 'omni-working' has recently been coined [5], and some guidance is now available on the best way to balance the at-home/in the office requirement.[7] Research has found that it is helpful to divide work tasks into four categories and then to consider which are most well-suited to home working and which not (Table 13.5).

Table 13.5 Four categories of types of work from Trevor and Holweg article.

Focused Creative Tasks, such as writing code or designing a brochure, require little teamwork and are easily supported by technology. They are the easiest to transition to virtual work.	Coordinated Group Tasks, such as town halls, routine project work, regular review meetings, and group information-sharing, may be largely standardised but still require human interaction. These are more difficult to accomplish with remote participants, but it is possible with communication technology.
Individual Procedural Tasks, such as entering data or processing claims, can be performed without interacting with others. Consequently, for remote work, only supervision became more difficult.	Collaborative Group Tasks, such as product development, creative problem-solving, and strategic planning, are the most social type – and important elements of innovation processes. The inherently collaborative nature of such tasks is the core challenge that drives the debate over hybrid work.

The first category is that of focused creative tasks, such as designing a brochure. These, the research suggests, are some of the easiest to transition to virtual work because they require little teamwork and are easily supported by technology. When I first read this, it seemed strange. Surely creativity benefits from ideas being 'bounced around' with others? But this is a different understanding of creativity, the clue being in the mention of technology. Already many designers work on their own, calling on sophisticated design tools and elements to support them. As the future unfolds, it is possible that this will become a field dominated by individuals working with the vast resources made accessible by artificial intelligence. There is very little point travelling to another environment to undertake this work, and being instructed to do so can breed resentment.

The second category, individual procedural tasks such as data entry, also lend themselves to virtual, remote or home working.

The other two categories, coordinated group tasks, such as project work and collaborative group tasks such as product development or strategic planning, were found to have been the hardest to transition to virtual working. These are the kinds of tasks that benefit from time spent together in the office. We can redefine these as team tasks, tasks that require the coordinated input from a number of different people to create something or that require collective, creative thinking where ideas bounce and build.

While the invention of the video meeting has facilitated much, it is a much poorer communication environment than being face-to-face. For example, it is harder to read facial expressions, it's harder, if not impossible to communicate by eye with another, bodies cannot be meaningfully swivelled or angled, hand and arm gestures are limited and groups find it really hard to coordinate their contributions. The loss of all this non-verbal communication and social coordination activity has a huge effect on a group's ability to feel, think, or move 'as one', which is what team working at its best can feel like. So, these tasks do really benefit from face-to-face time. This is what organisations need to be concentrating on when they bring people together. Then 'coming into work' should become rewarding to people. Interestingly, these potential benefits are not immediately obvious to people as we shall see in the case study below.

Case Study of Hybrid Working Challenges

Recently I was asked to work with a team that had very successfully transitioned to remote working during the Covid lockdown period, but now the organisation was requesting a minimal monthly in-office presence, less than a day a week, and was meeting resistance. Initial interviews with team members revealed a number of reasons for the resistance. Some people who had been recruited during the pandemic and had not at that time been expected to attend the work building lived some considerable distance away from it. Amongst the team many felt overburdened already with work and that this demand just reduced their time to actually do the work; in other words, that the cost of coming in was counterproductive in productivity terms. Many expressed frustration that people with whom they would like to have conversations, from other work teams, were not in the building on the same days. It did not help that the team was comprised of two previous teams who had been merged not long prior to the lockdown and that the team manager, being based on another continent, wasn't always able to be physically present on the 'inhouse' days. Instead, they continued to contribute to discussions via Zoom.

It was also evident that there were some difficulties with team functioning stemming from the previous merging of teams, with undercurrents of 'sides' and 'loyalties' at play. In all, the team absolutely exemplified the dangers identified by Trevor and Holweg [2] of a weakening corporate or team identity and culture. It was clear that a day in the office held little attraction or perceived value.

An initial team day was arranged. The emphasis of this first event was on having a good time together in an effort to boost a sense of relatedness, as well as creating valued outcomes. The day was structured around the SOAR model of appreciative inquiry. The first session focused on creating a timeline of successes over the previous six years and of identifying the team strengths that had supported this. This exercise had many benefits including helping newer recruits connect to the sources of pride in the team and generating positivity in the room.

We next moved on to identifying the opportunities for the team, in terms of both exciting and profitable work. From there the discussion moved on to identifying aspirations for the future. We spent some time imagining and sharing best possible futures, as in the dream phase of appreciative inquiry, followed by an open space to develop ideas for actions. These were ratified in a final round. The day was evaluated against desired outcomes, and on all dimensions, scores had shifted to the right and clustered up, all of which indicated a more shared and common view amongst team members of their strengths, successes, understanding of the opportunities for growth, sense of what success looks like and sense that there are ideas for how to move things forward.

Individual commitments to action by team members centred around being proactive about offering availability to others in slacker periods; being cognisant of the need for attention to relationships as well as tasks; being more sociable; boosting their own and others' mood and positivity; and recognising differences of perspective in the group. All these actions would help alleviate some of the downsides of remote working. The event also had an impact on mood, with people commenting at a lunchtime round and at the close of the event that they felt emotions such as optimism, hopefulness, curiosity and awe. The event was seen as a good use of time spent together face to face. It reminded people of some of the pleasures and benefits of working together on joint activities.

The organisation decided on a further event a few months later. The pre-event interviews revealed that team members were still struggling to see the value in 'in office' days. While this event had a number of objectives, shifting this perception was a key desired outcome. After some preliminary activity, the model outlined in Table 13.4 was introduced to help the group work out the best use of the time in the office. My ambition was that they first identify the various team and individual tasks, and then match these to the four quadrants. At this point something interesting happened. The group pushed back against the exercise, rejecting the offered model as not being appropriate to their situation. In response I inquired into what might be a more helpful way of engaging with this thorny issue. This led to a good conversation from which emerged the realisation that they needed to approach the compulsory in-office days with a different mindset if they were to get value from them.

Further inquiry allowed us to understand that the mindset required, as characterised by them, was that of being open to interruptions and thinking of office days as 'Collaboration Days'. Labelling is a very important linguistic activity, and this relabelling allows the days in question to be thought about differently. The idea of collaboration conjures up different images to the idea of 'office working'. It's small shifts like this in language, naming and thinking that can liberate people from embedded patterns of behaviour, creating the potential for new things to emerge.

Having identified this mindset shift, they were then able to identify some specific ideas about how to best use the days; for example: ad hoc discussions of issues or problems; one-to-one conversations; showcasing work to colleagues; knowledge-sharing, discussing project opportunities and planning the project pipeline; learning from project successes; holding concept meetings, for example to revise a workflow when initiating a project; and for organising collaboration days with other teams. This was a great list of self-generated valuable ways to use their time together.

It was also felt that it would be helpful to include email periods throughout the day to give people specific timeslots to attend to emails. And also, to declare the day a 'no Zoom day'. A couple of team members took responsibility for planning the next in-house day to incorporate some of these ideas.

Six months later, an update from the team leader reported that the team was working better as a team and the collaboration days in the office were seen as critical to solving problems best tackled in person. Newer team members, it was reported, particularly appreciated the Zoom-free, person-to-person, light-on-email, project-planning days. This encouraging feedback suggests that the 'in office' days were now being used to much greater collective purpose and were beginning to generate their own momentum.

All this goes to show that a shift to hybrid working requires a 're-experiencing' of the benefits of being together and a shift in mentality about both what counts as work and the workplace. Rows of partitioned desk are of less use than meeting rooms and other breakout spaces. The emphasis when people are together in the office needs to be on conversation and communication. Documents should be sent in advance so the time together can be used to question and to compare perceptions, build understanding and promote consensus, clarity, motivation and commitment. In this way the office becomes more of a social and collaborative hub.

A good hybrid working ambition is to ensure that every day spent in the office is worth it, for everyone. As demonstrated by the case study above, this will not happen by accident. Hardworking, efficient people like those who made up this team can easily experience days in the office as a waste of precious time. The performance and productive payoffs of time together are not always as immediately evident as those of banging on through writing a report, or similar activities. As in this case study, appreciative inquiry-informed team days that ensure tangible and experiential benefit to people can help the transition. Indeed, having everyone together in the office may be a great opportunity to use appreciative inquiry to make productive use of the time.

Conclusion

In this chapter we have looked at the growth of hybrid, remote and virtual working. We've looked at how appreciative inquiry–informed activities can help with some of the challenges of remote working. We have outlined some key considerations when conducting an appreciative inquiry event in a virtual environment. And we have introduced a model for hybrid working. Finally, a case study explored the role of appreciative inquiry in helping to create an environment that encourages the best use of office-based working.

Learning Points

1. Appreciative inquiry approaches can help alleviate some of the effects of remote working.
2. Appreciative Inquiry summits can be run successfully online.
3. Hybrid working arrangements need conscious thought to be successful.

Discussion Questions

1. Discuss your experiences of remote working. What seemed to be the benefits and costs? What helped?
2. Why is maintaining a strong sense of organisational identification and culture important?
3. How might the perspective of leaders, middle management and staff differ on the importance of time in the office?

Teaching Exercise

1. Design two appreciative inquiry–informed exercises to incorporate into online team meetings or an online appreciative inquiry summit.

Helpful Resources and Further Reading

See the online platform Deckhive for a way of using tangible tools online. https://www.acukltd.com/deckhive.

Sterling-Wilkie, G. (2021). *From Physical Place to Virtual Space: How to Design and Host Transformative Spaces Online*, BMI Series in Dialogic Organizational Development. BMI Publishing.

Stirling-Wilkie, G. (2023). *Omni-Working: Work Effectively in all Ways from all Places*. Academy for Relationships.

Notes

1. MIT reported research based on work done by Professors Trevor and Holweg at the University of Oxford's Said Business School (see Ref. [2]).
2. All of this information and more can be found in the positive emotions card pack at theppshop.store.
3. There are many strengths card packs available, including a selection at the theppshop.store.
4. See deckhive.com, for example.
5. See Ref. [4].
6. This section pulls information from *The Guardian* reference in Ref. [1].
7. See the Gallup article referred to in Ref. [3].

References

1. Geddes, L. (2023). What have the past three years taught us about hybrid working. The Guardian Explainer. 10 March. 12.02.
2. Trevor, J. and Holweg, M. (2022). Managing the new tensions of hybrid work. *MIT Sloan Management Review* 64 (2).
3. Wigert, B. and Robison, J. (2020). Remote workers facing high burnout and how to turn it around. http://Gallup.com. Accessed November 2023.
4. Stirling-Wilkie, G. (2021). *From Physical Place to Virtual Space: How to Design and Host Transformative Spaces Online*, BMI Series in Dialogic Organizational Development. BMI Publishing.
5. Stirling-Wilkie, G. (2023). *Omni-Working: Work Effectively in all Ways from all Places*. Academy for Relationships.

14

Reviewing and Evaluating Practice

Commissioners, not unreasonably, like to know they are getting value for money. To this end it is appropriate to evaluate the impact of our interventions. This poses some interesting challenges for an appreciative inquiry intervention. Generally, to measure change it is important to take a baseline measure. But if 'the question is the intervention', does the very attempt to achieve a 'prior to our intervention' measure become, by definition, nigh well impossible? And then there is the question of what to measure? Often organisations want to use measures they already have baked into their system: staff surveys, absence rates, turnover rates and so on. These are usually gross, crude measures. But often the areas in which we hope to have effect are specific, subtle and local. For example, we might be attempting to positively influence the quality of communication, of shared understanding or of morale and motivation. Then there is the idea at the heart of appreciative inquiry, that perception is reality. In other words, that change has occurred if people perceive change. Following this logic, measuring change is not about taking objective measurement, it's about tracking changes as perceived by those involved.

This chapter first explores the purpose of evaluation from an appreciative inquiry perspective. It then looks at how many activities labelled 'evaluation' are actually 'reflective rituals' that achieve very little that is useful to the primary players. It goes on to consider how a fairly standard organisational process, 360° feedback, can be wrapped in an appreciative envelope and its impact transformed through the inclusion of a preliminary appreciative conversation. The chapter then offers a case study that illuminates how to help a group expand their understanding of the nature

---

Practical Appreciative Inquiry: A Toolkit for Applying Appreciative Inquiry to Organisational Challenges, Opportunities, and Aspiration, First Edition. Sarah Lewis.
© 2025 John Wiley & Sons Ltd. Published 2025 by John Wiley & Sons Ltd.

and purpose of reviewing and evaluating so they are able to embrace an appreciative review process.

Why Evaluate Activity?

What is the point of evaluating our activity and interventions? First and foremost an evaluation is usually intended to demonstrate change, ideally improvement. But evaluation can serve other purposes. For example, Malene Dinesen [1] argues that when undertaking an evaluation the ambition is to generate internal commitment, meaning that the members of the organisation undertake the evaluation to help develop their practice so that they can do their job in the best possible way. To achieve this, she suggests, it is helpful to give up a number of ideas, for example the idea that an evaluation is a process conducted by an individual of the work of others. Rather, evaluation becomes a co-created process conducted by the evaluator and the participant(s). The process of evaluation starts at the very beginning of the intervention when the ambition for change can be interrogated for ideas about where, if successful, the desired changes and improvements might show up. In this way, the intervention and the evaluation of it are intimately connected.

It can be seen, then, that an effective evaluation needs to start with a genuine wish to create a change in practice. By co-creating evaluations with people and by working together to decide what should be evaluated, meaningless measurement points [2].[1] can be avoided. The importance of this can hardly be overstressed: if change is all about perception, as I would argue it is, then the ambition of evaluation is to direct people's attention to what they need to be looking at to see the impact of their activity. Given this, it is clear that evaluation cannot be regarded, as it frequently is, as an isolated objective process that does not influence the field being observed: it absolutely does. From this perspective it becomes clear that in any particular intervention, instead of somehow collating universal truths, we are looking for 'locally generated truths for that time and context'.[2] The evaluation needs to be meaningful to those involved if it is ultimately to create better practice. The primary audience for an effective evaluation thus becomes the participants in the process. This perspective can run into conflict with other audiences who may also want to get the measure of what is going on.

This confusion of interested parties can mean that many activities that aren't really an evaluation may be labelled as such. For example, sometimes evaluations are conducted as a 'reflective ritual', [3][3] which means they are conducted just to enable the group to say, or prove, that it undertook one.

Meaningless Measurement Points and the Reflective Ritual Review

As an example of a ritual review based on meaningless measurements, we can consider the evaluations that organisations are frequently required to carry out to satisfy external requirements from a higher authority. Organisations often put a lot of organisational effort and energy into completing these externally designed, driven and controlled processes. These documents are often many pages long requiring hundreds of predetermined questions to be completed from a menu of limited answers along a scale such as 'completely' to 'not at all'. For example, I have occasionally been involved in delivering publicly funded projects that required evidence of impact. The desire to ensure value-for-public-money-spent is legitimate, but the outcomes recorded were highly divorced from the life of the activity and were, I believe I can safely say, regarded by all involved solely as a bureaucratic necessity to secure present and future funding.

Anecdotally it does seem as if, particularly for public sector and grant-funded bodies, this kind of paperwork has grown exponentially over the last 20 years. But when evaluations are performed to satisfy management or authority and people spend their resources on something that does not create new knowledge or useable results for them, they disconnect, and evaluations become something negative that people try to avoid participating in. This can breed frustration internally with the whole idea of evaluation.

Undertaking an evaluation as a reflective ritual helps convince some audiences that the institution or organisation is serious about its work, but it tends to have little impact on practice and often brings little learning or development. In such situations, there is a lack of will to apply learning from the evaluation to future activity.

Appreciative-Informed Evaluation of Leadership or Management

There are many ways to conduct appreciative management performance reviews, from using the appreciative inquiry 5D model [4, 5][4] through to the best-self exercise [6, 7].[5] Sometimes, however, we have to work within the constraints of existing practice.

An evaluative practice commonly found in organisations is that of assessing managers' performance through a 360° feedback process that uses a

Likert[6] scale against a series of items or questions. Often undertaken prior to designing a development programme that will address the reported areas of poor performance, the performance assessment is made by those around the manager on a number of criteria deemed important for the execution of the role. The unspoken part of the question in many of these measures is, 'Dear recipient, in your mind, measured against managers you have known or the ideal you have in mind, how good is this person at, for example, communicating clearly? Rate them on this 5-point scale from very poor to very good'. No matter how good the competency scale criteria people are provided with to help them, essentially everyone is using their own ruler. Yet the process proceeds as if the rulers were standardised.

The results are duly collated, and the report produced. Then the manager discusses the results with the person who is going to help them develop their action plan for improvement. At this point the psychological bias towards negative information kicks in and all the attention goes to the perceived areas of shortfall or deficit while any areas of abundance or exceptionalism are ignored as not offering any room for growth. So strong is this tendency that, even coming at these feedback conversations from a positive, appreciative perspective, it can prove very hard to shift people's attention to their areas of excellence, where they have topped out on the score board, so focused are they to improve their scores in the next round of the exercise.

Appreciative Process for Management Performance Assessment

Chella [8] suggests a process that allows for an appreciative assessment of managerial performance. Although it was designed as a stand-alone process and is an ideal to aim for, it can be used to improve the chances of conducting a productive, impactful, motivating management assessment when involved with a 360° feedback process. It all starts with a conversation.

In the process outlined, the emphasis of the initial conversation is to demonstrate appreciation of the manager and to form a relationship with them. There is a focus on understanding the manager's context, their history so far, their aspirations as a manager, and on demonstrating an appreciation of what they have achieved. This conversation allows the conversational partner to understand the manager's resource base and to identify what has worked for them in the past that has brought them to their current position. It can also be used to gain their perspective on their current performance and what they bring to the challenge.

A further benefit of this early conversation is that it can be used to identify the person's strengths. Many effective leaders have what is commonly known as a 'spiky' profile, meaning they have peaks of exceptional strengths, but equally, they are likely to have deep canyons of weakness. If third-party feedback needs to be incorporated into the process, then having gathered information, created perspective, boosted mood and formed a good relationship, this can be a good point to bring it into the conversation.

In this case start first with the high-scoring items exploring what enables the manager to demonstrate high skill in this area. The conversation can then relate these observations back to their beliefs about the role and job of a manager, their ambitions, their history and their strengths. Having thoroughly explored how their strengths contribute to their high performance, it may well be possible to spot when the feedback about unsuccessful behaviours is an indication of strengths in overdrive, or misapplied strengths, for example. In this case the discussion can move to exploring how to use their strengths with more skill or how latent strengths can be activated to help with specific areas. By reframing 'areas of weakness' as 'areas of strengths challenge', a whole different tone of conversation is created, and many avenues of exploration of ways forward become apparent.[7] Still, there may be areas of low competency scores that are just that, areas in which the person can draw on neither existing skills nor strengths to help.

Before engaging with any such item, it is worth questioning how important this area actually is to team performance and relationships rather than just assuming it must be addressed. But assuming it is important, the next step is to see if there is an easy way to address the issue, such as through job-crafting, delegating or strengths-swapping within the team.

A conversation of this nature is likely to release considerably more energy and motivation for improvement than one focused exclusively on a leader's intractable weaknesses. Following this process, the finalised development plan should include many more actions that are directed to using established strengths more effectively, and making better use of team resources, than those directed at correcting areas of weakness head-on.

Case Study: Introducing Appreciative Peer Reviews to a Regional Health Team

This case study is drawn from some recent work and focuses particularly on the challenge of conceptualising an appreciative evaluation. The invitation to work with the organisation was framed as a desire to bring appreciative inquiry to the workplace. When possible and appropriate, I prefer to help and support an organisation to hold an appreciative inquiry, rather than just 'teach' the methodology. The commissioner and I searched for a way in. An area that fell under the remit of quality improvement was suggested. At the time, most quality improvement activity within the part of the organisation with which I would be working was based on a review of performance against past objectives, usually involving self-assessment using a lengthy tick-box form which was completed on behalf of all by one person. In general, the various services that made up the specific children's and mental health service function found being reviewed more demoralising than energising, suggesting that much of the activity was an example of reflective ritual, with all its downsides, as identified above.

When a national requirement that service delivery teams undertake an annual peer review was introduced, we realised it presented an opportunity to design a new and specifically appreciative review process. A peer review is where a team's activity and performance is reviewed by another, within an ambition of service improvement. Hence this desired peer review process could be framed as an evaluation. An assembled steering or planning group identified this as an opportunity to approach the review challenge differently, seeing it as something that could potentially have a positive impact on service and also positively affect staff morale. It was agreed that appreciative inquiry was an appropriate methodology that might be able to both satisfy the national body and deliver meaningful evaluative peer reviews that led to positive change.

At the beginning of the assignment neither I nor anyone involved had much idea what this appreciative peer review process would look like: we were going to have to design it ourselves. To get us started I looked at some work undertaken by others in the field about how to do an appreciative evaluation to inform our discussions [9, 10, 11].[8] From these articles I drew up this initial diagram which looked at the possible purpose of a review process, which I shared with the steering group at our initial development day (Figure 14.1).

The top left quadrant is where, for example, a driving test assessment sits. The ambition is a control of the standard of drivers on the road, and this is

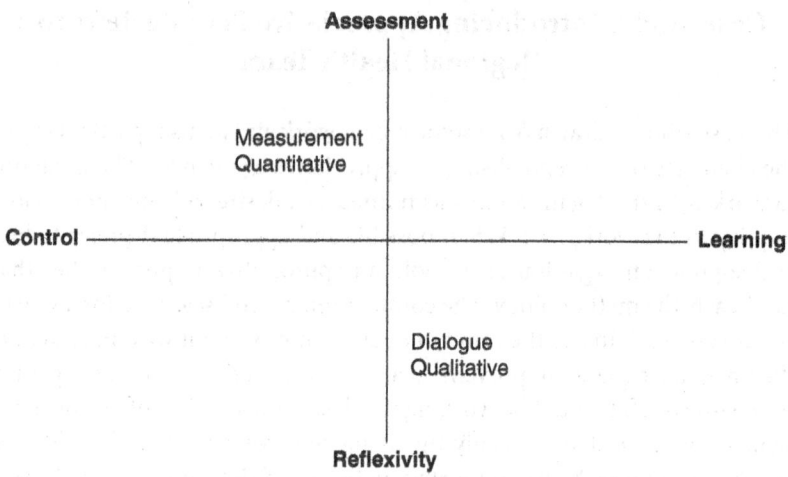

Figure 14.1 Possible purposes of a review.

achieved through quantitative measurement: there are a series of tangible activities the learner driver has to be able to complete successfully. In the bottom right corner is something quite different and much less familiar based on reflexivity and learning and involving qualitative dialogue and reflection.

By using the two axis of *approach to evaluation* (assessment-reflexivity) and *purpose of the evaluation* (control-learning), it was possible to expand understanding of the 'space' of reviewing or evaluation beyond just that of quantitative measurement (top left quadrant), which is the most familiar to most people and was the standard approach in the organisation. Reflexivity was a reasonably familiar term for many in this group. It means to reflect on your practice, with a view to improving. Interestingly, the assessment-reflexivity axis can be seen as running from an assessment undertaken by an external observer to self-observation, connecting back to the previous section about the varied nature of evaluation running from reflective ritual to impactful discovery.

Once we'd got our heads around this, I presented a further diagram (Figure 14.2) to enable us to explore what review might mean from a different angle. This time we looked at what kind of assessment or evaluation ours might be.

This model brings in the idea of past and future orientation and substitutes development for reflexivity. The top left-hand quadrant is about passing or failing exams, as in the previous model. It's about assessing what

Reviewing and Evaluating Practice 213

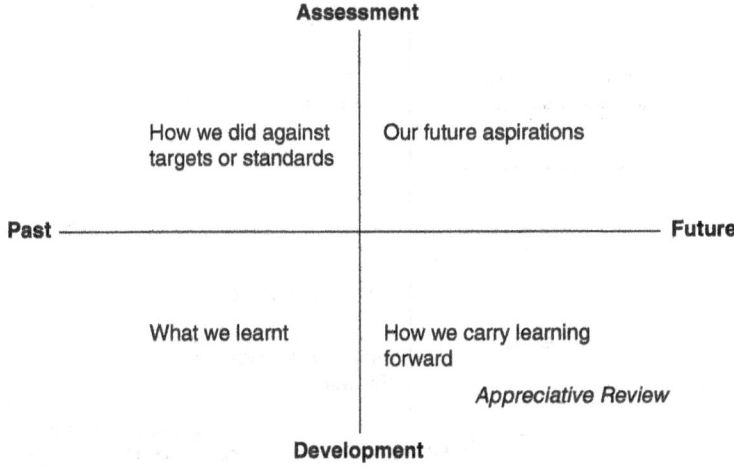

Figure 14.2 Possible review foci.

standard someone is at right now, due to their past learning, and whether it meets the criteria to be awarded some badge or other.

The bottom left-hand quadrant is focused on past development and can be characterised as being about the process of learning over time. Unlike the top left-hand quadrant, it does not require a standard to have been met so much as progress to have been made. Graded exams in educational settings, where there is scope for different levels of learning to be exhibited and rewarded, might fit here. This type of evaluation might also be particularly applicable in skills development. For example, I'm interested in whether my forehand in tennis is improving, but I'm not looking to take an exam in it. In this quadrant or form of evaluation, the progress criteria is continually present, and the information against which I can assess whether I am improving is flowing back to me continuously as I hit and miss shots.

The right-hand side of the diagram is more interesting; now the focus of the review activity is future-oriented. The top right-hand quadrant is a space to note our future aspirations, against which at some point we can be assessed. I want to pass my driving test, I want to get my coaching qualification, I want to be able to put 'spin' on my shots and so on. In future we can review progress against such objectives. The bottom right-hand quadrant, being both developmental and future oriented, suggests that the focus is to be able to carry learning forward and to continue learning. As you can see, this was identified as the quadrant in which a systemic appreciative review

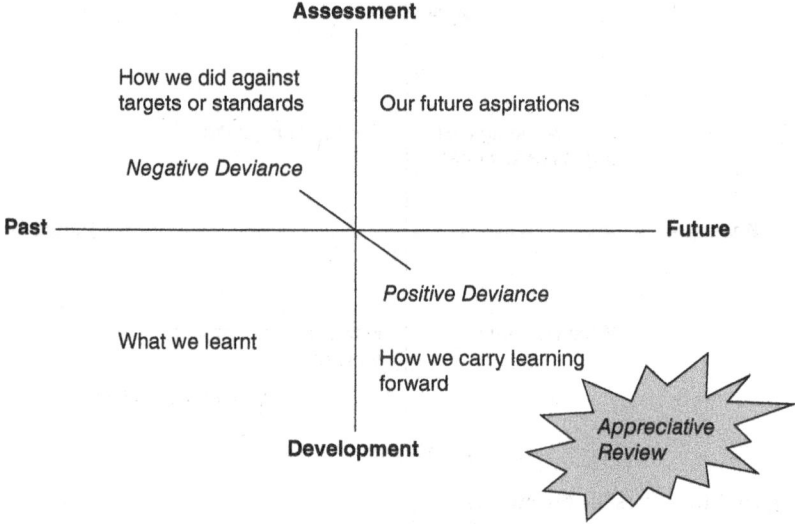

Figure 14.3 Adding in the positive/negative deviance dimension.

would fit. In the next figure presented, I developed the model further by adding the positive/negative deviance axis (Figure 14.3).

Evaluations on the upper left-hand side aim to establish that some minimal standard has been reached and so are often focused on spotting negative deviance. Failure to reach a standard counts against 'passing' the assessment. For example, in our driving test, we fail if we cannot do a three-point turn smoothly, but we do not get extra marks for a fantastic 'reversing round a corner' execution. In other words, in these situations, positive deviance, that is, exceeding the standard, does not necessarily attract much interest. However, in the opposite quadrant, there is a focus on positive deviance. In this quadrant what is working well, or has worked well in the past, and examples of exceptional performance are experiences from which we can learn for the future. This is the territory of appreciative inquiry.

The point of taking the group through this journey of exploration was to create an account of how an appreciative inquiry–based review, where the main focus is on reviewing what has gone well, is as much of an evaluative process as one that looks at what has gone wrong.

The discussion around this was animated. For people who have grown up in an exam system and who are used to performance appraisals that are focused on the goals that have not been achieved, the idea that you can focus on the good and still be reviewing and evaluating performance is challenging. There was an early recognition that the national body would need to be introduced to this line of thinking for them to see that the proposed appreciative peer review would meet their quality assurance requirements.

The next challenge was to design an appreciative peer review process. To do this we worked in a co-creative way with the people who would be peer reviewing each other. We took them on a journey of understanding where positive evaluations sat in the evaluation landscape, as outline above, introduced them to appreciative inquiry as a process and a set of principles and both developed and ultimately road tested a design with them. The principles in the table below emerged to support our design (Table 14.1).

In this way our proposed approach offered something different to the dominant view within the organisation, and its wider network, of how change happens. Below are a couple of examples of how these principles worked in practice.

Table 14.1 Design principles for the project.

Seek out examples of positive experiences to identify the core values, beliefs, strengths and aspirations that are at the heart of the service functioning at its best.
Use the discovery stories as a springboard to create aspiring visions of the future.
Work with the whole system, from the beginning, to co-create change.
Understand change as an emergent property of a system.
Ask questions to generate growth, engagement and creativity.
Create a 'pull' motivation for change.
Recognise that positive emotions create more sustainable energy for change.
Create and recreate positive affect.
Recognise the importance of narrative and story to the creation of accounts of the past and possibilities for the future.
Recognise the importance of relationship and patterns of communication in co-creating change that is owned by, and desired by, the whole system.
Recognise that the group event itself can create change by affecting people's sense of themselves and their colleagues, their world and their system, and that this change is as important as the 'plans for future change' that emerge from the event.
Recognise that 'good' and 'change' are context-specific.

1. Co-creation

We spent time ensuring that as many people as possible were involved from the start. We held an open invitation face-to-face introductory event to explore appreciative inquiry and peer review, including magic moment questions, discovery questions and personal strengths identification. In this way we aimed to give anyone who was interested a tangible experience of an appreciative inquiry process.

2. Whole system

We invited everyone to the training events, and the steering board meetings were open to anyone in the system who wanted to be involved. We involved commissioners and providers and worked hard to make events accessible to the many different professions including medical, paediatric etc. We included parent and carer organisations of the vulnerable client group from very early in the process. The benefits of this approach were that we never had to overcome resistance to change or to sell it to anyone, beyond the initial period of system engagement.

3. Self-organisation

The reviews were run in a self-organised way, that is, they were organised and delivered by the teams involved amongst themselves to suit different availabilities, readiness and time constraints. This was very powerful: it built relationships between teams, it allowed many excellent facilitation skills to be exercised in service of helping colleagues learn about, and develop, their service and it produced a lot of cross-fertilisation of great practice in a very organic way.

See Table 14.2 for an overview of the whole project process.

The process wasn't perfect, and the intended repeated iterations were somewhat disrupted by the challenge of the emergence of the Covid virus. Even so, beneficial outcomes could be identified from undertaking the peer reviews this way. One was that all the reviews produced an inspired 'dream' or set of aspirations for the future of delivery in their area, and most identified quick-win actions, often directly related to the involvement of the wider system (e.g. the parents or carers). Some examples were redesigning information leaflets, redesigning initial responses, redesigning service pathways and establishing a rapid phone response.

Table 14.2 Project process.

Initial stakeholder orientation. Initial introduction to AI, models of evaluation and initial consideration of how to design an appreciative evaluation process.

Webinar delivered and recorded for those unable to attend above meeting.

Steering group formed – process of data capture for evaluation planned and baseline measure of group effectiveness completed by all teams.

Training of the service delivery teams in appreciative inquiry, followed by a half day to co-create an appreciative peer review process.

Creation of minimal paperwork to support reviewers in performing an appreciative peer review.

Simulation training of peer reviewers in undertaking and experiencing appreciative peer reviews.

Six peer reviews undertaken.

Two follow up 'booster' sessions.

Celebratory event.

Creation of report with impact evaluation.

One of the most exciting outcomes, at least from my perspective, was that some project members took the methodology into other parts of the system. Equally inspiring, someone who wasn't even part of the project watched the webinar and applied appreciative inquiry to a performance review, very successfully.

The intervention had direct impacts on staff well-being. Those involved reported feeling more valued and positive, and some said that they had found benefit from applying the methodology not only in their professional but also their personal life. Some parents also reported benefiting from being included in the peer reviews, saying, for example 'it was almost a bit therapeutic'.

The initiative stimulated greater connectivity across the system, such as the establishment of new forums to facilitate better interagency and inter-area working and parent support groups.

Team members reported learning from reviewing each other, both from their colleagues' current practice and their aspirations. By exploring each other's contexts, teams came to better understand how and why there were regional variations in service delivery patterns. As opposed to the reflective ritual review processes that many had previously been involved in, the staff involved reported that they found the process accessible, not just another set of boxes to go through. They felt that it was relevant, that there was little preparation needed and that it was a good use of their time.

The senior staff involved agreed that it was a good use of time and that it aligned with the service's objectives. Indeed, they became some of the process's keenest advocates. As I left the project, teams were working on how they could share resources better, have influence on junior general practitioners, and other key first identifiers, and hold more regular conversations with doctors generally. They planned to hold an area joint conference to include service users. In addition, the appreciative inquiry process is now thoroughly embedded in the system and is organically expanding to other National Health systems in the area.

These outcomes, and more, are accredited by those involved as being direct consequences of undertaking appreciative peer reviews. Those who had previously undertaken more conventional peer reviews were extremely clear about the degree of aspiration, motivation and action generated by doing them differently. I hope it is evident how this is a future focused, developmental evaluation process that delivered against project objectives while avoiding being driven down the road of assessment of failures to meet standards.

Conclusion

In this chapter we have looked at the challenge of considering evaluative and assessment processes, and undertaking practice, from an appreciative inquiry perspective. To explore this we have noted the danger of evaluations becoming reflective ritual reviews and have considered what enables evaluation to be a valuable and useful exercise. We looked at one scenario of bringing an appreciative perspective to a standard process, 360° management assessment and another case study where an appreciatively informed peer review process was able to be developed from scratch.

Learning Points

1. Evaluation is a process located along a number of axes.
2. Selection can be made of an appropriate evaluation process against the desired impact of the evaluation.
3. Standard evaluation processes can be modified to be more appreciative in orientation, to good effect.
4. In practice, it's helpful to enable people to see the connection between evaluation as assessment of the past conducted from a negative deviance perspective and as the development of future activity from a positive deviance perspective.

Discussion Questions

1. How you do you generally understand evaluation?
2. What might people find challenging about the idea of an appreciative evaluation?
3. How might you help people understand the value offered by an appreciative evaluation of practice or an intervention?

Teaching Exercise

1. Engage the class in designing a peer review process for the module, focusing on how the module (all elements, the learning, the relationships) will affect their future practice and impact. The key question being 'How will we carry learning into the future?' This can be expanded to inform future iterations of the module.

Helpful Resources and Further Reading

Stellenberg, M. (2010). *Evaluation of Appreciative Inquiry Interventions: Longer-Term Impact, Critique and Reflection Across Case Studies.* Deutschland: Lambert Academic Publishing.

The key papers from https://aipractitioner.com/ and other references in the footnotes, particularly footnote 12.

Notes

1. Dinesen, quoting Ref. [2].
2. Dinesen above, quoting Ref. [2], page 51.
3. Dinesen, quoting Ref. [3].
4. See particularly Ref. [4] for a very full account of using appreciative inquiry for coaching or, more recently, Ref. [5].
5. A description of this exercise can be found in Ref. [6], and there is an account of it in Ref. [7].
6. This is a technical psychology term applied to the frequently encountered 5- or 7-point assessment scale. Sometimes these are numbered; other times a scale of descriptors is used such as 'not at all' to 'completely'.

7. For more on this interesting area, you might like to see my chapter Positive Leadership and Change in Ref. [7], which discusses the challenge of psychopathic leaders, and strengths leadership, amongst other aspects of leadership.
8. For this I called on Dinesen, as above and Ref. [9].

References

1. Dinesen, M.S. (2009). Systemic appreciative evaluation: developing quality instead of just measuring it. *AI Practitioner* 11 (3): 49–55.
2. Petersen, V.C. (2004). *Hinsides regler – selvorganisering og ledelse med ansvar*. København: Børsens Forlag.
3. Dahler-Larsen, P. (1998). *Den rituelle reflektion – om evaluering i organisationer*. Odense: Odense Universitetsforlag.
4. Orem, S.L., Binkert, J., and Clancy, A.L. (2007). *Appreciative Coaching: A Positive Process for Change*. San Francisco: Jossey-Bass.
5. Lewis, S. (2021). Appreciative inquiry coaching in the workplace. In: *Positive Psychology Coaching in the Workplace* (ed. W.A. Smith, I. Boniwell, and S. Green), 515–528. Springer.
6. Cameron, K. (2008). *Positive Leadership: Strategies for Extraordinary Performance*. San Francisco: Berrett-Koehler.
7. Lewis, S. (2011). *Positive Psychology at Work: How Positive Leadership and Appreciative Inquiry Create Inspiring Organizations*. Chichester: Wiley Blackwell.
8. Chella, G. (2020). Appreciating before assessing: the true sign of respect in coaching and leadership development. *AI Practitioner* 22 (1): 14–20.
9. van de Wetering, A. (2010). Appreciative auditing. *AI Practitioner* 12 (3): 25–30.
10. Webb, L., Preskill, H., and Coghlan, A. (2005). Bridging two disciplines: applying appreciative inquiry to evaluation practice. *AI Practitioner* 2005: 1–3.
11. Jacobsgaard, M. and Norlund, I. (2011). Embedded (e)valuation. *AI Practitioner* 13 (3): 68–71.

15

Supporting Planned Change Processes

When organisations decide they need to make changes in the way they work, for instance changing their culture or transforming their IT system, they often default to a planned change approach. This approach is usually based in the diagnostic organisational development mindset we discussed in Chapter 1. Typically, to facilitate the change, specialists are brought in to advise on or manage the situation, and the process of initiating a top-down organisation-wide change intervention begins. This approach views change as a problem of data and logic and makes change look manageable, sequential and what I can only describe as 'tidy'. It also leads straight to the 'how to get buy-in' and 'how to overcome the resistance to change' conversations, concern about which can suck up a lot of top-management energy.

In this chapter we will look at some of the challenges commonly associated with planned or imposed change. We will look at how appreciative inquiry can help and in particular explore the role 'opening-up hope,' explained below, plays in remotivating staff. We will identify and explore some particular principles that support working in an appreciative way with ongoing planned change processes and will look at some research into how diagnostic and dialogic approaches can work together. We conclude the chapter with two case studies that illuminate how appreciative processes can be applied in planned change situations.

Practical Appreciative Inquiry: A Toolkit for Applying Appreciative Inquiry to Organisational Challenges, Opportunities, and Aspiration, First Edition. Sarah Lewis.
© 2025 John Wiley & Sons Ltd. Published 2025 by John Wiley & Sons Ltd.

The Challenges of Wholesale Large-Scale Planned Change

When wholesale, large-scale planned change is announced people's attention is initially grabbed by the evident high cost to them: the disruption, the inconvenience, the uncertainty and other perceived threats. It is these instinctive reactions that fuel the 'resistance to change' conversation. This in turn can quickly descend into a binary dispute where each side feels obliged to amplify their view: so management hide their doubts and concerns, expressing only their belief in the great outcomes just over the horizon, while staff focus exclusively on bringing to management's awareness the challenges and obstacles staring them in the face. Neither story reflects the complex and nuanced aspects of the planned change, and the danger is that the gulf grows between two entrenched and disconnected accounts.

In this situation people often give up trying to actively influence the change process, becoming passive, demotivated and demoralised, waiting only to be told what to do. While waiting they become less and less effective as they find it hard to know what to do for the best on a day-to-day basis. They are no longer sure what to be doing *now* to help create a great future; they know only that what they have been doing is apparently not what they will be required to do in the new set-up. In addition, they start to make their own sense of what is going on, what the intentions of the change might be, which are unlikely to align with those expressed by management. Frustration can grow on both sides. In due course the organisation notices and misinterprets this reaction as 'lack of buy-in' or 'resistance.' In this way, while a planned change approach has attractions for managers, it also has some pitfalls.

Appreciative Inquiry and the Generation of Hope

Despite not being the chosen mode of change, appreciative Inquiry still has something to offer an organisation by working with those who are beginning to feel disenfranchised and helpless to influence their own future.

Imposed change can often induce a sense of hopelessness, so one of the key requirements is to regenerate a sense of hope. Hope in my opinion, is the singularly most important positive emotion necessary to pull people from apathetic inertia into becoming proactive again in their own futures. The specific mode of hope that needs to be created is that of opening-up hope [1]. Opening-up hope can be seen as the necessary precursor to the more familiar goal attainment hope [2].

Opening-up hope is a co-created, shared relational, emotional experience. This experience of generalised, but as yet untargeted, hope can be characterised as the ability to believe that the future will be different from the past in ways not yet specified and somehow freer than the past or the present [3]. It is this opening-up hope that allows groups paralysed by uncertainty to start to step into the unknown. Such hope cannot be commanded into existence by imprecations to, for instance, 'Buck up!'. It can only be generated or released. The positive, relational and generative focus of appreciative inquiry processes help create this more diffuse yet powerful hope motivation. It reconnects people to their desire to influence their own future and enables them to find a way to be part of the change process.

1. How discovery interviews help

Discovery interviews are a process that feeds new information into the system, allowing new conceptualisations to emerge. As a group of people share stories of themselves at their best, many of which will be previously unknown to the majority of the group, something begins to shift in the group's conception of themselves. It can be experienced as almost a tangible rearrangement of the atoms in the room. Essentially, as person after person reveals hidden strengths, determination, tenacity, moral courage, effectiveness, values and abilities and other virtues, people begin to re-evaluate the nature of the group of which they are a member and the potential of the group to achieve change. Hope, goals, dreams, possibilities, imagination and creativity are all interlinked and interdependent and can be powerfully held together by narratives generated during an appreciative inquiry.

2. The role of the dream phase

The dream phase of appreciative inquiry is key to the generation of hope. By encouraging people to create images of positive, attractive futures conjured from exploration of the best of the present, and then inviting them to explore in an experiential way how that future could be, a desire to create that future begins to emerge. Through appreciative inquiry dreaming, people begin to believe that there is life beyond their present circumstances; essentially, they begin to believe, 'it doesn't have to be like this'. Once they start to experience this motivation people start to have both ideas about and energy for doing things now to make other things happen in the future. In this way dreaming of the future and experiencing hope are inextricably intertwined.

In a broader sense appreciative inquiry acts to switch people's attention, helping them focus on different aspects of the imposed change. Achor [4] estimates that we are able to attend to 1 out of every 100 'bits' of information that come our way. We filter out the remaining 99% without even noticing. For many of us our default filters are set on noticing problems, errors, mistakes, faults and flaws, and so we unintentionally filter out success. It is of course important to notice these things. But if these are all we notice, then our world becomes full of nothing but errors, mistakes and flaws. And during times of change, without conscious effort, it is easy to slip into the mindset where everything is wrong.

To counteract this we need to consciously seek out things that are right, and beyond that, to amplify them. That is, we need to take the weak signals that exist of things that are working, that are improvements, that are signs of quality, that demonstrate commitment or important values and to boost them through active and deliberate amplification processes [5].[1] Through the use of appreciative questions people and groups can be guided to redirect their attention and focus away from the things they can't influence to those they can.

There is an art to bringing in the value of appreciative inquiry into planned change. In my experience, joining with a planned change project feels as if I am being asked to work with a moving train of change, where the direction and mode of advance has already been decided. So instead of shaping a change intervention from the beginning, I need to work at the interstices, in the gaps that emerge in the planned change process. In working with this challenge, there are some principles to support engagement and interaction that I have found useful as outlined in Table 15.1.

Some General Principles for Bringing Appreciative Inquiry to Planned Change

Of the principles outlined here, there are a few that I would particularly like to expand upon [6].[2]

1. Work with what you are offered

It may not be possible to negotiate to get the whole system in the room. So instead the ambition is to work with whom you can, where you can and when you can, taking advantage of the opportunities that arise to help

Supporting Planned Change Processes 225

Table 15.1 Some principles for engaging with planned change projects.

Work with what you are offered.

Adapt processes to fit the opportunities.

Encourage awareness of possibilities of local influence and control.

Help people use the best of the thinking behind appreciative inquiry.

Volunteerism – people are being pushed around enough already; try to make any specific events you are able to run optional (and very attractive!).

Co-creation – always ask 'Who else can we usefully involve in this?' Encourage leaders to take questions to their teams in a co-creative (e.g. not just consultative) way. The idea of 'drawing on the collective intelligence of the group' often helps with negotiating more involvement by lower-level staff.

Positivity – focus on creating positive affect; it really helps create resilience during a difficult time.

Strengths – people are more energised, engaged, motivated etc. when they can use their strengths to achieve their objectives.

Hope and optimism – using appreciative techniques helps people focus on the best of the past and their hopes for the future.

Proactivity – encourage people to take responsibility for how they are engaging with the change and the effect they are having on others around them.

Leaders' face – be mindful always of leaders' face. They are (usually) doing their best to do the best for the organisation, and they are doing it the only way they know how.

Story and choice – unhelpful stories often emerge during change about the motivation for change in general and to explain leaders' behaviour in particular.

Amplifying success – in change people get so focused on what isn't working they lose sight of the fact that they are still achieving things. Bringing these to the fore helps with morale, pride etc.

---

people reconceptualise change as an emergent phenomenon that they can influence, even as planned change is unfolding all around them. By using your appreciative questioning style, your positive focus on strengths and your ability to create good affect you can help people focus what they *can* do and what they *can* influence, rather than what they can't.

2. Encourage awareness of possibilities of local influence and control

Usually the idea that top management has got it all planned out is a myth. Top management doesn't have brain space to attend to every last detail. If people want good decision-making in their own area, they need to seize the initiative and start presenting ways forward. Steven Covey's [7][3] circles of concern, control and influence can be helpful here. By encouraging groups to challenge their unquestioned assumptions about the control and influence they have, you can expand their sense of what aspects of the change they can effect. Once again appreciative inquiry is great for this. It is these conversations that start to rekindle hope, optimism and the motivation to engage.

3. *The principle of positivity*

Encourage people to recognise the importance of frequent positive mood boosts. Many rewarding experiences disappear during change as people go 'heads down' and pleasurable interactions can lessen. Also, some people act as if there must be a moratorium on good experiences during difficult times, that to be seen laughing would be disrespectful of others in some way or a display of unwarranted frivolity. On the contrary, good experiences help us cope with, and even better, remain proactive during, difficult times. Particularly important in this situation are the positive emotions of hope and optimism. In my experience these can be early casualties of planned change. Using appreciative questions can effect an instant mood boost.

4. *The principle of story and choice*

The stories we tell about what is going on reflect our sense of reality. But there is always more than one version available. Unhelpful stories often emerge during change about the motivation for change in general and to explain leaders' behaviour in particular. These are often stories of blame, inadequacy, deficit and deceit, nefarious motives and so on. By bringing overlooked or neglected aspects of life into view, we can widen perspectives on what is happening and why. We can remind people that there are many truths about a situation and that situations are often paradoxical: that is, contradictory things can be true at different times and places within a context. We can remind them that they have a choice about the story they choose to tell, both to themselves and to others, and that the telling of stories has impact for action. See the case study below for an illumination of this.

5. *Look after the leader*

And finally, it is a good idea to look after the leader, however misguided you may think some of their actions. They are usually doing their best, and they are doing it the only way they know how. We need to recognise the good intent, effort and energy going into trying to change things, and often to help others recognise this too. As we help people perhaps being adversely affected make sense of what is going on, we need to help them recognise that the situation for their leaders may be more nuanced and complex than the current story about them and their motives allows.

In these ways we can blend our dialogic, appreciative work in with the ongoing diagnostic change interventions, to good effect.

The Blended Approach Is Best

To explore the sources of successful change two researchers [8] interviewed 47 people, some leaders, others not. They asked their interviewees to share 'two stories of a change you were involved in, one that was a success and another that was a failure'. This gave them 91 stories that related to 79 unique cases of organisational change. In other words, some stories referred to the same change event. Importantly, they were able to confirm if the change that was claimed to be successful actually was by collecting hard data about the outcomes of the change against its objectives. This allowed them to develop a definition of success: transformation to a new organisational state that is achieved in a way that is positively perceived by the people involved.

In another line of inquiry, they asked the people who had been affected by change how they and their colleagues had talked about the change and the stories that they had told about it. In this way the researchers also inquired into the shared meaning-making going on amongst organisational members during the change process.

When they looked at their data, the stories of change, they identified both diagnostic and dialogic approaches to change and found that change was most successful when leaders switched back and forth between the two approaches as the change unfolded. Sometimes this was by deliberate choice, other times, as earlier researchers [9–11][4] have found, this strategy emerged as they adjusted their original plans. This was particularly true for those that started down the road of diagnostic change but oscillated to dialogic processes at some point in the process.

They identified that a typical change pattern like this might involve, for example, a change being initiated as a *diagnostic* process, to identify and clarify problems, and then switching to creating *dialogic* environments to facilitate learning. This produced new ideas and innovations that could be fed into the planned process. Switching process like this allowed organisational members to offer ideas, innovations and new possibilities that became part of the change leadership. This back-and-forth is described as an oscillating pattern of change.

One factor that affected the likelihood of this dual pattern of intervention being adopted was the leadership mindset. Leaders who inquired into both 'What is true?' (e.g. the facts of the situation) and 'What are people saying is possible?' (e.g. the sense people are making of the proposed changes or the change experience) were most likely to adopt the oscillating pattern of change. That is to say, leaders with this mindset were interested in understanding how people were experiencing and making sense of the change, as well as more objective measures of progress. To describe this dual-oriented mindset the researchers coined the term 'concurrent inquiry'.

This gives us a situation where the change leadership holds two approaches in mind at once, and the change process adopted switches between the two modes of intervention, diagnostic and dialogic, in response to awareness of the sense being made of the change in the organisation. This combination of concurrent mindset and ability to switch between change approaches proved to be the most effective process in terms of change success, with a success rate of between 89% and 93%. The cases that were initially diagnostic in nature were marginally more successful than those that were originally dialogic in nature. While of the solely diagnostic change efforts only 33% were successful, the 67% failure rate echoed once again previous research findings on the lack of success of solely diagnostic change processes [12–14].[5] By contrast, in the few cases where a dialogic approach was used throughout, the success rate for them was 86%, almost as good as the combined approach.

One fascinating sidebar finding was that resistance was present in all cases, both in those deemed successful (present in 41% of cases) and those classified as failure (50%). The researchers suggest that these resistance accounts can be reconceptualised as being not signs of a problem per se, but as a feature of change that makes clear that the meanings being co-created between organisational members are not updating in ways that are supportive of the change. This observation invites dialogic intervention to positively affect organisational sense-making, and in most of the cases of successful change that is what happened: the resistance narratives were recognised as a source of valuable insight for leaders, and, following dialogue, accommodations to the plan were made as a result.[6] The successful response to resistance to change was to inquire into it, rather than to push back against it; this latter is a response frequently observed as organisations, in their frustration, start to insist that everyone 'get on the bus or get out'. The case studies below, as well as those in the original paper, illuminate these ideas in action.

Case Study: From Push to Pull

This was an organisation that owned and ran care homes for the elderly and those with disabilities. They had recently adopted a comprehensive organisational support IT system as part of a future-proofing digitalisation programme. Access portals had been installed on computers in the various homes. As the executive team saw it, this was a huge benefit that had been provided, but it was proving very difficult to get some of heads of home to adopt it.

The executive team commissioned an appreciative inquiry team development day. Working through an appreciative inquiry process, we arrived at the dream phase where it was decided that we would articulate the dream through interview. We set it up so that it was two years in the future, their best hopes had come to pass, and I was a journalist interviewing them for an article about their recent success. In their dream the heads of the various homes were using the software that had been provided to plan the rota, manage annual leave and so on, and the executive team were accruing the advantages: real-time data for responsive decision-making.

The design phase is where we aim to identify what change is needed now to create the future. In this instance we used the 'creating the ladder of change' technique. Essentially this means that we locate ourselves in the imagined future and, looking back (in our imagination), identify how the various changes came about. Our conversation went something like this:

'Looking back, who were the first people to adopt the new IT system?' I asked.

'Some of the younger, newer heads of homes were quite quick to get it, but there were a few of the older heads who just wouldn't', answered a member of the executive team.

'How did you work with them?'

'We just kept telling them that they had to, that it was part of their updated job description. We had to let some go in the end'.

'Okay, that's sad. Let's see if we can find a ladder for them. Had they used computers much before at work?'

'No, it was a new, much overdue, improvement. We gave them all training, but they just weren't using it'.

'Did they use work-type computer programmes, you know, Word, Excel, out of work do you think?'

Pause for thought, 'I don't know, maybe not'.

'So, at a guess, not the most computer-literate people, then. They were facing a big learning curve by the sound of it, what was in it for them?'

'We kept telling them it would give us better data'.

'Hmmm. . . and how did that help them do their job?'

Another pause, 'Well I suppose it didn't, in the short run'.

'So, they faced a steep, uncomfortable, deskilling learning curve which would give them no obvious benefit?'

'I hadn't thought of it like that'.

'So, what was it going to do for them?'

'It would save them time; they wouldn't have to spend hours doing the rotas and so on manually'.

'Would I be right in thinking that this staff timetable planning was one of their core management tasks?'

'Yes, it took up a lot of their time, it's very complicated in homes with 30 or more staff, many part-time, and annual leave and whatnot'.

'A challenging task, a key responsibility that distinguishes them from their staff, that they might take pride in doing well? And now they're being told not to bother, a computer can do it'.

'Hah. I hadn't thought of it like that, but once they'd got used to it, it would save them time'.

'And how was that going to benefit them?'

'Excuse me?'

'What could they do with all this extra time?'

'I don't know, whatever they wanted'.

'If I were them and you didn't know, and I didn't know, what having all this extra time would mean, I might be worrying I wouldn't be needed so much. I might be feeling I was in danger of being made redundant'.

As you can see it was a sticky conversation. As is typical in a top-down change, the executive team had invested a huge amount of time, energy and hope in this initiative and had created a great story for themselves of the benefit the investment would bring. What they were trying to do was to sell this change to the heads of homes from the executive team perspective. My hypothesis was that the heads had created a different story that recognised their own vulnerability, which was more closely related to their experience and more compelling to them. They weren't buying the management account. What was needed, exactly as was suggested by the research above, was an inquiry into the heads of homes' resistance, geared at the creation of a 'pull' motivation about the change for them.

It took a while from this point but, with thought, they were able to name some things that the heads of homes might value time for: planning and organising events and outings for residents, being able to give staff members more development time, local fund-raising events for special projects and so on.

It became clear that instead of trying to sell the benefits of this transition to working on the computer from the executive perspective, they needed instead to help these heads of home build their own dreams of what having more time would make possible in terms of their dreams and aspirations for the home they ran, which would create the motivation and energy to engage with the new technology. They would also need a lot more support than computer-literate staff to build confidence in using the programme and would need reassurance that even if this was a cost-cutting exercise, their necks weren't on the line.

It was no reflection on this particular team that all this was not apparent to them. We can all become locked in our own world view. As light dawned that the unanswerable question 'What was in it for them?' was key to moving from the unsuccessful push motivation to a potential pull motivation, they resolved to hold an appreciative inquiry type conversation with the heads of homes.

Case Study: Impact of a Two-Hour Workshop on Change Practice

A publishing house asked me to run a series of two-hour workshops for managers on aspects of management and appreciative inquiry. Unusually, I was able to conduct some follow-up interviews to assess impact. This is one of the stories of how a manager put what they had learnt into practice.

Within the organisation, certain parts of the production process were to be outsourced. This had implications for most people involved in production even if they weren't sure what they were. The possibility of redundancy hung unspoken in the air. One manager I interviewed after the training event explained how he called on a number of aspects of appreciative practice to help his people through this experience.

For example, he deliberately used visioning (dreaming) to help people imagine a future beyond the immediate, worrying present. He said that appreciative inquiry offered a 'good framework to help people see liberating possibilities', as distinct from the mundane tasks of the change, and therefore options for future behaviour.

He invited experienced people from projects that were further along in the outsourcing programme to come into meetings to talk to his people. This changed how the conversation went. In this way he amplified the good stories of the past to help the present. He also recognised the relational aspect of change.

He also worked with his production staff to visualise the outsource companies' experience, drawing on their own experience when in a supplier role to their clients. This helped them understand the danger of all conversation being triggered by negative things and so the whole experience of interaction becoming very negative. He encouraged his people to think what made for a good client/supplier relationship. In this way he was using discovery, working to improve the positivity ratio and recognising the importance of the relational aspect of the engagement, not just the transactional.

He reported that this use of appreciative practice moderated the possible negative aspects and outcomes of this change in production. It 'helped people keep ticking along'. His manager commented that his people seemed less stressed than other teams and were not leaving, that there was less churn in his section. He was pleased other people noticed and this gave him confidence. We might also note that a financial benefit accrues to reduced churn. This is an example of an adaptive use of appreciative inquiry to ameliorate some of the negative effects of imposed change.

Conclusion

In this chapter we have considered how appreciative inquiry can help with planned change initiatives. This has included looking at the problems of planned change and some principles to help bring appreciative inquiry to the challenge. We have reviewed some very interesting recent research that supports a dual approach to change and have explored two examples of how this can be done.

Learning Points

1. Appreciative inquiry can help with some of the unintended consequences associated with planned change.
2. There are some principles of practice to help with bringing appreciative inquiry to planned change.
3. Research suggests that adopting a concurrent inquiry mindset and oscillating between diagnostic and dialogic approaches is the best route to achieving successful organisational change.

Discussion Questions

1. What can and can't be compromised about the appreciative inquiry methodology when applying it to ongoing planned change projects?
2. Why is the oscillating approach to change so much more effective than a solely diagnostic approach?
3. Why was it so difficult for the managers in the first case study to see the change from the heads of homes' perspective?

Teaching Exercise

1. Take the first case study and ask groups to imagine that they were able to organise a whole-system event with the executive team, heads of home and staff. How would they design the event to help create an organisational pull motivation to adopt the new technology (assume an assurance of 'no redundancies due to technology changes' has been given in good faith).

Helpful Resources and Further Reading

Lewis, S. (2016). *Positive Psychology and Change: How Leadership, Collaboration and Appreciative Inquiry create Transformational Results*. Wiley Chapter 3: Helping people engage positively with change, 51–75.

Bushe, G.R. and Lewis, S. (2023). Three change strategies in organization development: data-based, high engagement and generative. *Leadership & Organization Development Journal* 44 (2): 173–188.

Notes

1. Bushe's original terms are 'fanning and amplifying' in Ref. [5].
2. I have also addressed this challenge in Ref. [6]. Chapter 3: Helping people engage positively with change, pp. 51–75.
3. While this idea originates in his book, *The Seven Habits of Highly Effective People* (Ref. [7]), you can find the basic idea all over the web.
4. Malcolm Higgs and Deborah Rowland did some great research into how change actually happens which is presented in a very digestible way in Ref. [9]. However, I also highly recommend the original research papers that seem to contain more details and present the information in a more condensed manner, for example Refs. [10, 11]. Their research is also presented in Lewis [6], *Positive Psychology at Work*, chapter 5.
5. See the Hastings and Schwarz article for many further references. To which I can add Ref. [12], which undertook a systematic review of the impact of long-term planned change papers published between 1980 and 2014 and concluded there was little substantive impact from the work, confirming perhaps the much-quoted Kotter assertion that '70% of change efforts fail'. This figure came originally from work by Hammer and Champy, originators of the 'Business Process Re-engineering' methodology, which, for younger readers, enjoyed a moment of ascendency in the 1990s. See Refs. [13, 14].
6. The paper I am referring to, Hastings and Schwarz, is a dense, academic read. However, in the latter part of the paper the case studies used to illuminate findings really bring all this to life and are highly recommended to give further insight into what oscillating looks like in practice.

References

1. Carlsen, A., Hagen, A.L., and Mortensen, T.F. (2012). Imagining hope in organizations. In: *The Oxford Handbook of Positive Organizational Scholarship* (ed. K.S. Cameron and G.M. Spreitzer), 288–303. Oxford University Press.
2. Snyder, C.R., Rand, K.L., and Sigmon, D.R. (2002). Hope theory. In: *Handbook of Positive Psychology* (ed. C.R. Snyder and S.J. Lopez), 257–276. Oxford University Press.
3. Rorty, R. (2000). *Philosophy and Hope*. New York: Penguin.
4. Achor, S. (2011). *The Happiness Advantage; the Seven Principles that Fuel Success at Work*. London: Virgin Books.
5. Bushe, G. (2001). Five theories of change embedded in AI. In: *Appreciative Inquiry: an Emerging Direction for Organizational Development* (ed. D. Cooperrider, P.F. Sorenson, T. Yaegar, and D. Whitney), 117–129. Stipes Publishing L.L.C.

6. Lewis, S. (2016). *Positive Psychology and Change: How Leadership, Collaboration and Appreciative Inquiry create Transformational Results.* Wiley.
7. Covey, S.R. (1991). *The Seven Habits of Highly Effective People.* Provo, UT: Covey Leadership Center.
8. Hastings, B.J. and Schwarz, G.M. (2022). Leading change processes for success: a dynamic application of diagnostic and dialogic organization development. *Journal of Applied Behavioral Science* 58 (1): 120–148.
9. Rowland, R. and Higgs, M. (2008). *Sustaining Change: Leadership That Works.* West Sussex: Jossey-Bass.
10. Higgs, M. and Rowland, D. (2005). All changes great and small: exploring approaches to change and its leadership. *Journal of Change Management* 5 (2): 121–151.
11. Higgs, M. (2010). Change and its leadership: the role of positive emotions. In: *Oxford Handbook of Positive Psychology and Work* (ed. P.A. Linley, S. Harrington, and N. Garcea), 67–80. Oxford University Press.
12. Barends, E., Janssen, B., ten Have, W., and ten Have, S. (2014). Effects of change interventions: what kind of evidence do we really have? *Journal of Applied Behavioral Science* 50 (1): 5–27.
13. Kotter, J.P. (1995). Leading change: why transformation efforts fail. *Harvard Business Review* 73 (2): 59–67.
14. Hammer, M. and Champy, J. (1993). *Business Process Reengineering.* London: Nicholas Brealey.

16

Health and Well-being at Work

It is only relatively recently that we have been concerned about the effect of work on people's health and well-being. Fredrick Taylor [1] the first management consultant guru, took a very mechanistic view of people, perhaps no surprise given that he was by training an engineer, regarding people as essentially components of the machine. His belief was that the nature of the work was unimportant to workers, who were concerned only with the relationship between effort and pay.

One hundred years of psychological discovery, sociological investigation into organisations and advances in medical diagnosis later and we understand much better the systemic influence of mind and matter, brain and body. Yet the way we think about organisations has not fully kept up with these advances. Many working in organisations still retain a model of them as places (and spaces) where an understanding of people as essentially no more than rationally and logically functioning parts of a well-oiled machine is both correct and sufficient.

In this chapter we will be exploring how appreciative inquiry impacts positively on well-being in a number of areas. We'll start by briefly outlining what is known about stress factors in work design and then focus in on the area of psychosocial work hazards. Next, we'll explore interventions from an appreciative perspective at the individual level, noting their limitations. We'll explore organisational toxicity to understand factors at the organisational level that affect well-being, and we'll look at how appreciative inquiry can effect change in emotional states and relationships, as well as at a system functioning level, to boost well-being. Finally, at the team level, we'll look at appreciative inquiry's contribution to psychological safety and the

---

Practical Appreciative Inquiry: A Toolkit for Applying Appreciative Inquiry to Organisational Challenges, Opportunities, and Aspiration, First Edition. Sarah Lewis.
© 2025 John Wiley & Sons Ltd. Published 2025 by John Wiley & Sons Ltd.

well-being benefits of strengths. A brief case study of an appreciative inquiry into working with respect with an organisation experiencing unwanted levels of reported fear of bullying and harassment will conclude the chapter.

People at Work

The Taylorist approach outlined above is adhered to perhaps more in hope than belief (sometimes it feels as if it would be so much easier if people were emotionless automatons), and we now know it to be mistaken. The human body (not to mention soul) responds to the nature of particular jobs as well as to the emotional tenor of interactions and workplace climate. It has been known for nearly 50 years that a lack of autonomy, role overload or lack of role clarity, unclear lines of accountability and other elements of job or organisational design all contribute to more or less stressful places to work [2, 3]. Thanks to more recent research we now also know that an unhealthy ratio of negative to positive experiences and emotional states, and an inability to exercise our strengths can also contribute to poor mental and physical health.[1]

The opposite to wellness at work is ill-health, mental or physical, caused by, or exacerbated by, work or working conditions. The shorthand collective term for this is usually stress. Both the organisation itself, the way it works, its culture, systems and processes, and any particular team, the leader, the team relationships, the communications and so on, can create stress for people. These can broadly be identified as workplace psychosocial hazards, as they have been under six key areas by the Safety Executive in the UK. See Figure 16.1 below.

It is broadly this field of hazards we are going to concern ourselves with, which is not to ignore that many fields of work also include physical dangers and stressors. It is perhaps worth noting here that research on safety at work has demonstrated that the creation of a living, embedded, actively policed by all safety culture is pretty much a prerequisite to making sure safety guidelines are followed. And of course, appreciative inquiry can be used to help develop this.

Interventions to improve psychosocial well-being and to reduce hazards can be made at three levels: the organisational, the team and the individual. A lot of in-house wellness programmes are focused on boosting the individual's well-being and/or their resilience to stress. I have taken part in a number of wellness weeks, delivering presentations with

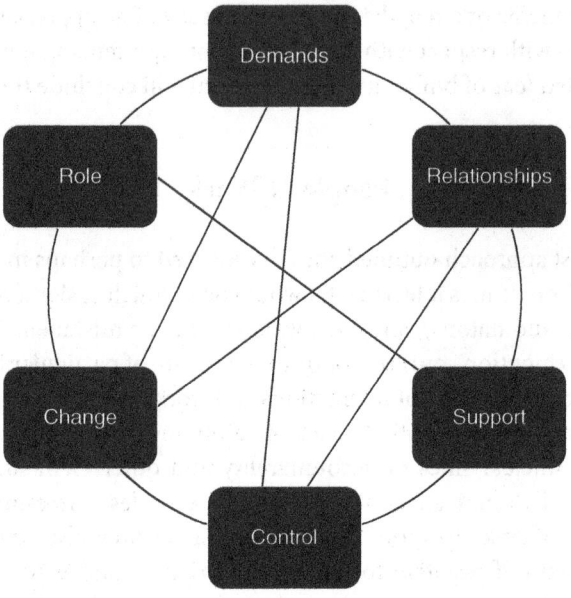

Figure 16.1 Pyscho-Social Workplace Hazards.

titles such as 'Feel Better at Work,' or 'Well-being at Work'. I try to use these opportunities to alert people to how they can better manage their own emotional states, understand and use their strengths and create positive relationships. During the session we do energiser exercises and positive emotion exercises to boost mood, explore the nature of flourishing, introduce the idea of constructive responding [5], which is essentially the research name for inquiring into the good news, and use discovery interviews to discover our strengths. I also provide further information and top tips.

People always report enjoying the session and perhaps their well-being is improved momentarily. Maybe they leave with some better ideas about how to look after themselves, but at heart we both know the issue is not so much them as the place they are working. Wilde [6], amongst others, has noted how these kinds of interventions, along with mindfulness [7] or yoga sessions, while often helpful, essentially lay the blame and need for change at the individual's door, blaming them for their normal reactions to systemic factors that are outside their control. She also points out, very interestingly, that such interventions may encourage and develop skill in disengaging from damaging contexts for self-preservation. While helpful to the individual, such tactics would work against the need to work collaboratively to achieve change.

How Organisational Cultures Can Become Toxic

To achieve sustainable improvements in well-being at work interventions need to be made at the environmental level: I want to look at what happens at the organisational level that makes so many of them unhealthy places to work and how appreciative inquiry can help by exploring them through the lens of organisational toxicity which can be defined thus:

> Organizational toxicity is the widespread, intense, energy-sapping, negative emotion that disconnects people from their jobs, their co-workers, and organizations. Painful emotions that are inevitably part of organizational life become toxic when others respond to them in harmful and destructive ways. Organizational toxicity has pervasive negative effects, undermining individuals' confidence, hope and self-esteem and damaging their morale and performance, both at work and outside [8].

It is interesting to note that many words here describe the negative end of dimensions of organisational life that appreciative inquiry is designed to positively affect: energy, emotions, confidence, hope, self-esteem, morale and performance, suggesting it may well be the antidote. However, let us explore the idea of toxicity, which is derived from a medical perspective, a bit further for the insight it gives into what might explain what we see in organisations and ideas of how to best intervene.

Wilde's analysis starts from the observation, drawn from early medical thought, that everything is poison and there is poison in everything.[2] It's all, she suggests, about the dosage. I read this to mean that when working with toxic organisations we aren't working to get rid of something which is integral to organisational life; instead we are working to get something back below the threshold of toxicity. An example of a spillover into toxicity might be when corrective feedback becomes critical feedback, and when that becomes a large part of someone's organisational experience, leading to a loss of confidence, negative emotional states etc.

The effect of any poison does not necessarily stop if the poison is removed. Poisons interact with a living entity to alter it in ways that often cannot easily be reversed. A well-known example is paracetamol. A little can be helpful. A lot can be fatal. And enough can cause liver damage even if the intake has been stopped before the point of death. Interestingly, even if people survive the initial few days after a near-fatal overdose, antidotes must be administered if death is to be avoided shortly thereafter. We can argue a similarity with critical feedback: a little might be helpful, a lot could cause a person, at the very least, to quit work. But even if there is a reduction in the critical feedback, the person might not immediately revert to their once confident state: the anxiety about getting it wrong, the unwillingness to take risks or speak up, the desire to stay out of the limelight etc. may well continue.

The model in Figure 16.1 offers us some ideas of domains into which to focus appreciative inquiries. For example, Wilde mentions doing inquiries into 'How are control and support enabled in the workplace?', finding that the conversation stimulated by questions like this led to much more useful conversation than those focused on the seemingly intractable problems of stress reduction. She notes that, in a double win, the appreciative inquiry process itself bolsters employees' sense of control and support.

The Importance of Relationships and Emotional States

Much distress in organisations is caused by painful emotions, which are often embedded in relationships. Relationships do not always run smoothly in life, and that includes at work. Painful emotions are a part of life and are as ever-present in organisations as elsewhere. The dosage turns toxic when the response to such pain is harsh, insensitive or indifferent and so does not repair the damage. This is toxic at an organisational level because these difficult emotional states, exacerbated by the inappropriate response to them, take up organisational psychological resources in dealing with and managing them; these resources are not then available for pursuit of the organisational goals.

Appreciative inquiry works directly on emotional states. As we have seen, positivity, meaning positive emotional states and experiences, is key to the appreciative inquiry process; and it's not just a nice to have. There is plenty of research demonstrating the benefits of feeling good to health and well-being. Happier people experience greater well-being; that is, they tend to have stronger immune systems and better cardiovascular health [9]. They tend to have lower vulnerability to infection, faster recovery from illness and slower courses of advancing disease. Positive emotions 'undo' the physiological effects of negative emotions; that is, they bring heart-rate and blood pressure back to the baseline up to 20 seconds faster. Some leading positive psychologists [10] brought together over 200 studies conducted on 275 000 people worldwide in a landmark metastudy. They found happier people, those with higher levels of well-being, are healthier with a tendency to live longer and are less accident prone. They are more successful, more productive, more creative, faster thinking, harder-working, higher earning, more caring and altruistic, more socially engaged and luckier.

To this data we can add the specific effects of high-energy emotions like excitement, zest and enthusiasm that shift our mood and our physiology fast. Laughter, for instance, is one of the quickest ways to activate the healing effect of positive emotion. Just a few minutes of laughter a day can reduce stress and improve heart rate, muscle activity, digestion and the immune system [11, 12].[3] In addition, from an organisational perspective, happy employees equal lower costs. Although many of us could probably guess that happy employees are healthier, Gallup's global health study managed to quantify the average cost of an unhappy employee: they take significantly more sick leave, staying home on average of 1.25 days more a month, equivalent to 15 extra sick days per year [13].[4] Happiness and resilience are a reflection of the ratio of experiences of positive to negative events and emotional states in someone's life, against their coping capacity. And while we want to boost their coping capacity, we want also to improve the positivity ratio of experiences and emotional states.

System-level Health and Well-being Intervention

As a system-level intervention, appreciative inquiry can do more than just help individuals feel better; it can tip a system into a different way of relating that replace old habits and behaviours with more adaptive and positive ones. For example, when I've done appreciative inquiries into performance and motivation it has rapidly become clear that it's not the annual performance appraisal and the recording forms, however carefully designed, calibrated and well-baked into the yearly cycle they are, that makes the difference. It turns out it's about relationships and conversations on an ongoing basis. Telling people this, as one could, would not have the motivating effect of a communal discovery. It's this that leads to changes in behaviour and relationships.

Appreciative inquiry is a relational process. It is extremely clear how important positive relationships and social support are to well-being. A different Taylor [14] identified social support as the most significant and reliable psychosocial predictor of health outcomes, with effects on health on a par with smoking behaviour. Indeed, the message that comes through loud and clear from all the research on happiness and psychological well-being is the positive difference that social support makes; and healthy relationships with others have been shown time and again to be the best, most consistent and strongest predictor of human happiness [15]. The key distinguishing factor of the happiest 10% of people is the quality of their social support network [16]. And, to follow the circle around, happier people cope with stressful events with less strain on their physiology and enjoy better health.

Interestingly, time perspectives [17] also have an effect on people and organisational well-being (Table 16.1).

This is particularly relevant in times of organisational change which can unintentionally induce both an overfocus on what was wrong in the past, and, paradoxically, amidst the disruption of change, an overly rosy view of how great it was in the past. So, while one group might cast the past as having been somehow 'wrong' to justify the change (past negative), another may be busy creating the 'golden age' myth of a time when everything and everyone worked well in the absence of this level of management interference (past positive). The greater challenge though is the spread of a present-fatalistic mindset. In this state people feel hopeless and express beliefs that immutable outside forces control their lives. Both past-negative and present-fatalistic mindsets are associated with strong feelings of depression, anger, anxiety and aggression. In addition present-fatalistic orientation is related to a perceived lack of control, negative affect and a great degree of emotional distress and hopelessness.

Table 16.1 Zimbardo and Boyd theory of time perspective.

Time perspective	Key characteristic
Future oriented	Thinking about the implications of decisions and actions taken now for the future
Past positive oriented	Reminiscing
Past negative oriented	Rumination
Present hedonistic oriented	Enjoying the moment
Present fatalistic oriented	Believing that all is inevitable and nothing one does makes a difference
Future transcendental oriented	Believing in life after death which enables a calm acceptance of the inevitability of death and can afford a different relationship to today's painful challenges

Clearly, as we explored in the previous chapter, appreciative approaches can help to encourage a move away from these time perspectives towards a genuine exploration of the positives from the past that may be useful in the future, and a grounded positive future-oriented mindset to help guide our actions today. In this way, by affecting how people and groups relate to time, we can help boost people's well-being with appreciative processes.

Psychological Safety in Teams

Much psychological distress at work is created at the team working level. A key component of well-being in teams is a sense of psychological safety which is in turn directly related to team outcomes. The perception of being safe, psychologically speaking, appears to explain why some people are more engaged at work, better able to share information, better able to extend themselves in their roles and are more innovative than others. People who feel psychologically safe are more likely to notice issues and speak up [18]. The impact of low psychological safety in an organisation or team is silence, withdrawal and suspicion. Interestingly, psychological safety, along with learning, is higher in groups with a sense of mastery and autonomy, both of which relate to the psychosocial hazard of control, than for teams that have either been given instructions on their performance goal or have no such instructions. By creating psychological safety and a sense of mastery and control (doing it for ourselves!), appreciative inquiry can work at the team level to reduce the psychosocial hazards that contribute to workplace stress and ill-health.

While teams within an organisation can vary in their climates of psychological safety, it's worth noting that some effects labelled 'organisational trauma' have been shown to have a negative effect on psychological safety at the organisational level, for example repeated restructuring, large-scale redundancy initiatives and public reputational damage with media or regulatory shaming [19]. Once again appreciative inquiry is a strong contender to be included in activities to start rebuilding the sense of psychological safety that is necessary for productive futures after such traumatic events.

Appreciative inquiry is also a strengths-based process. Broadly speaking strengths can be defined as well-developed, habitual ways of behaving that when expressed through positive endeavours are seen as good, beneficial or admirable. So 'cowardly' does not appear as a strength, but 'courage' does. Note though that courage can of course be expressed through heroism on the battlefield or heroism as a Mafioso or drug baron. Despite this, courage is generally regarded as a positive attribute while cowardliness is not. So, strengths have a general moral value of being 'good things'.

The various different theorists in the field also agree that using our strengths is experienced as life-enhancing or affirming. Or, to put it another way, when we are feeling at our best, we are probably using our strengths and conversely, all else being equal, using our strengths is likely to boost our positivity. Using our strengths is relatively effortless. Using our strengths is an energising, self-reinforcing, life-affirming and positive experience which energises and improves mood and is associated with increased engagement at work and absence reduction. Using our strengths can be good for our well-being and health in more specific ways.

For example, it has been found that various character strengths such as hope, kindness, social intelligence, self-control or perspective can buffer against the negative effects of stress and trauma, preventing or mitigating disorders in their wake [20], while the strengths of love, hope, gratitude, curiosity and zest are particularly correlated with psychological well-being [21]. Research shows that when people use their strengths they feel happier and more confident, are less stressed, more resilient and more engaged in their self-development. When combining our strengths with others' and assisting them to use theirs, we build stronger and more co-operative relationships, enabling greater collaboration and teamwork.

Toxic organisational cultures and working practices can produce some predicable outcomes: bullying, exclusion, harassment and retaliation, all of which can have very detrimental effects on physical and mental health. These are not only bad for the individuals concerned; to be a witness or bystander can also be problematic with both vulnerable to experiencing a level of trauma [22]. Applying the toxic dose metaphor, Wilde notes that research suggests a base line measure of 4–10% of the work population ever experiencing bullying directly and finds that, this level, while distressing for those involved, does not appear to be destructive of the functioning of a community. At this level individual 'toxin handlers' offer active compassionate interventions; kind and brave people in other words help those affected to recover. And moving people around, a tactic I have often observed in organisations, can sometimes solve an isolated problem. The real trouble starts at 15% or above as the whole system becomes, as it were, poisoned, and organisational functioning becomes dominated by fear of rejection rather than a concern for the work to be done. The fear acts to inhibit compassion and the self-healing process breaks down.

The case study below describes working with an organisation worrying about the level of reported fear of bullying and so making an early attempt to address the threat. This intervention is not perfect (whichever is?) but will hopefully give an idea of how to work with these kinds of issues from an appreciative perspective.

Case Study: Working with Respect

An organisation issued a staff survey that came back with a low positive response to the statement, 'I would feel able to report bullying/harassment without worrying that it would have a negative impact on me' for a particular department. This had not changed in the three years since the previous survey. In response, the organisation established a focus group to examine how the situation could be improved. I was asked to run a three-hour session for 16 staff. At that stage it was thought by the organisation best to hold this session first and then possibly another for management later. While this can be seen as a less than ideal way to set up the work, it also has some benefits.

The identified desired outcomes were an opportunity to discuss and examine the issue in a constructive and supportive way, and to produce a distilled code of behaviours that support working with respect and diminish the likelihood of bullying and harassment behaviour. While honouring this commitment, my ambition was to help people identify when they were able to work with others in ways that felt respectful and to imagine what needed to be different to allow the factors that supported such working relationships to flourish. Areas of specific interest might include respectful ways of giving praise or recognising good work and of addressing performance difficulties.

Initially I interviewed a few of the people who would be in the group, asking such questions as, 'What are some of the best experiences you have had of being treated with respect by colleagues or other stakeholders (outsiders)?', 'Tell me something of your personal experience around bullying and harassment, if any', 'What in the present ways of working, the culture, would you say supports working with respect? What works against it, contributing to the possibility or likelihood of bullying and harassment behaviour?', 'Have there been any significant changes in the organization that have contributed to the amount of either working with respect or bullying and harassment?' And of course, 'Tell me what would be a really useful three hours of your time? What would we achieve? What would success look like?'

I hope you can see that, as well as giving them a chance to share their story, if any, about bullying and harassment behaviour in the organisation, I was focused on working with respect as my appreciative topic of inquiry; I was also interested to see if there had been any recent organisational changes that might have contributed to the staff survey data. I was also working to co-create a design for our three hours together. This topic was a new area for me, and I was feeling my way in how to approach it from an appreciative perspective while also honouring their experiences (Figure 16.2). Please see below the outline for the session.

It was evident initially that people were anxious about the form the discussion would take. Hence the necessity of spending a good hour on establishing the context and the aspiration for the session and introducing the appreciative approach. For this I drew a figure eight with bullying and harassment in one circle and working with respect in the other. Emphasising that they were connected phenomena and that the ambition was to grow one circle and shrink the other. All of this was in the service of explaining how we were still talking about undesired behaviour even as we focused on desired behaviour.

We also spent a lot of time on agreeing how to work together. Clearly modelling how we wanted the organisation to work, that is, with respect, in our mini-session was of paramount importance. And time was needed to explore what that meant to this group of people in this context. It was important to extend respect to those not present. This was agreed upon and helped make it clear that the session was not going to be a 'grousing' or 'name and shame' session. All this preparation enabled people to engage fully with the rest of the session.

First, we held a discovery interview into best experiences of working with respect in the organisation. This was followed by exploring why good people can behave badly. The intention here was to shift conceptions and discussion from 'that person's a bully' to a more nuanced 'in this context, this behaviour and dynamic is present.' The first essentially labels someone as a bad person, not a great starting point. The second places them in a context and views behaviour as a product of person and context, giving far more scope and possibility of change – more hope in fact. As you can see, in this exercise we explored the very organisational factors we talked about above: stress, pressure, measurement systems, organisational patterns, lack of management development, lack of understanding of others, and how they can create an environment that produces abusive behaviour. It was noted that the department in question was under immense pressure during a huge organisational transformation that was ongoing. The event then moved to activating resources and identifying causes for hope, and then ideas for what next.

Working With Respect Focus Group

Overall Objective: To move towards increasing the potential for people at the organisation to create effective, productive and respectful working relationships, and to diminish the creation of working environments characterized by bullying and harassment.

Specific Aims: By the end of the day the group should have:

> Identified what characterises respectful working relationships at the organisation
>
> Discovered what works in shifting relationships characterized by bullying or harassment towards working with respect here or elsewhere
>
> Identified some of the things in the wider context that affect people's behaviour in the workplace
>
> Identified what can be done to improve things to work on more fully in the second session
>
> An increased confidence that the overall objective of reducing bullying or harassment behaviour and increasing working with respect behaviour is achievable
>
> Enjoyed being together and felt supportive and supported throughout the morning
>
> Worked together with respect

Workshop format

Hello and Welcome!

> Welcome, context and aspirations
> *link to future activity e.g., next group meeting, Clear statement of organisational position*
>
> Essential housekeeping
>
> What is an AI approach *(brief overview)*
>
> Outline introduction to process for morning
>
> Working together today *(ground rules)*
> *– with a particular emphasis on working together with respect – respect both for those present and absent 'no talking about me without me" for example (for absent managers)*
>
> Baseline measurement against the objectives *(sticky dots – quick and easy)*

Introductions

> *In groups of 4*
> *– who are, why volunteered, what hoping to contribute, what hoping morning will achieve. Collation of answers – resources in the room/aspirations for morning*
>
> *(all this will take at least an hour – and highly important for setting tone, atmosphere etc.)*

Figure 16.2 Facilitator's agenda for session.

> Break (10 mins)
>
> Learning from the best
> > Different fours Quick positivity booster – what I love most about working for this organisation (or something in this vein). Then discovery interviews about best working relationships. Collate info
>
> Learning from the best cont.
> > In larger groups – 2x5, 1x6 – experiences of 'difficult' or bullying and harassment behaviour that has been successfully resolved. What made the difference? What shifted that allowed the pattern to change? (discovery interviews) Pull info from groups together.
>
> Why do good people sometimes behave badly?
> > Concentric circle map on wall from individual to society. Brainstorming, post-its, factors that influence behaviour. (Intention is to broaden story from 'bad people' to – stress, pressure, measurement systems, organisational patterns, lack of management development, of understanding of others etc.)
>
> Break (10 mins)
>
> What resources do we have to build on going forward?
> > A pulling together of what has been discovered so far. Plus anything not yet identified. Which of these offer the most leverage for making a difference in the future? We might also feed in ideas like facilitated conversations between people. We may be able to identify immediate support strategies for people clearly coping with stressful situations on a daily basis
>
> What hope for the future?
> > Final round – one thing about today or about this organisation in general that gives you real hope that this situation can be improved
>
> What next?
> > Summary of what happens next
>
> Finish

Figure 16.2 (Continued)

At the finish people reported feeling more confident in both their and the organisation's ability to increase working-with-respect experiences and to reduce bullying and harassment experiences. They felt that by sharing how to create good experiences, and how to deal effectively with bad ones, they had access to increased resources both personally and as part of the extended group. In other words, it gave a boost to their sense of self-efficacy. They reported hope and optimism that things would improve in the future and reported feeling more resilient. In this way this appreciatively oriented inquiry into a potentially difficult topic, where it would have been easy to evoke further feelings of abuse and hopelessness, had instead boosted their psychological capital [23],[5] so contributing to increased well-being.

Conclusion

In this chapter we have noticed that individual interventions to support well-being have a limited effect in organisations that have tipped into toxicity. We have considered what might contribute to this organisational toxicity and what the effects might be for organisational members. We have looked at how appreciative inquiry can offer some antidote properties by reconfiguring and resetting systems, as well as by positively influencing the core facets of psychosocial workplace hazards. We have noted that there are ways of conducting appreciative inquiries into difficult, well-being impairing topics, and presented an inquiry into working with respect in a context of an unacceptable fear of bullying as an example.

Learning Points

1. Causes of workplace-induced ill-health can be present at the individual, team and organisational levels.
2. The metaphor of toxicity provides a helpful way of thinking about how organisational culture contributes to poor mental health amongst its workforce.
3. Individually targeted wellness interventions have limited impact in an organisation that has slipped into a toxic state.
4. Appreciative inquiry is a wellness supporting intervention that can also be specifically targeted at areas of toxicity in organisations.

Discussion Questions

1. How well does the toxic dosage metaphor work to explain adverse organisational phenomena?
2. What does the case study illustrate about how to bring appreciative inquiry to a difficult area? And how could the intervention have been improved?
3. What have been your personal experiences of 'wellness initiatives' in the workplace and how effective or not have you found them?

Teaching Exercise

1. Assume you have access to the whole organisational system. Design an intervention to inquiry into 'Grace under Pressure'

Helpful Resources and Further Reading

Lewis, S. (2014). How positive psychology and appreciative inquiry can help leaders create healthy workplaces. In: *Creating Healthy Workplaces* (ed. C. Biron, R. Burke, and C. Cooper). Gower.

Lewis, S., Passmore, J., and Cantore, S. (2016). *Appreciative Inquiry for Change Management Using AI to Facilitate Organizational Development*, 2e. London: Kogan Page chapter 16 case study: rapidly transforming conflict into co-action at a South African coal mine, 232–248.

Wilde, J. (2016). *The Social Psychology of Organizations: Diagnosing Toxicity and Intervening in the Workplace*. London: Routledge.

Notes

1. For more on this see Ref. [4].
2. Here Wilde is quoting Paracelsus (1493–1541).
3. This information is from Ref. [11]. Available at https://www.thepositivepsychologyshop.com/collections/free-white-papers/products/white-paper-by-langley-group-7-ways-to-apply-positive-psychology-at-work. See also Ref. [12].
4. Gallup's global health study (2008) is quoted, but not properly referenced, in Ref. [13].
5. 'Psychological capital' is a term first used by Youssef-Morgan and Luthans (Ref. [23]).

References

1. Taylor, F. (1912). Scientific Management. In: *Organisational Theory*, 4e (ed. D. Pugh) (1997), 203–221. Penguin London.
2. Hackman, J.R. and Oldman, G.R. (1976). Motivation through the design of work: test of a theory. *Organizational Behaviour and Human Performance* 16 (2): 250–279.
3. French, J.R.P. and Caplan, R.D. (1972). Organisational stress and individual strain. In: *The Failure of Success* (ed. A. Marrow). New York: AMACOM.

4. Lewis, S. (2014). How positive psychology and appreciative inquiry can help leaders create healthy workplaces. In: *Creating Healthy Workplaces* (ed. C. Biron, R. Burke, and C. Cooper). Gower.
5. Gable, S.L., Reis, H.T., Impett, E.A., and Evan, R.A. (2004). What do you do when things go right? The intrapersonal and interpersonal benefits of sharing positive events. *Journal of Personality and Social Psychology* 87 (22): 228–245.
6. Wilde, J. (2016). *The Social Psychology of Organizations: Diagnosing Toxicity and Intervening in the Workplace*. London: Routledge.
7. Purser, R. (2019). *McMindfulness: How Mindfulness Became the New Capitalist Spirituality*. Repeater.
8. Maitlis, S. (2008). Organizational toxicity. In: *International Encyclopaedia of Organization Studies* (ed. S. Clegg and J. Bailey). Los Angeles: Sage Publications Ltd.
9. Diener, E. and Diener-Biswas, R. (2008). *Happiness: Unlocking the Mysteries of Psychological Wealth*. Malden, MA: Blackwell Publishing.
10. Lyubomirsky, S., King, L., and Diener, E. (2005). The benefits of frequent positive affect: does happiness lead to success? *Psychological Bulletin* 131 (6): 803.
11. Langley, S (2015). Seven ways to apply positive psychology at work. http://Langley.com (accessed November 2023).
12. Yim, J. (2016). Therapeutic benefits of laughter in mental health: a theoretical review. *The Tohoku Journal of Experimental Medicine* 239 (3): 243–249.
13. Stewart, H. Benefits of having happy employees. Happy Blog. 23 April 2023. www.happy.co.uk.
14. Taylor, S.E. (2011). How psychosocial resources enhance health and well-being. In: *Applied Positive Psychology: Improving Everyday Life, Health, Schools, Work and Society* (ed. S.I. Donaldson, M. Csikszentmihalyi, and J. Nakamura), 65–77. New York: Psychology Press.
15. Bormans, L. (ed.) ((2012). *The World Book of Happiness*. London: Marshall Cavendish Editions.
16. Diener, E. and Seligman, M.E. (2002). Very happy people. *Psychological Science* 13 (1): 81–84.
17. Zimbardo, P. and Boyd, J. (2010). *The Time Paradox: Using the New Psychology of Time to your Advantage*. London: Rider.
18. Wilde, J. (2016). *The Social Psychology of Organizations: Diagnosing Toxicity and Intervening in the Workplace*. London: Routledge.
19. Kahan, D.M. (2019). What's really wrong with shaming sanctions. In: *Shame Punishment*, 497–517. Routledge.
20. Peterson, C. and Park, N. (2011). Character strengths and virtues: their role in well-being. In: *Applied Positive Psychology: Improving Everyday Life, Health, Schools, Work and Society* (ed. S.I. Donaldson, M. Csikszentmihalyi, and J. Nakamura). New York: Routledge.

21. Park, N., Peterson, C., and Seligman, M.E.P. (2004). Strengths of character and well-being. *Journal of Social and Clinical Psychology* 1: 118–129.
22. Einarsen, S.V., Hoel, H., Zapf, D., and Cooper, C.L. (ed.) (2020). *Bullying and Harassment in the Workplace: Theory, Research and Practice*. CRC Press.
23. Youssef-Morgan, C.M. and Luthans, F. (2009). An integrated model of psychological capital in the workplace. In: *Oxford Handbook of Positive Psychology and Work* (ed. P.A. Linley, S. Harrington, and N. Garcea). Oxford University Press.

Index

Italic page numbers refer to *figure* and **Bold** page numbers reference to **tables**.

abundance, 129, 209
abusive behaviour, 246
accountability, 57, 94, 237
achievements, 27, 51–52, 90–91, 120, 153, 156–157, 186, 191
action planning, 46
activity, 21–22, 46, 49, 117, 146, 147, 196–197, 220–202
  evaluating, 207
  political, 80
affiliations, 117
aggression, 242
amplification processes, 224
anger, 242
anticipatory principle, *25*, 27, 179
anxiety, 10, 89, 123, 163, 240, 242
appreciative/appreciation, 181
  approach, 51
  architecture, 71–72
  coaching process, 162
  conversations, **43**, 43–44
  discovery interviews, 159
  intervention, 50, 180
  interviews, 193
  management performance, 208–209
  peer reviews, 211–215
  practice, use of, 232
  practitioner, 51–52
  questions, 44
  review process, 206–207, 211
  simultaneity principle, 179
appreciative inquiry, 49, 72, 86, 91, 117–118, 211, 214–215
  to aid project development, 121, *121*
  approach, 76
  aspects of, 231
  benefit of, 130
  broader sense, 224
  challenges for, 206
  commission, 50–55
  critiquing, 12–14
  definition of, 3, 18–19
  development of, 3
  discovery phase of, 161
  diversity, equality and inclusion, 58–63
  domains, **238**
  dream phase of, 161, 184–185, 201, 223–224
  ethical practice, 57
  5D, 18, *19*, 38, 130–131

Practical Appreciative Inquiry: A Toolkit for Applying Appreciative Inquiry to Organisational Challenges, Opportunities, and Aspiration, First Edition. Sarah Lewis.
© 2025 John Wiley & Sons Ltd. Published 2025 by John Wiley & Sons Ltd.

appreciative inquiry (cont'd)
  frequently encountered pushbacks against, 55
  and generation of hope, 222–224
  generative nature of, 137
  and improvisational theatre, 135
  indication, 35–36
  interventions, 59, 101–102, 195
  mental and physical health benefits of positive emotional states, **192–193**
  mode of practice, 6
  narratives generated during, 223
  organisational problems, 7–8
  origins of, 4–5
  vs. other change methodologies, 5–7
  perspective, 49, 124, 206
  positive energy and motivational impact, 4, *4*
  positive images of future, 191–193
  as practice, 11–13, 23, 30, 55–57, **58**, 129
  practitioner, 49
  principles of, 57, 183–184
  real magic of, 145
  relational and generative focus of, 223
  relational process, 241–242
  skill, 134
  SOAR model of, 201
  strengths-based process, 243–244
  team development, 229
  thinking, 190
  in transformational change, 30–31
  value of, 224
  volunteer principle in, 45–46
appreciative inquiry summit, 90, 92, 100, 144
  5D model of, *19*, 39
    defining topic of inquiry, 18–19
    designing for better futures, 22–23
    destiny, 23
    discovering best of present, 19–21
    dreaming of future, 21–22
  anticipatory principle, *25*, 27
  constructionist principle, *25*, 29
  description of, 18
  narrative principle, *25*, 26–27
  poetic principle, 24, *25*
  positivity principle, *25*, 28
  simultaneity principle, *25*, 27–28
  wholeness principle, 24–26, *25*
appreciative leadership, 88–90, 92, **93**, 96
  in action, 93–96
  appreciative inquiry event, 87–88
  conversations, 89–92
  description of, 86
  leading through uncertainty, 93
  mindset required for appreciative inquiry, 88
approach to evaluation, 212
ARE IN model, 39, *39*
artificial intelligence, 31, 199
aspirations, 4–5, 19, 21, 71, 78–80, 122, 124, 126, 132, 152–153, 181, 185, 191–193, 218
autonomy, 23, 181, 190, 237, 243

banking organisation, 136–137
behaviour, 69–70, 210, 246
  abusive, 246
  desired, 246
  domain of, 166
  hurtful and harmful, 182
belonging, 65, 89, 117
blue sky thinking, 21, 132
body language, 123
Boston Map exercise, 146, 152
brainstorm/brainstorming, 131–132, 170
bullying, 237, 244–249
burnout, productivity without, 194

Index

case study
  appreciative leadership in action, 93–96
  appreciative peer reviews to regional health team, 211–218
  community system I- IPOD appreciative intervention, 80–82
  creativity for business growth, 136–137
  hybrid working challenges, 200–203
  merged organisation, 145–153
  organisation adapting to market changes, 136
  positive approach to difficult issues, 109–111
  project team-based large-system change, 121–126
  from push to pull, 229–231
  two-hour workshop on change practice, 231–232
  using appreciative inquiry to enhance diversity, equality and inclusion, 62–63
  using SOAR to Return to Power Zone, 75–80
  working with respect, 245–249
  working with stuck team, 179–186
change. *see also* planned change process
  create motivation for, 159–160
  disruptions of, 74
  interventions, 143–144
  ladder of, 185
  language, 122
  leadership, 228
  measurement of, 185
  motivation for, 226
  organisational, 109–111
  pattern, 227
  philosophy of, 86
  potentialities and possibilities for, 159–160
  power for, 20
  process of, 18, 24–25
  real power of, 133
  relational aspect of, 232
  resistance to, 228–229
  stories of, 227
  transformational, 30–31
client/supplier relationship, 232
coaching. *see also* PRISMM coaching
  qualification, 213
  relationship, 160
co-creation, 35, 39, 89, 135, 137, 216
cognitive diversity, 101
cognitive schema, 118
collaboration, 13, 71, 136–137, 202, 244
collective sense-making, 24, 92, 125
commissioning process, 54
  roles in, 52, **52**
  suggested solutions, 55, **55**
  traditional and appreciative inquiry approaches, 52, **53–54**
'common' project management, 116
communication, 142, 203
  challenges, 142
  channels, 170
  environment, 200
  patterns of, 77, 143, 152
  processes, 153
  skills training, 142
community
  action programmes, 81
  leaders, 81
  project management, 81
competence, 73, 74
  within organisation, 102
complex organisation, *147–149*
conscious attention, 196
constructionist principle, *25*, 29
context-specific evaluation processes, 185
contraindications, 34–36
conventional peer reviews, 218

conversation, 51, 77, 79, 91, 100, 106–108, 134
   an appreciative stance, 42
   appreciatively oriented, 43, **43**
   depreciative perspective, 42–43
   and energy, 87
   generative, 43
   inquiry-based, 43
   quality of, 41–44, 59
   statement-based, 43
   types of, *42*
coordinated group tasks, 199
coping capacity, 241
corrective feedback, 158–159, 239
   appreciative approach to, *159*
'creating the ladder of change' technique, 229
creative/creativity, 26, 103, 129, 133–135, 137, 140, 144
   of appreciative inquiry, 132
   benefits, 199
   for business growth, 136–137
   contribution, 135
   description of, 128
   design phase, 133
   discovery stories, 130–133
   emotional states of, 22
   as generativity, 128–129
   ideas and energy, 129–130
   impact on, 130
   inquiring into, 133–135
   opportunity for, 27
   stimulating process, 131
   thinking, 137
cynicism, 35, 140, 142

decision-making, 13, 22, 34, 40, 46, 56, 87, 91–92, 95, 105, 150, 157, 229
depression, 242
design
   and destiny, conflation of, 186
   principles for project, 215, **215**

desired behaviour, 246
destiny, 18, 23, 133, 152, 186
diagnostic change, 227–228
dialogic change processes, 227–228
dialogic organisational development, 7, 29, 80, 117–118, 144
   definition of, 8–11, 14
digitalisation programme, 229
discovery conversation, 106, 121, 130–132, 151, *167*
discovery interviews, *20*, 100, 106, 110, 120–121, 124, 125, 131–133, 163, 183, 190–191, 193, 223, 246
discovery questions, 103, 216
discovery stories, working generatively with, 131–133
disruption of change, 242
diverse facilitation teams, 63
diversity, 118–120
   cognitive, 101
   of experience and knowledge, 101
   and performance, 119, *119*
dreaming, 21–22, 27, 28, 38, 121, 132, 134, 223–224, 232
dysfunction, 94, 140–143, 175, 176, 186

emotional/emotions, 191
   distress, 242
   high-energy, 241
   negative, 240–241
   painful, 240
   positive, 241
   states, importance of, 240–241
empowerment, 30, 162, 186
energising experiences, 71, 73
energy, 4, 4, 21–22, 28, 36, 72–73, 77, 87–88, 129–131, 140–145, 152, 153, 162, 163, 165, 184–185, 208, 210, 231, 239, 241
'energy-pumping' approach, 6
engagement, 45, 73–74, 196, 244
   across organisational boundaries, 56

employee, 7–8
  positivity, 161
  rules of, 104, 146
  staff, 197–198
  stages of, 36
  system, 216
  trust and, 8, 35
enterprise resource planning project, 91
equality diversity and inclusion
  appreciative inquiry to enhance, 62–63
  description of, 58
  psychological safety, 59–60
  in workplace cultures, 59
evaluation, 12–13, 109, 214
  activity of, 207
  ambition of, 207
  appreciative-informed, 208–209
  approach to, 212
  context-specific processes, 185
  effective, 207
  improvement-oriented, 157
  purpose of, 212
event
  facilitator plan for, 41, 46, 50–51, *107–108*, 146, 170
  invitation, *164*
evidence-based practice, 11–12, 14
exceptionalism, 209
executive team, 229–230, 233

face-to-face events, 101, 196, 200, 216
facilitators, 34, 41, 46, 50–51, 61–62, 78, 136–137, 146, 163
  agenda, *247–248*
  influence of, 41
feedback, 99, 157
  amplifying, 157–158
  corrective, 158–159
  experience, 100
  form of, 157
  positive, 158

5D, 18, *19*, 38–39, 130–131
  appreciative inquiry cycle, 130–131
  cycle, 55–56, 134
  defining topic of inquiry, 18–19
  designing for better futures, 22–23
  destiny, 23
  discovering best of present, 19–21
  dreaming of future, 21–22
  model, 62, 70
flourishing, 75, 80, 82, 176, 238
  definition of, 74
  organisational (*see* organisational flourishing)
free-choice principle, 45
freedom within constraints, 71–72
fund-raising events, 231
future, attractive images of, 160

generative/generativity, 23, 26, 43, 44, 78, 128–129, 137, 153
  questions, 134
  talk, 130–131
'get up and move' exercise, 151
good relationship, 176, 210
group conversations, 196

harassment, 237, 244–246, 248
hazards, 35, 236–237, 243, 249
health and well-being at work
  description of, 236–237
  organisational cultures, 239–240
  people at work, 237–239
  psychological safety in teams, 243–245
  relationships and emotional states, 240–241
  system-level health and well-being intervention, 241–243
  working with respect, 245–249
helping-based practice, 11
high performing teams, social dynamics of, 176, *177*, 186
home-working, 194–195, 198

Index

hope, 79–80, 103–105, 163, 244, 248
   emotional states of, 22
   generation of, 222–224
   positive emotions of, 226
   sources of, 162
hopelessness, 222, 242, 248–249
HR manager, 91, 123
hybrid working, 190, 198, 202–203
   ambition, 203
   challenges, 200–203
   getting best from, 198–200

I-IPOD. *see* Innovation-Inspired Positive Organisational Development (I-IPOD)
Imagination, 6, 125, 129, 131, 132, 134, 223, 229
   power of, 21–22, 51
   use of, 118
improvement-oriented evaluation, 157
improvisational theatre, 135
incompetence, 111
increased impact, 71–72
individuals, 9, 23, 29, 43, 69, 74, 92, 140, 145, 162, 184–185
   actions of, 89
   commitments, 201
   energy, 143
   psychological capital, 99
   reflection, 196
   remote working for, 190
   resilience of, 102–103
   resourcefulness, 107–108
   toxin handlers, 244
   well-being, 237–238
inexperienced consultants, 11
informal conversations, 152
inform practice, principles to, 157, 196
in-house wellness programmes, 237–238
initiative-developing conversations, 152–153

innovation, 129, 136, 140
   description of, 128
   discovery stories, 130–133
   emotional states of, 22
   as generativity, 128–129
   ideas and energy, 129–130
   inspired, 71–72
   thinking, 137
Innovation-Inspired Positive Organisational Development (I-IPOD), 69–70, 80–82, *81*
inspiring strategy, *70*, 71
intellectuals
   apparatus, 60
   book-learnt knowledge, 61
   curiosity, emotional states of, 22
   knowledge, 60
interconnectedness, 145
interdependence, 10, 176
intervention, 36, 50, 86, 238
   diagnostic and dialogic, 228
   diagnostic phase of, 179
   dual pattern of, 228
   evaluating, 207
   modes of, 228
   problem solving, 50
interview format, 179, *180*

kindness, 105, 244
knowledge, 11, 13, 36, 43, 49, 73, 110, 120, 125, 144–145, 184, 186, 208
   codified forms of, 61
   domains of, 71
   intellectual, 60
   imperfect, 100
   of 'reality' or 'truth', 24
   practice, 71
   sharing, 202
   tacit, 60–62
   transfer, 99
   translating, 12

leaders/leadership, 46, 116–117, 123, 175
  ability, 78–79
  appreciative-informed evaluation of, 208–209
  attention, 90
  behaviour, 226
  burden of, 88
  change, 228
  conversations, 89–92
  minds, 90
  mindset, 86, 88, 228
  moments, 110
  personal resources of, 124
  powerful focus of, 72
  priorities of, 110
  psychological capital, 110
learning, 20, 61, 69, 74, 89, 92, 99, 100, 111, 146, 158, 163, 212–214, 217
  awareness of, 70
  environments, 30
  levels of, 213
  organisational, 5
legacy systems, 91
Likert scale, 208–209
listening, 41, 51, 62, 76, 77, 185–186
local influence and control, 225–226
lockdown, 189–190, 200
logic-based problem-solving, 7
look after the leader, 226–227, 238

management, 222, 225–226, 230–231
  appreciative-informed evaluation of, 208–209
  aspects of, 231
  performance assessment, 209–210
  process, 106–107
  style, 105
managers, 11–12, 21, 46, 76, 78, 94–96, 109–110, 116–117, 122–124, 157–158, 209–210, 231–233
market changes, organisation adapting to, 135–136

marketplace sharing process, 196
market share, 136–137
media/regulatory shaming, 243
memory, 134, 170, 172, 191
mental flexibility, emotional states of, 22
metaphors, 26, 78, 95, 116–117, 125, 244
middle managers, 94
mindfulness, 21, 238
mini-appreciative inquiry, 52
models, of practice
  5D, 18–23, *19*, 22–23, 38–39, 55–56, 62, 70, 130–131, 134
  I-IPOD, 69, 80–82, *81*
  PRISMM coaching, 156–162, *160*
  SOAR, 69–70, 74–80, *75*
mood, 77, 111, 159, 161, 183, 191, 195, 201, 210, 226, 241, 244
motivation, 4, 5, 23, 27, 41, 46, 88, 90, 141, 142, 160–162, 195, 203, 206, 223, 226, 231
  and energy, 162, *195*
  for improvement, 210
  intrinsic, 23
  maintaining, 194–195
  pull, 28, 121, 125
  push, 28
  techniques to help maintain, **195**
moving to action, *160*, 162
myths, attached to appreciative inquiry, 36–38

narrative principle, *25*, 26–27
negative emotions, 37–38, 179, 185, 239, 240
non-verbal communication, 200

off-putting, 38
omni-working, 198
online appreciative inquiry, *197*
online project management, 115–116
opening-up hope, 221–223
optimism, 42, 79–80, 103–106, 225–226, 248

Index

organisational flourishing, 69–70, *70*
  appreciative architecture, 71–72
  appreciative inquiry for, 70, *70*
  appreciative practices, 70–71
  definition of, 69–70
  energising experiences, 73
  increased impact, 72
  strengths and organisational power zone, *73*, 73–74
organisational/organisation, 9–10, 21, 35, 100, 120, 150, 153, 167, 189, 201
  ability, 99
  adapting to market changes, 135–136
  behaviour and actions, 140
  boundaries, 56
  challenge for, 91, 140
  change, 7, 88, 109–111, 221, 227, 246
  connect, 56–57
  culture, 49–50, 135–136, 239–240, 244
  development, 9–10
  distress in, 240
  energy, *144*
  evidence-based, 11–12
  feature, 101
  forms, 143
  growth and development, 60–62
  identity, 197–198
  leader in, 89
  life, 170, 239
  needs, 102
  reaction, 35
  realities, 118
  resilience, 100–102
  sense-making, 228
  sources of pride, 151
  structure chart, 145
  structures and culture, 52
  thinking, 50
  toxicity, 236, 239
  trauma, 243
  values, 167
  working practices, 244
oscillation, patterns of, 179
outcomes, 8, 10, 13, 24–25, 35, 40–41, 46, 74, 82, 90, 96, 109, *109*, 140, 145, 198, 216–218, 227, 232, 243–245

passion, 28, 59, 61, 92, 100, 130, 163
path of possibility, 21–22
perception, 6, 51, 88, 90, 134, 184–185, 201, 203, 207, 243
performance, **168–169**. *see also* performance culture
  appraisals, 214–215
  coaching approach, 157
  diversity and, 119, *119*
  improvement, 101, 156
  review, 217
  space, 146–147
performance culture, 157, 172
  amplifying feedback, 157–158
  corrective feedback, 158–159
  positive, *165–166*
performance management, 159
  conversations, 177
  culture, 162–172
personal interest, *70*, 72
personal resilience, 99, 102–103, 111–112
personal well-being, 102
planned change process, 52, 143, 232
  appreciative inquiry and generation of hope, 222–223
    discovery interviews, 223
    dream phase, 223–224
  blended approach, 227–229
  description of, 221
  general principles for appreciative inquiry
    look after leader, 226–227
    possibilities of local influence and control, 225–226
    principle of positivity, 226
    principle of story and choice, 226
    work, 224–225

large-scale, 222
  principles for engaging with, 224, **225**
  from push to pull, 229–231
  two-hour workshop on change practice, 231–232
poetic principle, 24, *25*, 179
positive emotions, 22–23, 28, 33, 144, 150, 175, 190–191, 222, 226, 238, 240–241
positive energy, 4, *4*, 22, 71, 77, 102, 162–163, 184–185
positive feedback, 158
positive leadership, 181
positive/negative deviance dimension, *214*
positive performance, *70*, 71, *165–166*
  culture, *171*
  management, 71
positive psychology, 4, 12, 20–23, 30, 71, 159, 175–176, 185–186, 249–250
positivity
  creating activities, **178**
  experience of, 176
  principle, *25*, 28, 226
possible review foci, *213*
practical support, *70*, 72
practice
  activity, 207
  appreciative-informed evaluation of leadership/management, 208–209
  appreciative peer reviews to regional health team, 211–215
    co-creation, 216
    self-organisation, 216–218
    whole system, 216
  appreciative process for management performance assessment, 209–210
  description of, 206–207
  design principles, 55–57
  domains of, 71
  knowledge, 71
  measurement points and reflective ritual review, 208

preparation interview, *106*
principles, of appreciative inquiry, 25, 70, **196**. *see also specific types*
  anticipatory principle, *25*, 27
  constructionist principle, *25*, 29
  description of, 18
  narrative principle, *25*, 26–27
  poetic principle, 24, *25*
  positivity principle, *25*, 28
  practice design, 55–57
  reflecting, *58*
  simultaneity principle, *25*, 27–28
  volunteer, 45–46
  wholeness principle, 24–26, *25*
PRISMM coaching, *160*
  appreciative, 159–162
  description of, 156
  performance culture, importance of, 157
    amplifying feedback, 157–158
    corrective feedback, 158–159
problem-solving, 7–8, 10, 19, 41, 50, 99, 101, 130, 142, 145, 152–153
productive energy, 143–144, 153
product portfolio, *148*, 152
professional development, 136–137
project
  manager, 11–12, 21, 46, 76, 78, 94–96, 109–110, 116–117, 122–124, 157–158, 209–210, 231–233
  plans, 117, 202
  process, 216, **217**
  teams, 115–118, 121–126, 218
  working, complex demands of, 115–116
project-craft, psychology of, 115–118
project management, 115, 121
  applying appreciative inquiry to, 120–121
  appreciative approach to team member diversity, 118–120
  approaches, 116
  methodology, 117

project management (*cont'd*)
  project team-based large-system change, 121–126
  psychology of project-craft, 115–118
  system of, 122
psychological/psychology
  capital, 102–105, **103**
  contracting, 146
  discovery, 236
  process, 120
  safety, 34, 59–62, 120, 123, 236–237
  strengths, 104
  well-being, 242
  withdrawal, 103
psychometrics, 177
psychosocial, 241–242
  hazards, 236–237, 243
  well-being, 237–238
  workplace hazards, 249
pull motivation, 5, 27–28, 121, 125, 186–187, 231, 233
purpose, 90, 118, 145–146, 151, 181, 182, 202, 206–207, 211, *212*
  of evaluation, 212
  statement of, 184
push motivation, 28, 231

questions, 5, 7–10, 28, 34, 43, 50–51, 59, 63, 71, 73, 76–78, 81, 90, 124–125, 134, 161–
  generic appreciative inquiry, 45, *45*
  quality of, 44–45, *45*

realisation, 4, 22, 26, 62, 185, 197–198, 202
reality, 3, 21, 24, 26, 29, 91–92, 117, 131–132, 134, 159, 206, 226
reciprocal expertise affirmation, 120, 122
'redefining of success' exercise, 111
reflective rituals, 206–208, 211, 212, 217–218
reflexivity, *212*, 212–213

regional health team, 211–215
rehearsed talk, 130–131
relationships, 133–134, 145, 175, 201
  build and strengthen, 89
  cancelling conversations, 89
  domain of, 166
  enhancing conversations, 89
  importance of, 240–241
  and motivation, 195
  patterns of, 77, 143, 152
  tolerating conversations, 89
relaxed mental roaming, 132
relief, sense of, 184
remote working, 190
  achieving high productivity without burnout, 194
  challenges of, 190–195
  creating positive, aspirational images of future, 191–193
  downsides of, 201
  flexibility of, 194
  home model of, 189
  identifying and working with strengths, 193–194
  maintaining motivation, 194–195
  positive emotional states with discovery interviews, 190–191
  recrafting work, 194
  supporting work relationships, 195
  on workplace, 197–198
reorganization, 141
research-produced knowledge, 11
resilience for people and organisations, 99, 103–105
  appreciative inquiry and, 100–103
  boosting effects of strengths, 104–105
  description of, 99
  disruption of organisational change, 109–111
  organisational, 100–102
  personal, 102–103

positive approach to difficult issues,
    105–109
social capital on, 102, *102*
strengths and, 104, *104–105*
resilient relationships, *70*, 71
'resistance to change' conversation, 128,
    130, 216, 221–222, 228
responsive decision-making, 229
review, 22, 49, 102, 105, 208, 211–218
rules of engagement, 146

safety culture, 237
self-assessment, 123, 211
self-control, 244
self-efficacy, 103–104, 111, 248
self-observation, 212
self-organisation, 34, 55–56, 216–218
self-preservation, 238–239
sense, 9, 91, 118, 129
    of certainty, 117
    of commitment, 56
    of mastery, 243
    of well-being, 104
service, 89, 92, 110, 111, 211, 216–218, 246
    delivery patterns, 217
    exercise, 150
    users, 218
silo-busting, 153
silo mentality
    appreciative inquiry, 144–145
    description of, 140
    merged organisation, 145–153
    nature of organisational energy, 143–144
    organisation, dysfunctional, 141
        adverse effects of silo-working,
            141–142
        downsides of silo-working, 141
        dysfunction of silo-working,
            142–143
silo-working
    adverse effects of, 141–142
    disbenefits of, 144

    downsides of, 141
    dysfunction of, 142–143
simultaneity principle, *25*, 27–28
skills, 14, 18, 37, 71, 74, 79, 92, 120, 142, 216
    development, 213
    shortages, 94
social
    capital, 99, 102, *102*
    constructionist perspective, 6–7
    groups, 21
    intelligence, 244
    isolation, 181
spotlighting values, *160*, 162
staff
    engagement, 197–198
    members, 181
    well-being, 217
stakeholders, 10, 13, 77, 83, 144, 183, 245
stories/storytelling, 9, 26–29, 40, 44, 50,
    51, 72, 80, 93, 95, 110–112, 124,
    128, 151, 161–165, 180–184, 223,
    226, 230, 246
    in appreciative inquiry, 27
    and belief systems, 6
    and choice, principle of, 95, 226
    discovery, 131–133, *132*
    dynamic nature of, 27
    of leadership, 110
    of positive experiences, 20
story-sharing, pyramid structure of, 164
strategic planning, 62, 199
strategic priorities, 150
strengths, 51, 58, 77–81, 83, 92, 110–112,
    131, 145, 177–178, 210–211,
    237–238, 243–244
    identifying questions, **178**
    identifying and working with,
        71, 193–194
    and organisational power zone, 73–74
    positive psychology research into, 23
    relationships, 89
    and resilience, 103, 104, *104*

Strengths, Opportunities, Aspiration and Results (SOAR), 69
  based questions, 78
  model of strategy development, 74–75, *75*
  process, 74
  to return to power zone, 75–80
stress, 28, 80, 81, 100, 105, 191, 207, 232, 236–237, 240, 242–244
structural differences, 62
structured dialogic processes, 80–81
stuck team, working with, 179–186
success
  criteria of, 183–184
  definition of, 227
  root causes of, 151
  shared stories of, 151
switching process, 227–228
synergenesis process, 131–132, *132*
system engagement, 216
systemic consulting, 159–160, 172
systemic oppression, 62
system-level health, 241–243
system summit process, *70*, 71

tacit knowledge, 49, 60–62
Taylorist approach, 237
teams
  building event, 125
  configuration, 175
  creating positivity, 177–178
  definition of, 176
  description of, 175
  event, agenda for, *182*
  identity and culture, 200–201
  member diversity, 118–120
  performance, 61, 210
  psychological safety in, 243–245
  relationships, 210
  strengths in, 177
  stuck situation, 178–186
  successful, 176
teamwork, 19, 81–82, 176, 181, 183, 244

thinking, 8, 9, 21, 25, 50–51, 55–56, 87, 89, 117–118, 190, 193, 199, 241
time perspectives, 242, **242,** 243
'time to think' model, 76
toxicity, 236, 239, 249
toxic organisation, 236, 239, 244, 249
toxin handlers, 244
traditional leaders, 88, 90
transformational change, 30–31
'tribes' challenge, 117, 125
trust, 28, 78, 80–81, 123, 145, 151, 176

uncertainty, 9, 86, 109–110, 222–223
  admission of, 95
  leading through, 93
  principles for leading through, **96**

video meeting, 200
virtual appreciative inquiry, 190, 196, **196**
virtual working, 199, 203
  appreciative inquiry online, 196–197
  description of, 189–190
vision, 9, 30, 37, 44, 51, 76, 122, 129, 133, 145, 161, 184
voluntarism principle, 46
volunteer groups, 153

'walk and talk' activity, 78, 197
weak cultures, 197–198
well-being, 236, 240
  boost, 236–237
  and health, 244
  individual's, 237–238
  intervention, 241–243
  levels of, 241
  psychological, 242
  psychosocial, 237–238
  sense of, 104
  staff, 217
  in teams, 176, 243
wholeness principle, 24–26, *25*, 144–145, 183–184

wholesale large-scale planned change, 222
whole system, 5, 29, 35, 40, 51, 75, 80, 82, 88, 100–102, 122, 138, 163, 216, 244–245
'wicked' problems, 8, 11
work. *see also* working/workplace
  categories of types of, **199**
  cultures, 115
  people at, 237–239
  relationships, 195

working/workplace, 202–203, 211
  climate, 237
  cultures, 59
  environment, 194
  from home challenges, 190, **191**
  with respect, 245–249

yoga, 238

Zoom, 197, 200, 202